February 2000

To Madeleine,

With warmest
wishes.

Karen Stein

Margaret Atwood Revisited

Karen F. Stein

University of Rhode Island

Twayne Publishers
New York

Twayne's World Authors Series No. 887

Margaret Atwood Revisited
Karen F. Stein

Twayne Publishers
1633 Broadway
New York, NY 10019

Library of Congress Cataloging-in-Publication Data

Stein, Karen F., 1941–
    Margaret Atwood revisited / Karen F. Stein.
        p.   cm. — (Twayne's world authors series ; TWAS 887. Canadian
    literature)
    Includes bibliographical references (p.   ) and index.
    ISBN 0-8057-1614-9 (alk. paper)
    1. Atwood, Margaret Eleanor, 1939–   —Criticism and
    interpretation.   2. Women and literature—Canada—History—20th
    century.   I. Title.   II. Series: Twayne's world authors series ;
    TWAS 887.   III. Series: Twayne's world authors series.   Canadian
    literature.
    PR9199.3.A8Z896   1999
    818'.5409—dc21   99-33696
                                                                              CIP

This paper meets the requirements of ANSI/NISO Z3948-1992 (Permanence of Paper).

10 9 8 7 6 5 4 3 2 1

Printed in the United States of America

For Arielle and Lisa

Contents

Note on Sources   *ix*
Preface   *xi*
Acknowledgments   *xiii*
Chronology   *xvii*

> *Chapter One*
> Margaret Atwood, Storyteller   1
>
> *Chapter Two*
> Northern Gothic: The Early Poems, 1961–1975   9
>
> *Chapter Three*
> "Home Ground, Foreign Territory":
> Atwood's Early Novels   41
>
> *Chapter Four*
> Lost Worlds: Three Novels   64
>
> *Chapter Five*
> Victims, Tricksters, and Scheherazades: The Later Novels   86
>
> *Chapter Six*
> Firestorms and Fireflies: The Later Poems, 1978–1995   110
>
> *Chapter Seven*
> Scarlet Ibises and Frog Songs: Short Fiction   125
>
> *Chapter Eight*
> Poets and Princesses: An Atwood Miscellany
> Literary Criticism, Reviews, and Children's Books   145

Notes and References   *153*
Selected Bibliography   *162*
Index   *167*

Note on Sources

Parenthetical citations from Atwood's published works correspond to the following editions:

AC   *The Animals in That Country* (Boston: Little, Brown, 1968).

AG   *Alias Grace* (New York: Doubleday, 1996).

BE   *Bluebeard's Egg* (New York: Ballantine, 1990).

BH   *Bodily Harm* (New York: Bantam, 1983).

CE   *Cat's Eye* (New York: Doubleday, 1989).

CG   *The Circle Game* (Toronto: Anansi, 1978).

DG   *Dancing Girls and Other Stories* (New York: Bantam, 1989).

EW   *The Edible Woman* (New York: Bantam, 1991).

GB   *Good Bones* (Toronto: Coach House, 1993).

HT   *The Handmaid's Tale* (New York: Ballantine, 1987).

IN   *Interlunar* (Toronto: Oxford University Press, 1984).

JSM   *The Journals of Susanna Moodie* (Toronto: Oxford University Press, 1970).

LBM   *Life Before Man* (New York: Ballantine, 1990).

LO   *Lady Oracle* (New York: Ballantine, 1990).

MBH   *Morning in the Burned House* (Toronto: McClelland and Stewart, 1995).

MD   *Murder in the Dark* (Toronto: Coach House, 1983).

PP   *Power Politics* (Toronto: Anansi, 1971).

PU   *Procedures for Underground* (Boston: Little, Brown, 1970).

RB   *The Robber Bride* (New York: Doubleday, 1993).

SF   *Surfacing* (New York: Ballantine, 1987).

SV   *Survival: A Thematic Guide to Canadian Literature* (Toronto: Anansi, 1972).

SW   *Second Words: Selected Critical Prose* (Boston: Beacon Press, 1984).

THP   *Two-Headed Poems* (Toronto: Oxford University Press, 1978).

TS   *True Stories* (New York: Simon and Schuster, 1981).

WT   *Wilderness Tips* (New York: Bantam, 1996).

YAH   *You Are Happy* (New York: Harper & Row, 1974).

TF   Unpublished material from the Margaret Atwood Papers, Thomas Fisher Rare Book Library, University of Toronto, Ontario.

Preface

Margaret Atwood is an extraordinary writer. Her poems and fictions are lucid, engaging, witty, and provocative, appealing to a wide audience of general readers as well as academics and other writers. She is a supreme storyteller, keenly attuned to current issues and cultural phenomena. Her texts encompass social and political critique, allusions to other literary works, and intertexts of cultural documents such as the Bible, Canadian and Greek myths, and fairy tales. Her texts question social, political, and literary ideas, beliefs, and conventions as they delight, inform, intrigue, and sometimes irritate.

Atwood arrived on the literary scene in the mid-1960s at the juncture of several important cultural phenomena, especially a resurgence of Canadian nationalism and of North American feminism. Her unique combination of talent, energy, and personal history equips her to join the ongoing political discourses dialogue and to interpret this cultural moment to a growing audience. Because of her interest in feminism, human rights, and Canadian nationalism, she has become a public figure as well, although she endeavors to keep her life and family private.

This study aims to provide an overview of her texts and to situate them in the context of a contemporary Canadian and North American milieu. Its focus is on central themes in her work, especially the paradoxes and possibilities of storytelling, sexual politics, and quest. Her stories stretch the boundaries of traditional genres as the protagonists narrate stories of journey that call into question conventional sex-role stereotypes and interrogate the limits and contradictions of narrative.

This book looks at Atwood primarily as a storyteller and secondarily as a Canadian and a feminist. Each of these categories is a contested one. My purpose here is to raise, rather than to answer, a range of questions that stem from this categorization and to welcome readers into the worlds of Atwood's writings.

Chapter 1 sets out central themes and motifs of Atwood's work and provides some biographical background. Atwood defines writers as tricksters, setting the stage for her work. An important subject of her fiction is storytelling itself. Her protagonists are storytellers, witnesses to a world that is often confusing and dangerous. Most of these protago-

nists undertake journeys that may lead them to insights, although the
texts resist closure, preferring ambiguity.

Chapter 2 discusses poetry published up to 1975, the date of publication of *Selected Poems 1965–1975*. The voice in these poems is that of a
victim, a woman struggling to survive and to tell her stories in a harsh
Northern climate. The season is winter, and the mood is Gothic.

Chapter 3 reads the early novels, *The Edible Woman, Surfacing,* and
Lady Oracle, as Gothic fiction that both describes the female narrators'
quests for identity and at the same time parodies the conventions of
Gothic fiction and the possibility of such quests.

Chapter 4 reviews the next group of three novels. *Life Before Man*
purports to be a realist novel, but it questions the limits of realism. *Bodily Harm* stretches the boundaries of the detective thriller. *The Handmaid's Tale* is a near-future dystopia. These novels expose political dangers but eschew political solutions. Instead, the protagonists choose the
role of witness, reporter.

Chapter 5 looks at three novels, *Cat's Eye, The Robber Bride,* and *Alias
Grace,* that celebrate storytelling and examine its paradoxes. Time and
its relation to memory, and the formation of an artist are also central
themes.

Chapter 6 looks at the poems from 1976 to 1995, *Two-Headed Poems*
(1978), *True Stories* (1981), *Interlunar* (1984), and *Morning in the Burned
House* (1995). These poems question language; urge us to bear witness
to the pain and suffering in the world; and encourage us to find solace in
poetry, the imagination, and in human relationships.

Chapter 7 reviews the short stories, *Dancing Girls and Other Stories*
(1977), *Murder in the Dark* (1983), *Bluebeard's Egg* (1983), *Wilderness Tips*
(1991), and *Good Bones* (1992). Atwood is especially interested in the fictions characters invent about their lives and in the ways that these fictions may become traps locking them in uncomfortable situations or
self-fulfilling prophecies, leading to the outcomes they fear most. In
many of these stories the characters come to question the fictions they
have invented.

Chapter 8 reviews Atwood's four children's books and her nonfiction,
Survival, Second Words, and *Strange Things.* It ends with Atwood's voice
speaking about writing and reading.

Acknowledgments

It is a pleasure to thank those who have helped in the writing process. A Canadian Government Faculty Enrichment Grant helped initiate my research on Atwood. The University of Rhode Island has generously provided support in the form of a sabbatical, a URI Foundation Grant, and an Arts and Sciences Dean's Excellence Grant. The English Department provided assistance. Librarians at both the Kingston and Providence campuses were helpful in tracking down resources. My students have been both captive audiences and participants in the unfolding of ideas, most especially Hanan Abdullatif, Jacqueline Clark, Bill Hampl, Chihiro Masada, John Medeiros, Michael Pugliese, Genevieve Scott, Terri Selby, Nancy Teeter, Sandra Wall, and Robyn Younkin.

Margie Bucheit and Linda Shamoon convened writers' groups that provided thoughtful readings, most especially by Elena Gonzales, Karen Markin, Larry Rothstein, and Jon Sutinen. Tina Letcher read several chapters and asked provocative questions. Hugh McCracken provided encouragement.

Research for the book began at the University of British Columbia through the generous hospitality of the Centre for Research on Women's Studies and Gender Relations, the Department of English, the Library, and the Arts Computing Centre. Librarians at the Thomas Fisher Rare Book Library, University of Toronto, were also helpful. A community of Atwood scholars has been publishing the studies that helped to shape my ideas. Others have helped in a variety of ways. Robert Lecker gave me the opportunity to write about Atwood.

Margaret Atwood's assistant, Sarah Cooper, helped in organizing the facts of publication and obtaining photographs for the book cover and frontispiece.

Permission for general quotation from her work was granted by Margaret Atwood. Grateful acknowledgment is made to the following publishers for allowing me to quote from Atwood's works:

In Canada:

House of Anansi Press for permission to quote from *The Circle Game, Power Politics, Second Words,* and *Survival.*

Coach House Press for permission to quote from *Murder in the Dark* and *Good Bones.*

Key Porter for permission to quote from *Princess Prunella and the Purple Peanut.*

McClelland and Steward for permission to quote from *Alias Grace, Bluebeard's Egg, Bodily Harm, Cat's Eye, Dancing Girls, The Handmaid's Tale, The Edible Woman, Lady Oracle, Morning in the Burned House, The Robber Bride, Surfacing, Survival,* and *Wilderness Tips.*

Oxford University Press for permission to quote from *The Animals in That Country, Interlunar, The Journals of Susanna Moodie, Procedures for Underground, True Stories, Two-Headed Poems,* and *You Are Happy.*

In England:

Andre Deutsch for permission to quote from *The Edible Woman, Surfacing,* and *Lady Oracle.*

Bloomsbury for permission to quote from *Alias Grace, Cat's Eye, The Robber Bride,* and *Wilderness Tips.*

Jonathan Cape for permission to quote from *Bodily Harm, Cat's Eye, Dancing Girls, The Handmaid's Tale, Interlunar,* and *Murder in the Dark.*

Virago for permission to quote from *Bluebeard's Egg, Bodily Harm, Cat's Eye, Good Bones,* and *Morning in the Burned House.*

In the United States:

Ballantine Books for permission to quote from *Surfacing, Lady Oracle, The Handmaid's Tale,* and *Bluebeard's Egg.*

Bantam Books for permission to quote from *The Edible Woman, Bodily Harm, Dancing Girls,* and *Wilderness Tips.*

Beacon Press for permission to quote from *Second Words.*

Doubleday for permission to quote from *Alias Grace, Cat's Eye, Good Bones, The Robber Bride,* and *Wilderness Tips.*

Harper and Row for permission to quote from *Power Politics, Survival,* and *You Are Happy.*

Houghton Mifflin for permission to quote from *Bluebeard's Egg, The Handmaid's Tale,* and *Morning in the Burned House.*

Little, Brown for permission to quote from *The Animals in That Country, The Edible Woman,* and *Procedures for Underground.*

Simon and Schuster for permission to quote from *Bodily Harm, Dancing Girls, Lady Oracle, Two-Headed Poems, True Stories,* and *Surfacing.*

Workman Press for permission to quote from *Princess Prunella and the Purple Peanut.*

Chronology

1939	Margaret Eleanor Atwood born 18 November in Ottawa, Ontario. Siblings are Harold (b. 1937) and Ruth (b. 1951). Father, Carl Edmund Atwood, is a forest entomologist specializing in bees, the spruce budworm, and forest tent caterpillars. Mother, Margaret Dorothy (Killam), is a graduate in Home Economics from the University of Toronto.
1939–1945	Family lives in Ottawa in the winters and spends the rest of the year in northern Quebec and Ontario where father conducts research.
1946	Family settles in Toronto, where father teaches at University of Toronto.
1952–1957	Studies at Leaside High School, Toronto; contributes prose and verse to school literary magazine.
1958	Works at Camp White Pine, Haliburton, in charge of the nature hut, where she meets Charles Pachter, in charge of arts and crafts.
1957–1961	Honors English student at Victoria College, University of Toronto; studies with Northrop Frye, Jay Macpherson, Kathleen Colburn, Millar MacLure; submits literary work to college magazines, cowrites articles with Dennis Lee.
1961	"Double Persephone" wins E. J. Pratt medal. Wins Woodrow Wilson Fellowship on graduation.
1961–1962	Graduate studies in English at Radcliffe College, Harvard University; studies Victorian literature under Jerome H. Buckley. Gains her M.A.
1962–1963	Doctoral studies, Harvard University.
1963–1964	Works for a market-research company, Toronto; writes novel, as yet unpublished, "Up in the Air So Blue."
1964–1965	Teaches English literature at the University of British Columbia.

1965–1967   Continues doctoral studies at Harvard; completes all the requirements except for dissertation, "The English Metaphysical Romance," to focus on H. Rider Haggard.

1966   *The Circle Game.*

1967   Wins Governor General's Award for *The Circle Game.* Marries James Polk, fellow graduate student and American novelist.

1967–1968   Teaches English at Sir George Williams University (now part of Concordia University) in Montreal.

1968   *The Animals in That Country.*

1969   *The Edible Woman.*

1969–1970   Teaches creative writing at the University of Alberta.

1970   *Procedures for Underground; The Journals of Susanna Moodie.*

1970–1971   Travels in England, France, Italy.

1971   *Power Politics;* serves on the board of House of Anansi Press (until 1973).

1971–1972   Teaches Canadian literature at York University, Toronto.

1972   *Surfacing; Survival: A Thematic Guide to Canadian Literature.*

1972–1973   Writer-in-residence at University of Toronto.

1973   Separated from James Polk; moves to Alliston, Ontario, with Graeme Gibson, Canadian writer (*Five Legs,* 1969; *Communion,* 1971; *Perpetual Motion,* 1982). Awarded by Trent University the first of her many honorary degrees. Becomes involved in Writers' Union of Canada.

1974   *You Are Happy* (poetry).

1973–7195   Member of the board of directors of the Canadian Civil Liberties Association.

1975   Begins to contribute a comic strip called *Kanadian Kultchur Komix* featuring "Survivalwoman" to the left-wing nationalist magazine, *This Magazine,* under the name Bart Gerrard.

1976   *Lady Oracle;* City of Toronto Book Award 1977; Canadian Booksellers Association Award, 1977; *Selected*

Poems; daughter Jess (Eleanor Jess Atwood Gibson) born.

1977   *Dancing Girls;* receives St. Lawrence Award for Fiction; the Periodical Distributors of Canada Award for Short Fiction. *Days of the Rebels: 1815–1840* (history).

1978   Visits Australia for Writers' Week; *Two-Headed Poems; Up the Tree* (children's book); becomes contributing editor to *This Magazine.*

1978–1979   Lives in Scotland while Gibson teaches at the University of Edinburgh.

1979   *Life Before Man.*

1980   Family moves to Toronto; *Anna's Pet* (children's story, with Joyce Barkhouse; adapted for stage, 1986).

1980–1981   Vice-chair of Writers' Union of Canada.

1981   *True Stories; Bodily Harm.*

1982   *Second Words: Selected Critical Prose.* Edits *The New Oxford Book of Canadian Verse in English.*

1982–1983   President of Writers' Union of Canada.

1983   *Murder in the Dark: Short Fictions and Prose Poems; Bluebeard's Egg.*

1983–1984   Travels and works in England, Germany.

1984   *Interlunar.*

1984–1985   President of P.E.N. International's Anglo-Canadian branch; (P.E.N. promotes friendship among writers, supports freedom of expression, and pressures for the release of writers who are political prisoners.)

1985   *The Handmaid's Tale.* Governor General's Award, Los Angeles *Times* Award, Arthur C. Clarke science fiction award, runner-up Booker Prize and Ritz-Paris Hemingway Prize. MFA chair, creative writing, University of Alabama, Tuscaloosa; teaches course on Ontario Gothic literature.

1986   Coeditor with Robert Weaver of *The Oxford Book of Canadian Short Stories in English.* Berg chair, New York University, New York, creative writing. *Selected Poems II: Poems Selected & New, 1976–1986. The Festival of*

Missed Crass (children's musical). Writer-in-residence, Macquarie University, Sydney, Australia.

1988 *Cat's Eye.*

1989 Author of the Year, Canadian Booksellers Association.

1990 *Selected Poems: 1966–1984* and *For the Birds* (children's fiction). Order of Ontario and Harvard Centennial Medal. Film of *The Handmaid's Tale,* screenplay by H. Pinter.

1991 *Wilderness Tips.* Trillium Book Award.

1992 *Good Bones.*

1993 *The Robber Bride.* Canadian Authors Association Novel of the Year Award.

1995 *Morning in the Burned House; Strange Things: The Malevolent North in Canadian Literature.*

1996 *Alias Grace;* short-listed for Booker Prize, wins Giller Prize.

Chapter One
Margaret Atwood, Storyteller

Margaret Atwood inspires accolades. Fiction writer, poet, critic, cartoonist, editor, children's book author, lecturer, teacher, and active participant in literary organizations, she is perhaps the major figure in the contemporary flowering of Canadian literature. She has won numerous awards and also sparked literary controversies. Scholars and reviewers praise her wit, her brilliance, her moral vision, her verbal virtuosity. Her work, solidly grounded in the English and Anglo-Canadian literary traditions, appeals to both scholars and the general public; it has been translated into more than 20 languages, including Dutch, Finnish, French, German, Italian, Norwegian, Spanish, and Swedish. Peter Dale Scott writes that her "critical projects . . . can be seen as projects of total cultural renewal."[1] Her nonfiction book, *Survival* (1972), aims to legitimize the study of Canadian literature and to provide resources for teachers. She has long been a member of the Writers' Union of Canada, serving as its president in 1981–1982. She edited the *Canlit Foodbook* (1987) to raise money for writers who are prisoners of conscience internationally. Her 22 comic strips in *This Magazine* (1975–1978) feature "Survivalwoman," a superheroine who defends Canadian culture against Canadian bureaucrats and the United States.

Central among her wide-ranging interests is a fascination with storytelling. Her fictions simultaneously tell stories and comment metafictively on the narrative process, engaging readers with a provocative series of questions: What would happen if we heard the stories of marginalized, usually silent people, especially women? What stories do women tell about themselves? What happens when their stories run counter to literary conventions or society's expectations? What factors limit or enhance their storytelling? How may they become authors, authorities of their own lives? Can storytelling be liberating? What are the possibilities and limits of different forms of narrative, or of language itself? Do we write our stories, or do they write us? These questions reverberate through the Atwood canon, and indeed they echo throughout our lives, for storytelling forms the fabric of human consciousness.[2] Women's stories in particular have, throughout history, often contained

unauthorized and dangerous knowledge. Many of Atwood's protagonists are Scheherazades, narrating their stories to win over hostile listeners. For them narrative is a life-and-death concern.

To speak about Atwood we must place her in twentieth-century
Canadian social and historical contexts. A portrait of the Atwood family—the parents, Carl and Margaret Atwood; her brother, Harold
Atwood; Margaret Atwood; her partner, novelist Graeme Gibson; and
their daughter, Jess—appears in a half-hour videotape, *Atwood and Family*.[3] They are congenial and good-humored as they relax at their island
vacation home, swimming, canoeing, walking, and enjoying books, stories, and nature. Carl Atwood explains botanical lore to his granddaugh-
ter and Mrs. Atwood bakes pies and swims as Margaret's voice-over
reads appropriate selections from her tribute to her parents,
"Unearthing Suite" (*BE*). One feels that Atwood's family was a comfortable place to grow up and that she was encouraged to develop her tal-
ents and to be confident and self-directed. When director Michael
Rubbo finds Atwood enigmatic, she turns the tables and mischievously
enlists her family to tease him about his quest for her dark side.

Atwood was born in 1939 into a middle-class Anglo-Canadian family, and her childhood was divided between the city and the bush (the
wilderness). During the school year the family lived in the cities where
her father taught entomology or worked for government agencies. During the summers they lived in remote areas as he conducted field
research on insects such as the spruce budworm. The experience of life in
the bush without the popular distractions of urban society encouraged
Atwood to develop her imagination and to read extensively.

Atwood knew from an early age that she would become a writer. As a
child she wrote and illustrated poems, which she made into small books.
Some of the young Atwood's early works are still available to interested
readers. "Rhyming Cats," composed when she was five years old, is in
the collection of Atwood papers housed in the Thomas Fisher Rare Book
Library at the University of Toronto. Clearly the family appreciated and
encouraged these childhood productions and deemed them important
enough to save even though the family moved frequently.

As a student at Leaside High School in Toronto, Atwood wrote for
the literary magazine. At Victoria College, University of Toronto, from
1957 to 1961, she continued to pursue a literary career and to participate in the social and intellectual life of the college. She joined the
debating team and wrote for the newspaper and the dramatic society.

The 1960s inaugurated a renewed interest in Canadian literature and cultural productions, and Atwood has been an important participant in this cultural resurgence. When she was an undergraduate at Victoria College, a body of Canadian literature was gaining recognition. In 1955 Carl F. Klinck and Reginald E. Watters published the *Canadian Anthology;* in 1960 A. J. M. Smith's *The Oxford Book of Canadian Verse* appeared (Atwood would edit an updated version of this book in 1982). The university was a center for Canadian poetry, with a well-stocked library of Canadiana and several influential faculty members, including poet Jay Macpherson, critic Northrop Frye, and the recently retired E. J. Pratt. Sandra Djwa sums up key influences on Atwood's work: "the new feminism, a myth-centered [English and Canadian tradition of] poetry, Frye's criticism and the growing nationalism of the early sixties."[4]

Atwood and other young poets gave readings at coffeehouses such as the Bohemian Embassy, and conversation about literary topics was intense and enthusiastic. She recaptures this milieu in her story "Isis in Darkness" (WT). She wrote reviews, poems, and parodies for the college newspaper, *Acta Victoriana,* sometimes under the pseudonym Shakesbeat Latweed in collaboration with her fellow student, the Canadian author Dennis Lee. She spent the summer of 1958 as a nature counselor at Camp White Pine in Haliburton, where she became friends with Charles Pachter, who later produced artist books that combined her poems with his artwork.

In 1961, she graduated from college and won the E. J. Pratt medal at Victoria College for a group of poems, "Double Persephone." She also won a Woodrow Wilson Fellowship to continue her studies in English at Radcliffe College, Harvard University. There she studied Victorian literature under Jerome Buckley and early American literature under Perry Miller. She received her M.A. in 1962 and began work toward her Ph.D. in English, completing all of the requirements except for her dissertation, which was to focus on H. Rider Haggard and the English metaphysical romance. While at Harvard, Atwood found that the main poetry collection was housed in a library that women were not then allowed to enter. Instead, she read Canadian poetry, which was in the accessible Widener library.[5] Returning to Canada in 1963, she focused her attention on Canadian literature and on her own writing, continuing to write poetry and beginning the novel, as yet unpublished, "Up in the Air So Blue."

From these beginnings Atwood's career has evolved.

Atwood lives and writes in a world shaped by specific events and ideologies: World War II, the Cold War, the Vietnam War, the Civil Rights movement, the feminist movement, the rise of the New Left, the resurgence of Canadian national identity, and the contemporary literary and cultural debates about structuralism, deconstruction, postcoloniality, and postmodernity. Atwood's work responds to this political milieu, asserting either directly (as in her essay "Canadian-American Relations: Surviving the Eighties" in *Second Words*) or encoded in her novels a Canadian nationalism that challenges materialism and hypocrisy in both the United States and Canada. World War II is a significant background factor in Atwood's fictions as well. Most of the female narrators come from dysfunctional families marred by the absence of fathers who served in the war. In her novels (especially *The Robber Bride*) and her work with Amnesty International, Atwood expresses a strong antiwar conviction.

Atwood's love of story and its paradoxes is augmented by her interest in codes, games, and clues. She writes with a combination of caricature, comedy, satire, and seriousness. Her texts are richly textured tapestries, woven with strands of symbol, implication, metaphor, allusion, and image. Writing against the grain of literary conventions, she places women in the center of the story and uses strategies such as parody, irony, and satire to expand the limits of what can be said in different literary genres, for, as she explains, the most interesting works of art cross or stretch the boundaries: "Every . . . art form has a certain set of brackets around it. You can say 'this is what happens within this form,' and, 'these are some of the things that don't happen within it.' Some of the most interesting things happen when you expand the brackets."[6]

Her writings question, challenge, and disrupt the conventions of both literary traditions and social structures as well as Western philosophical dichotomies (binaries) such as fact/fiction or rational/irrational. They address recurring themes, including men's and women's roles, romantic conventions, the politics of power in daily life, victims and victimization, the conflicts within families, mother-daughter relationships, city and nature, emotional paralysis and release, the complexities of narrativity and interpretation, and the role of the storyteller. As Atwood continually reminds us, stories are always ambiguous and subject to interpretation. Her poem "True Stories" warns: "The true story is vicious / and multiple and untrue" (*TS*). Consequently, her texts resist closure, and they feature doubled characters and situations, mirroring, twinning, and other variations on the theme of multiplicity.

She combines realism with mythic subtexts to tell women's Gothic quest stories (see discussion of *Lady Oracle*). A key component of the quest is the search for a voice with which to tell their stories, for women's plots have traditionally centered on romance and passivity. Closely linked to the Gothic is the fairy tale, also a story of quest and transformation. According to psychological theory, fairy tale protagonists seek to ameliorate their fragmentation, their loss of the golden radiance of youthful innocence. Atwood cites the Grimm's fairy tales of danger and transformation as important influences. Sharon Rose Wilson's comprehensive *Margaret Atwood's Fairy-Tale Sexual Politics* documents fairy tale motifs in her texts, pointing out that she uses them parodically and ironically as well as seriously.[7]

Atwood's fiction and poetry encompass a wide range of concerns. A central one, examined in most of her fictions and in *Survival,* her thematic study of Canadian literature, is the problem of victimization; she finds that the marginalized (especially women and Canadians) are often cast as victims. Her female protagonists experience a duality of power and victimhood, for they are all simultaneously both victims and at least potentially powerful. But social constraints deform their power, so it is often expressed in distortion or excess. Although the conclusions remain ambiguous, many of the protagonists arrive (to different degrees) at knowledge of their power and thus are poised to achieve some measure of psychological awareness and personal transformation. Atwood maintains that she records actuality and that she offers her readers hope. Yet the hope may be paradoxical because her texts both propose and interrogate a counter narrative of optimism and mythic renewal.

Atwood is a satirist, a caricaturist with a deeply moral vision. In her collected essays, *Second Words,* she defines the novel as "a moral instrument" (*SW* 353). She explains: "*Moral* implies political, and traditionally the novel has been used not only as a vehicle for social commentary but as a vehicle for political commentary as well. The novelist, at any rate, still sees a connection between politics and the moral sense, even if politicians gave that up some time ago" (353). She is concerned with politics not only in the traditional sense of the governmental arena but across the gamut of daily life and human relations. She asserts: "By 'politics' I mean who is entitled to do what to whom, with impunity; who profits by it; and who therefore eats what" (394). And, indeed, eating is fraught with political overtones in Atwood's work.

Among her targets are a range of political and social institutions: sexism, consumerism, science, and romantic love ideologies. She finds many of contemporary Western society's cultural ideologies destructive. For example, her novels demonstrate that sexism locks both women and men into narrow roles, consumerism commodifies the natural world and people as well, and romantic love ideology creates false expectations. However, although the issues she addresses are social and political, she mistrusts politics. Therefore, the possible resolutions proposed by the novels are personal. Similarly, she resists the label of feminism, yet her work engages feminist issues and tells women's stories. Likewise, Marxists on the one hand point out that Atwood provides a Marxist analysis, and on the other fault Atwood for failing to suggest organized resistance. I believe Atwood avoids political solutions because she views them as part of the problem: victims who gain power often become victimizers themselves. Moreover, politics, or any other monolithic system, any single approach, is inadequate to deal with the complexities of human life. George Woodcock sums up her position cogently: whereas "even novelists with a politically revolutionary intent tend to proceed from the assumption that what is wrong with any modern society can be righted by . . . a more rational and scientific ordering of society. . . . Atwood proceeds from the assumption that the society which has emerged from a reliance on logic, and which defies the natural instinctual urges will be a sick one."[8] In her texts the city, a gray world, often stands for linearity, superficiality, and rigidity. To counter these limits, Atwood introduces subtexts—often embodied in imagery of a natural, green world—that allude to the realms of irrationality, illogic, emotion: myth, folk and fairy tales, Biblical allusions, and nature-centered spiritual systems.

In a talk presented in many venues in 1994, Atwood refers to writers as tricksters. In many cultures the trickster is a messenger, a teacher, a shape changer, an artist, a liar, a figure in touch with the life force. Tricksters delight in playing, in fabricating (making, lying), in crossing boundaries, in disrupting conventions. The trickster figure embodies contradictions, often using humor, parody, and satire to expose hypocrisy and pretension. As a writer she claims these roles for herself. This perspective gives rise to the doubleness of her vision and the concomitant plenitude of critical interpretations. Indeed, many of her characters share the trickster identity as well, sometimes posing as naive innocents whose befuddlement lays bare a range of political and social ills.

Many scholars analyze her double vision.[9] One collection, referring to Atwood's diversity of genres and perspectives, is called *Various Atwoods*. J. Brooks Bouson points to the contradictory conclusions arrived at by readers of Atwood's novels as evidence of the openness of Atwood's work. Camille Peri writes: "Atwood is a contrary woman: a nationalist who rankles nationalists, a feminist who rankles feminists." To this I would add: a political satirist who resists political solutions. She uses literary conventions to narrate her tales and at the same time to critique those very conventions and their underlying assumptions or, as Coral Ann Howells puts it, "the value structures and power relations coded into texts." Her fiction and poetry engage, often parodically, current literary, political, and scholarly debates. One ongoing contemporary debate concerns the position of women within the discursive community. One side of this debate, most strongly articulated by a group of French feminists (Luce Irigaray, Helene Cixous, and others), argues that because language already contains a set of power relationships that maintain patriarchal dominance, women must define themselves by subverting language, for example, "writing through the body" by devising experimental forms. On the other side, many Anglo-American critics assume that language is neutral and that realist narrative can reflect women's experience as well as men's. Atwood's position paradoxically incorporates both sides of the debate (thus challenging the theoretical polarity or binary). Although she writes realist fiction, she uses the strategies of metafiction, commenting on or questioning within the fiction itself realist narrative conventions such as voice, interpretation, or closed-end conclusions (Rao, Greene).

The preferred stance for Atwood protagonists is that of the engaged witness, the reporter, the storyteller. In almost every case a woman narrates the novels, and often telling her story is virtually a life-and-death matter, as in the case of Scheherazade. Stories may be entrapping or liberating for the protagonists. Throughout her novels, telling the story is a way to explore alternatives, to discover how to live, and to bear political witness. The narrators are victims, writers, ordinary women testifying to the extraordinary implications of our world through their stories. Many readers have noted Atwood's frequent allusions to the folktale "The Robber Bridegroom," in which the bride saves her life by telling a story. Marilyn Patton writes: "[T]he girl's story . . . parades itself as 'fiction' yet is about the most gruesome reality. . . . The reference to the story implies that telling tales may be a way of saving lives."[10] For Atwood, this tenet may be an imperative.

Atwood's fictions and poems demonstrate powerfully and poignantly that the stories we tell ourselves and each other may explain or obfuscate, entrap or liberate, lead us to safety or destruction, and bring us to the depths of despair or the heights of joy.

The world represented in Atwood's work is often a harsh place. Mothers, friends, lovers, and spouses are duplicitous: by turns they nurture, rescue, and threaten. Facing these situations, Atwood's storytellers inscribe their quests for autonomy in lucid, sometimes comic, often lyrical poetry and prose. In the short stories they may often remain trapped, perplexed, or caught up in fantasies. In the novels the protagonist usually works her way through to an insight or epiphany that may remove her from the victim position psychologically, yet the conclusions remain ambiguous. As her astonishing oeuvre evolves, Atwood's narratives explore the dilemmas of contemporary North American life with humor, irony, and paradox. Counterpoised to the surface realism of her texts are stories of mythic renewal, open-ended and rich with possibility. Readers continue to read Atwood for her stories, for her brilliant wit and wordplay, for her exploration of women's lives, and for her provocative engagement with literary conventions and with real problems of contemporary society.

Chapter Two

Northern Gothic:
The Early Poems, 1961–1975

Margaret Atwood's remarkable literary career encompasses all genres (essay, fiction, poetry, drama in the form of television scripts, literary criticism, children's books, political cartoons, and even an opera libretto); however, it was her poetry that first built her reputation. To read her early poetry (especially *Double Persephone, The Circle Game, The Animals in That Country, The Journals of Susanna Moodie,* and *Procedures for Underground*) is to be drawn into Atwood country, a stark and Gothic landscape, a harsh Northern geography of stunted islands, bedrock ridges, flooded forests, drowned worlds, frozen terrain, arctic wastes, and lakes that conceal drowned people. The poet of these books, however, is not a nature poet in the style of Mary Oliver, describing her impressions of particular scenes. Rather, she is a mythic poet, and landscape exists not as an identifiable locale, but as a mythic force in her work. Similarly, the characters in these early poems are archetypes rather than particular individuals. The protagonist who tells the story of her life here is likely to be a tourist or traveler, struggling to be comfortable in this harsh landscape. She is frequently alone, but even if other people are present they are likely to be estranged or hostile. Houses are not necessarily refuges, for disturbing omens and portents lurk in unexpected places: the landlady dominates the rented rooms, and mysterious messengers hang suspended outside the windows. The speaker may find herself descending through the carpet into watery depths below, or caught in labyrinthine museums at night. Cities are dangerously unstable, thin cement and steel veneers placed precariously over the untamed wilderness: the road is "a muskeg," or a "crust of ice that / easily might break" ("A Place: Fragments"). Aliens, exiles, tourists, invaders, and settlers, the people in these poems struggle to find their places in disquieting surroundings. Often, they must undertake journeys that test their mettle.

The cold Northern landscape is an important metaphor for many other Canadian writers as well, as Atwood points out in *Survival,* her thematic survey of Canadian literature. Indeed, literary critic Northrop Frye argues that Canadian identity itself is linked to place: the central Canadian question is not "who am I?" but "where is here?"[1] Moreover, according to Frederic Jameson the question of location has a more general application to the contemporary period, for he claims that the defining characteristic of contemporary Western culture is an inability to locate one's position.[2] We find that maps are useless, and we experience a general sense of historical discontinuity. Atwood's emphasis on maps, place, and spatial details is a reiteration of the question "where is here?" or part of an attempt to find an answer.

Thematically linked to this Atwoodian geography, a group of interrelated oppositions that structure much of her work are particularly salient in the poetry: surface and depth, city and nature, speech and silence, visibility and invisibility, the observer and the observed, rationality and irrationality, the real and the mythic, entrapment and freedom, life and death. Paradoxically, the protagonists seek connection but remain estranged; the invisible and silent are more potent than the seen and heard; characters are often paralyzed until they risk dangerous journeys through difficult terrain; and the most hazardous journeys are interior ones.

Landscape entails depth and the irrational, danger and power. City, on the other hand, stands for the repressive overlay of Western civilization, superficiality, and a stultifying rationality. Through a misguided wish for safety, characters attempt to create logically ordered urban worlds and thus cut themselves off from the land, becoming paralyzed, mired in the limited world of the real, the visible. In contrast, landscapes are both dangerous and liberating sites of journey, struggle, and ultimately confrontation with the self. For, as "Journey to the Interior" (CG) makes clear, the self remains uncharted frontier, the final quest.

In Atwood's texts the natural world repeatedly provides a touchstone or a test for the characters. Those who resist and struggle against it often fail; those who learn to read its meanings may gain power, but frequently at great personal cost. Often characters undertake quest journeys in harsh landscapes. Describing these quest journeys, Kathryn VanSpanckeren finds a recurring shamanic theme of "quests into the spirit realm . . . spirit journeys . . . dramatic descent to the underworld . . . a gaining of effective spiritual power and knowledge, and a return to the living."[3] Yet, although these travelers may sometimes gain power by breaking through the surface crust of the rational, the ordered, the linear, to access the irrational depths below, the outcomes of most of these journeys are ambiguous. Indeed, some of these journeys seem ironic or parodic.

The language of these highly crafted poems parallels the geography they describe: it is free verse, spare, condensed, minimally punctuated. The rhythms are subtly modulated, and the sound patterns are tightly knit to achieve a range of effects. Images are stark, often violent. For example, the first stanza of "A Place: Fragments" (*CG*) reads:

> Here on the rim, cringing
> under the cracked whip of winter
> we live
> in houses of ice,
> but not because we want to:
> in order to survive
> we make what we can and have to
> with what we have.

Situating us immediately in the poem ("here"), the language is spare, almost monosyllabic, avoiding rhetorical decoration, concentrating on one metaphor. Violent, cold, colorless imagery describes a desperate existence. The stanza's music is built mainly of a limited number of recurring consonants (w, h, m, c, r, t, n, v) and short vowels, thus dramatizing the contrasting long *i* in "ice" and "survive." Its rhythms emphasize winter's power and human struggle. Half of the lines end with unaccented syllables (cringing, winter, want to, have to). Monosyllables slow the pace of line seven, suggesting effort, while the spondee of "cracked whip" emphasizes winter's force. The landscape is primary; humans enter cringing, subjugated to its cruel terms. Winter cracks its whip, and we cower under the lash, making do with the limited resources available. We are in Atwood country.

Who inhabits this wintry landscape? A central narrative voice (although it may be embodied in different speakers) runs through the early poems, talking to us from a distance, usually in the present tense, telling variations of her tale of loss, alienation, quest. She is a marginalized person, often unseen, unheard, unnoticed. She frequently implies, "here I am, look at me," as she seeks to situate and point to herself. Like the Siren in *You Are Happy*, she tells and retells nightmarish or darkly humorous stories in a flat, affectless voice. She is often emotionally paralyzed, as frozen as the landscape she inhabits. As Frank Davey assesses

her, she "appears to be a spectator to her own life, standing outside both
this life and its temporal context."[4] As a result, "the principle of cause
and effect tends to disappear. . . . events become juxtaposed in space
rather than processually related. . . . [Characters] are introduced syntac-
tically as parallel subjects . . . inhabiting parallel but self-contained
experiences" (Davey, 146). This, then, is the central character of
Atwood's landscape, an alienated speaker, a victim-storyteller, insis-
tently reporting, imagining, and inscribing her tale. The emotional flatness, the distance from other people and from one's own experience, the
obsessive reiteration of details of place, and the emphasis on telling and
retelling stories all point to loss, lack, yearning. This is a world of dis-
juncture, dislocation, existential absurdity, and Gothic terror. In fact,
Judith McCombs describes the early poems as portraying a world of terrifying, claustrophobic Gothic, "interior Gothic," wilderness Gothic,
and the Gothic nightmare of the other.[5] Therefore, the poems produce
an eerie effect of distance, disconnectedness. The voice is that of the victim that Atwood defines in *Survival* as characteristically Canadian.

But, are the storytellers victims who are simply reporting what
exists? Or are they producing their victim positions in the imagining
and telling of their stories? Or, worse, is the situation reversed? Do the
tellers control the tales? Or do the tales control the tellers? As Eli Mandel observes, "there is a sinister suggestion that the stories . . . write the
lives of the story-teller."[6] These concerns echo throughout the Atwood
canon. The protagonists in *Selected Poems* have varying degrees of distance from and control over their stories. The narrator of *Power Politics* is
aware that she has created the entrapping situation she describes. But it
is in *You Are Happy* and later work that the convoluted and complex
questions of teller and tale are more fully explored.

Atwood's appearance on the literary scene fortuitously coincided with
a renaissance of Canadian literature and nationalist feeling as the nation
approached its 1967 centennial anniversary. Public interest in literature
was growing, and the newly established journal *Canadian Literature*
(started under the editorship of George Woodcock in 1959) provided a
receptive critical audience. The 1960s were a time of growth for Canadian poetry in English: 18 books of poetry were published in Canada in
1959, and over 45 in 1967.[7] In 1961, 3 new poets were published—
Atwood, Gwendolyn MacEwen, and Phyllis Gotlieb—and the number
increased to 17 in 1967. Every book published in those years received at
least one review. Since then the number of publishing Canadian poets
has continued to increase. Through her poetry, her reviews, literary crit-

icism, and other cultural work, Atwood has been in the forefront of this literary flowering.

Double Persephone (1961) is apprentice work, highly derivative, published privately the year Atwood graduated from college. In the next volume, *The Circle Game* (1966), she found her own voice, creating a uniquely Atwoodian world of Northern Gothic, a world where protagonists are locked in traps (sometimes of their own making) until they risk dangerous journeys through difficult, often interior, terrain. This book won the Governor General's Award, a notable achievement for a first volume by a young author. In less than a decade, between 1966 and 1974, Atwood published six volumes of poetry and two novels that solidified her reputation as they continued to explore and elaborate the Gothic world of Atwood country. In 1975, she compiled *Selected Poems 1965–1975,* a culmination of her poetic production to that date.

Double Persephone (1961)

During her college years, Atwood was already contributing poems to college publications and small literary journals. When she graduated in 1961 from Victoria College at age 21, Atwood printed privately a collection of seven poems, *Double Persephone* (TF 10). The project itself indicates the energy and determination that propel her career. The slim volume foreshadows the poet's future development and indicates her mastery of form, her technical facility, and her assimilation of wide-ranging English and Anglo-Canadian literary influences. The writer of these poems is a keen student of literature, yet, as is often true of first volumes, these are the poems of an apprentice, practicing the conventional forms to perfect technique. The lines carry echoes of the English poetic tradition and weave a tightly embroidered tapestry of sound patterns: slant rhyme, rhyme, alliteration, and assonance.

Thirty-five years later Atwood remembers the publication process: "My poems were . . . not very good, but . . . they showed a sort of twisted and febrile glimmer. . . . A group of them won the main poetry prize at the University [the E. J. Pratt Medal]. Madness took hold of me, and with the aid of a friend, and another friend's flatbed press, we printed them. . . . We had to print each poem separately, and then disassemble the type, as there were not enough a's for the whole book. . . . We printed 250 copies, and sold them through bookstores for 50 cents each. They now go in the rare-book trade for $1,800 a pop. Wish I'd kept some."[8]

Although it was a small volume by an unknown author, *Double Perse-phone* was well received, garnering three reviews.[9] Eli Mandel notes the influence of Jay Macpherson and comments on the book's "crisp, controlled formal gardens" and its "haunted and haunting" qualities. Peter Dale Scott finds the poems "more contrived than composed," but singles out "Persephone Departing" for its "simpler, but much more powerful understatement," while Milton Wilson praises its "precocious gloss and precision" but finds it "a bit lifeless."

The landscape here is a static, frozen one, and the poems mirror the world of frozen perfection they describe. In "Formal Garden" the protagonist reaches out to seize life but turns everything into marble, a sterile, although formally elegant construction. Touch, which ought to establish connection, produces distance, stasis.

Themes and motifs—form versus substance, life versus art, the Persephone story, the garden, touch as a means of connection or separation, the Gothic, humor, irony, and the doubling of characters and plots—recur in many of Atwood's works. Likewise, the emotionally paralyzed protagonist reappears in her fiction in various guises.

"Persephone Departing" is the best indicator of Atwood's evolving poetic skill, signaling the understated complexity and drama Atwood's later poems will achieve. Many Atwood heroines, like this powerful Persephone, will camouflage their strength and determination under a deceptive veneer of vulnerability. Persephone here is powerful and ambiguous; she contains within herself both maiden and crone.

The Circle Game (1966)

The Circle Game marks a dramatic advance, winning the Governor General's Award in 1967. While many of the themes echo those of *Double Persephone,* the poems here are more powerful, technically and thematically stronger. Pared down, unrhymed, minimally punctuated (although generously bedecked with parentheses), these poems are set in harsh landscapes and enclosed rooms. A stark and claustrophobic book, *The Circle Game* describes warring oppositions: isolation/connection, entrapment/freedom, life/death, nature/civilization. The book explores the devastating consequences of our human desire to impose order and logic on the world. Ultimately, a world based on logic and rationality is shallow and confining; consequently a deeply rooted irrationality wells up to threaten the fragile constructions we build to contain it. Paradoxically, the characters here are most vital and powerful when they submit to the forces of nature and the irrational: the speaker of the first poem has already drowned when we encounter her, and the last two poems are narrated by skeletons of dead people.

Atwood wrote these poems over a period of several years, revising and editing extensively as she tried to find a publisher for the book. The fall of 1964 was a period of heightened productivity, as she noted in a letter to her friend Charles Pachter. As she reviewed the poems she had written, more-powerful new poems emerged to replace them in the evolving collection. She sent Pachter, then a student at the Cranbrook Academy of Art in Michigan, a copy of "The Circle Game" that he set in type and illustrated with a set of lithographs. During his two years at Cranbrook he completed five such artist books.[10] Contact Press, which had first accepted, then rejected the first manuscript, called "Places, Migrations," agreed to publish the revised version and suggested the title *The Circle Game*.

Critical response to the book was favorable.[11] Tracing its evolution through successive manuscript drafts, Judith McCombs finds that it developed from a superficial book of "surface journey" to a complex and intricately structured book of archetypal "death and depth." Categorizing Atwood's early work as inscribing a "closed world," McCombs terms this book "a [Gothic] chamber of horrors" centered in the narrator (McCombs 1981, 37). In her introduction to *The Circle Game,* Sherrill E. Grace lists the book's themes: "the traps of reality, myth, language, and the pernicious roles we play, the cage of the self, and above all, the nature of human perception" (*CG,* 10). Canadian poet and novelist Michael Ondaatje describes Atwood's world as having "the form and violence of mythologies but none of the expected grandeur and costume" (29). He terms her "the quiet Mata Hari, the mysterious, violent figure who never explains."[12]

Many of the poems are simultaneously playful and serious, occasionally using surreal imagery to play variations on the possible relations between humans and the geography they uneasily inhabit. Cities represent the linear rigidity of reason, while the landscape contains the irrational, the mythic. Cameras and photographs recur, reiterating a range of artistic, psychological, and cultural dilemmas. How may an artist record life when the process of recording freezes the present moment and distances the writer? How accurate are the perceptions of any observer at any one moment? What is the impact of the observer's gaze on the observed?

The book's 28 poems comprise a "powerfully centered, symmetric, mirroring" structure, starting and ending with poems of the drowned world, and highlighting "The Circle Game" in the center (McCombs 1994, 65). The first half introduces the linear world of the city and contains almost all of the references to games, logic, and containment, while the second half focuses on poems of the frigid and threatening Canadian landscape, the paradoxically dangerous yet potentially liberating alternative to the city.

Games such as the children's circle game and the games of chess and playing cards are metaphors for the human need to impose the order that sooner or later becomes entrapping. In "An Attempted Solution for Chess Problems" the sister's solution fails, and the game ends in stalemate. The poem pits the player against the pieces, the house against the landscape, the upper floors of the house against the basement, the present against the past. The circle game of the title poem is joyless, repetitive, and suffocating.

"The City Planners" (36–37) argues that the rigid linearity of cities is destructive. Ultimately the land will triumph by undermining the carefully planned cities. Violent imagery of bruises and vicious coils reveals the city's instability and imbalance; the poem's echoes and off-rhymes (repeated *en* and *an,* as in "residential/offends/dent" "sanities/pedantic/sanitary/rational/slant/landscape/panic/bland") sharpen the focus on the city's conflicting energies. Excessive rationality threatens to explode as the poem moves from residential sanity to "panic . . . [and] bland madness" (37). Similarly, the couple in "A Meal" (42–43) learn that although they seek security they cannot evade the irrational, "the necessary cockroach" (43). The poem "A Place: Fragments" (87–91) reminds us that cities are fragile: "that man / walking on cement as though on snowshoes" knows that the streets are a veneer, a thin sheet of ice "that easily might break" (89). In the city, advertisements commodify human desire and strip it of life, as in "On the Streets, Love" (38–39). Atwood continues her critique of advertising's deadening effects in her novel *The Edible Woman.*

The book's claustrophobia and entrapment culminate in the centrally placed seven-part poem "The Circle Game" (44–55). Rituals and rules that seem to promise safety, protection, and enclosure become instead deadening constraints. Encompassing a cycle of the year and alternating between the children outside and the couple in their room, the poem is constructed like a series of concentric circles. The speaker seeks connection, yet her relationship with a distant and preoccupied partner is joyless and ritualized. Outside, children build forts and play circle games, but their activities are similarly joyless rituals. Inside, the speaker and her partner enact a series of estranging roles. Mirrors, cages, "the closed rules of . . . games," walls, forts, museums, and "prisoning rhythms" entrap them. Imagery of forts and trenches alludes to Northrop Frye's concept of the Canadian "garrison mentality," while the numerous mirror images suggest Canada's preoccupation with its search for identity.[13] The poem addresses the dynamics of sexual politics as well as national politics. The man and woman keep each other at a distance; he looks past her. Mirror and map imagery indicate the difficulty of perceiving accurately either the self or others. Frustrated by their paralysis and alienation, the speaker finally cries out for escape: "I want the circle / broken" (CG, 55).

Set against the poems of urban alienation are poems of landscape, linked to death and mythic power. These poems set up a relationship between the self and the landscape that Atwood explores throughout her work. Those who seek to order and control the world of nature fail; those who face its challenges may gain a perilous insight and power.

The first poem, the dramatic and frequently anthologized "This Is a Photograph of Me," challenges the reader to find the speaker drowned in the center. The first of Atwood's storytellers, a silenced and invisible woman, she is hidden, but invites—or dares—the persevering reader to discover her. Building from a matter-of-fact start to a dramatic climax, the speaker points out the blurred details of an old photograph but then notes parenthetically: "The photograph was taken / the day after I drowned." She explains that she is "in the lake, in the center of the picture, just under the surface," and continues: "if you look long enough, / eventually / you will be able to see me" (17). She does not describe the visible objects—a slope, a house, a lake, a branch—but, in contrast, takes 10 lines to point to the place where she lies invisibly, for the invisible is more highly charged and significant than the visible. Similarly, in "Camera" the speaker is a speck that has almost disappeared from the photo. Perhaps these poems tell us that women have become invisible in contemporary Western culture and ask that society acknowledge them. Or perhaps, as in A. M. Klein's poem "Portrait of the Poet as Landscape," the speakers are artists, invisible because an indifferent society does not recognize the value of poetry and artistic production.[14]

Photography recurs as a metaphor in Atwood's work, linked with other visual images such as mirrors and reflections. Such media record a visible surface at one point in time but cannot reveal the full measure of a subject, its depths, its fluctuations over time. On the contrary, photographs, mirrors, and reflections suggest the indecipherability of the subject, for as Lacan proposes in his theory of the Mirror Stage, the self can never perceive itself directly, but only as reflected in others; thus, these images represent the deferral of meaning, the ultimate inscrutability of the subject. Consequently, the photographer in seeking to fixate falsifies, distances, and freezes that which is observed. This is the danger of all art, a danger that Atwood seeks to avoid through a variety of strategies that resist closure and offer multiple possibilities.

"Journey to the Interior," like Emily Dickinson's poems of the haunted self, describes what may well be the most dangerous journey, the journey into the interior of the self, a more alien landscape than the external world. In Atwood's world there is never only one Truth, but many approximate truths. Thus, the speaker of "A Place: Fragments" finds that there is no one center, but many centers that "travel with us unseen." The poem asks how we can make sense of the world. Is it through order, through chaos, or through some balance of the two? Is there a key to the mysteries: "something not lost or hidden / but just not found yet / . . . something too huge and simple / for us to see" (90–91).

The speakers of the last two poems, "The Explorers" and "The Settlers," like the speaker in "This Is a Photograph of Me," achieve their power from union with the natural world. Ironically, the dead speakers are more vivid, more present, than the city dwellers locked in their grid-like enclave. Sherrill Grace writes: "perhaps the deaths described . . . are both necessary and propitious" (*CG,* 13) for the speakers merge with the landscape where children now play.

Although the next poetry volume, *The Animals in That Country,* elaborates many of the same themes—such as city and landscape, the rational and the irrational, the real and the mythic—it is somewhat less claustrophobic. In contrast to the "interior Gothic" of *The Circle Game,* its focus is more outward, there are more characters (a landlady, hunters and trappers, surveyors, a foundling), and relationships have more dimensions, even containing the possibility of love.

The Animals in That Country (1968)

By the time *The Animals in That Country,* her second volume of poetry, appeared, Atwood was already a rising literary star. Although her novels were as yet unpublished (*The Edible Woman* would appear in 1969, "Up in the Air So Blue" is still unpublished), she was writing short stories and TV scripts, and her poems were appearing in small literary magazines and in limited editions of artist books illustrated and typeset by her friend Charles Pachter. She won the first prize in the Centennial Commission Poetry Competition in 1967. John Robert Colombo invited her to join a group he was forming, "a national organization to further poetry in Canada" to be called the League of Canadian Poets, whose members were to include Earle Birney, Dorothy Livesay, Eli Mandel, Al Purdy, Robin Skelton, and Raymond Souster. She had completed her course work toward the Ph.D. at Harvard but set aside her dissertation to focus on her fiction and poetry.

Geography and landscape continue to pose questions of identity and meaning in *The Animals in That Country.* The book explores with humor and irony the human wish to make a mark in the world. Hunters seek their prey, surveyors blaze their signs, pioneers try to tame the unruly land, poets assert their voices. But time and nature foil most of these efforts. Those who deny the power of the land do so at their peril. The characters here—tourists, exiles, and invaders—face imperatives of journey and quest. They hope to gain totemic power through connection to the landscape. But through their wish to subjugate, delineate, and control, the colonizers often upset the natural order, with devastating consequences both for the land and for the would-be controllers. Giant tortoises and other animals are destroyed because of human manipulation of the natural environment. Pioneers who try to impose their linear vision on the curvilinear land end up deranged. Surveyors cut stumps and blaze their red marks, but time blurs the marks and leaches the blazes of meaning. These poems remind us that humans perch precariously on the planet, like roomers and renters in alien surroundings.

As we have already seen, along with many other Canadian writers, Atwood exploits the imagery of freezing and winter to describe life's dangers. As she observes in *Survival,* "there is a sense in Canadian literature that the true and only season here is winter: the others are either preludes to it or mirages concealing it" (49). Interestingly, her work itself has often been charged with emotional "coldness." Judith McCombs observes that "virtually every [male] Canadian reviewer" praises the aesthetic content, but finds the poems cold, even "inhuman." She wonders "would the same work, by one Martin Atwood, have evoked the same warmth-needing critical responses?" One reviewer, Mona Van Duyn, finds interesting the "distrust of the mind of man, the word, the imagination, even the poem."[15]

These poems negotiate the borders of realism and myth, as do many of Atwood's texts. On the one hand, a mythic vision of the world may lead to the hypocrisy of the foxhunters and bullfighters who imagine heroic and heraldic deaths for the animals they kill (as in "The animals in that country"). On the other hand, in "Notes from various pasts" the speaker is nostalgic for the wisdom that she associates with a past innocence and simplicity. But spiritual or shamanic vision is difficult to come by, for "the gods avoid revealing themselves" (24). In their quest for vision or for prey, hunters and trappers enact a complex ritual with the animals they pursue. Wishing to destroy, to smash, but also to celebrate and to gain knowledge of the alluring other, the trappers feel guilty both "because / they are not animals" and "because they are" (35). In "Arctic syndrome: dream fox" (48–49) the fox dreams of pursuing the hunter.

Poems of landscape predominate and frame the book. The first poem, "Provisions," about city dwellers unprepared for their journey, prepares us for more poems of confrontation with a harsh nature. Two ill-equipped travelers try to make their way across "the disastrous ice" carrying useless urban objects such as file cards and streetcar tickets. The concluding poem, "Axiom" (69), casts a love poem in the form of a geography project. Throughout the book enclosed spaces such as a rooming house and the Royal Ontario Museum open up to raise fundamental questions of history and survival. Even the landlady, a menacing figure in the poem bearing her name, becomes a threatening landscape herself as the tenant dreams futilely of escaping from her.

Several poems in this volume ("At the tourist centre in Boston," "It is dangerous to read newspapers," "A voice," and "Backdrop addresses cowboy") use landscape to explore the cultural, economic, and political relations between Canada and the United States. "At the tourist centre in Boston" challenges the image of Canada packaged for tourism, an airbrushed depiction of picturesque mountains and blue lakes. In contrast to the "unsuspecting" woman at the tourist center, readers of Atwood know that the unseen world below the water's surface is alive with portents and mysterious beings. "A voice" examines American and Canadian imaginative appropriation of the land. Walt Whitman may be the egocentric poetic voice that enters the landscape and whose expansionist, all-inclusive vision subsumes difference. Atwood's poem reflects the more fragmented and tentative stance characteristic of the Canadian and postmodern connection to the land, a stance fraught with contradiction and paradox.[16]

The antiwar poem "It is dangerous to read newspapers" describes the speaker's awareness that we are all, civilians as well as soldiers, implicated in the atrocities of war. A later volume, *True Stories,* will revisit themes of war and political terrorism. In "Backdrop addresses cowboy" the scenery, supposedly the silent background, gains a voice as the poem plays with the idea of reality and artifice and castigates the heroic cowboy film star for his disregard of the land. Instead of watching the "starspangled cowboy" in admiration, the backdrop asks "what about me," and calls attention to the selfish destructiveness of the cowboy mentality that perceives everything as a target.

The two longest poems, "Progressive insanities of a pioneer" and "Speeches for Dr. Frankenstein," are central statements of Atwood's credo, demonstrating the pitfalls of the rational, linear standpoint. "Progressive insanities of a pioneer" presents a settler who, like the city planners, fights to contain the natural world but loses the struggle. In *Survival* Atwood writes, "The Canadian pioneer is a square man in a round whole; he faces the problem of trying to fit a straight line in a curved space" (*SV,* 120). In this poem the pioneer arrives, declares himself the center of the world, builds fences, and plows the soil in rows. By imposing a rigid linear thinking on the open space he sets himself at odds with the natural world. Whereas in Genesis Adam named the animals and things of the world, in this poem, "things . . . refused to let him name them" (*AC,* 39). The pioneer tries in vain to build solidity when acceptance of fluidity would serve him better. He would do well to build an ark, but instead builds a house.

"Speeches for Dr. Frankenstein" depicts the artist's plight, the tragedy of creation. In creating the monster, the artist seeks to produce perfection. Because the creator is flawed, the work will be as well, and the artist rejects the imperfect creature. Atwood explains that the original *Frankenstein* story by Mary Shelley is "a creation parable, where God forsakes Adam: instead of taking care of the monster, Dr. Frankenstein deserts him because he can't face the grotesque creature that he's produced. But the monster's not *evil.* . . . He's totally innocent. . . . In my poem it's the monster who deserts his maker—not the other way around."[17] The power balance between them shifts, as the logical scientist grows gaunt while the sensitive creation grows more powerful and liberates itself. In the laboratory, the enclosed gray world of scientific logic and rationality, the scientist holds power, but outside, in the numinous, freezing Arctic landscape of the concluding stanzas, Dr. Frankenstein shivers and shrinks, while the "sparkling" monster gambols and dances on the ice.

Landscape here becomes a vehicle for describing relationships, for even the book's love poems are cast as geography. In "Attitudes towards the mainland" contrasting geographical outlooks characterize the couple: she tries to insist "on solidity," but he resists her descriptions and sees only a lake with drowned people. A frozen river stands for a time of stagnation; a hook locked in the ice looks forward to the "hook and eye" poem that initiates the turbulent love poems of *Power Politics.* Here, as in *The Edible Woman,* the politics of the hunt infect human relationships. The couple in "A pursuit" know that they "hunt each other" and "through the tangle of each other / . . . hunt ourselves" (66–67). The speaker of "I was reading a scientific article" explains that the lover is "a new planet. . . . a lost civilization. . . . a total universe" (65).

A love poem in the form of a geography project, "Axiom" concludes the book as the narrator explains the process of relationship in terms of exploration, the geography of land and sea. Whereas previously, in "Formal Garden" (TF) or "The Circle Game," touch was a distancing device, touch here is the medium of connection and knowledge: "my hands / where they touch you, create / small inhabited islands" (69). Touch figures prominently, placed in the central stanza, establishing relationship and connection. Linked to geography, touch enables the narrator to be at home in the world. Thus, *The Animals in That Country* travels from its starting point, a difficult journey over frozen terrain ("Provisions"), to conclude with a loving connection framed in terms of geographical discovery.

Journey in a difficult landscape (both external and internal) is the subject of the next book of poetry, *The Journals of Susanna Moodie.* Within this framework Atwood interrogates paradoxes of language, identity, and the complex relationships of the immigrant to the land.

The Journals of Susanna Moodie (1970)

The Journals of Susanna Moodie takes the form of a fictive diary written by an actual nineteenth-century English settler in Canada. In Atwood's retelling of her story, Moodie becomes the archetypal immigrant, a prototype of the Canadian experience as she negotiates the polarities of bush and town, England and Canada, rational line and irrational curve, enclosure and escape, so as to be at home in language and in the world.

During the period of 1965 to 1966 when Atwood had returned to Harvard University to resume her doctoral studies, a "vivid" dream that she had written an opera about Susanna Moodie prompted her to reread Moodie's narratives of her experiences, *Roughing It in the Bush* and *Life in the Clearings,* and so to find personal affinities with her. Away from her native country, struggling to succeed in the alienating environments of the United States and the male-centered academic world of Harvard, Atwood was then experiencing conflicts similar to Moodie's. Over the next year and a half, she wrote a series of poems that rewrite and respond to Moodie's story, using the nineteenth-century woman's voice to express her own conflicts. According to Atwood: "It was the unsaid in her work that I found compelling. . . . As for Susanna herself, I suppose she was my youthful Ms. Hyde, and I was the Ms. Jekyll through which she manifested herself . . . a negative to my positive, or vice versa. She was appalled by the wilderness, I by the city, once upon a time. Both of us were uprooted. Both of us were far from home, both anxious, both scrabbling for cash, both under pressure. Both knew the space between what could be said safely and what needed to be withheld from speech. I said for her what she couldn't say, and she for me. It's often over such distances, such emptiness and silence, that the poetic voice must travel."[18] And, just as Moodie interpreted the mid-nineteenth-century English woman immigrant's experience for her audience, Atwood interprets the experience of late twentieth-century middle-class Anglo-Canadian women for hers.

Summing up this book, Jerome H. Rosenberg finds that it "embodies Atwood's most concentrated use of the Canadian past to comment on the Canadian present."[19] He reads the book as "a clarion call for community," but finds that the community Atwood asks for "is a cold community" grounded in reason rather than "love and compassion . . . and . . . human warmth" (50). Indeed, Moodie's vision is a stringent rather than warm one, but I find that these poems warn of the dangers of unmitigated reason and urge acceptance of the irrational, however unsettling and perilous that may be.

Charles Pachter writes that when Atwood sent him a manuscript of *The Journals of Susanna Moodie* he was "stunned by its beauty and power. . . . I realized everything I had done up until that moment must be a rehearsal for this" (Pachter, xx). He produced a prototype for an artist's book using different styles and sizes of type combined with original lithographs, collages, and drawings. Because the costs of producing this book were considered prohibitively high, *The Journals of Susanna Moodie* was first published by Oxford University Press with paper collage illustrations by Atwood. Years later Pachter borrowed money to produce 120 copies of his version hand printed by two Spanish master printers, the Bello-Sanchez brothers. In 1984 the printed book toured in an art exhibition commemorating the bicentennial of the arrival of Loyalist immigrants from the United States to Ontario. In 1997, a facsimile version of Pachter's edition appeared, published simultaneously by Houghton Mifflin and Macfarlane Walter and Ross. In the foreword to this book, David Staines writes that Pachter's "images complement and complete the poem, the text and the visual image functioning interdependently as a new and integrated work of art" (Pachter, xv).

Although this book continues to explore the complicated relationships of settlers to the landscape, its tightly knit storytelling structure and its use of a historic persona as narrator depart from her previous books of poetry. Atwood finds in Moodie's life a deep-seated "schizophrenia" that she attributes to all (nonaboriginal) Canadians, faced with a difficult land. Her afterword describes Moodie's self-division, her two voices, the "poetic" voice that writes about flowers and pretty scenes, and the darker voice of nightmares, struggles, and blood.

Who was the historic Moodie? Born Susanna Strickland in 1803 to a literate and prosperous English family that fell on hard times with the death of her father, she gained a reputation by writing poetry and essays for small literary journals. In 1831 she married Lieutenant J. W. Dunbar Moodie. Because of their difficulties supporting themselves in England, husband, wife, and young daughter came to Canada in 1832 to settle on the north shore of Lake Ontario near Port Hope. Moodie found it difficult to adjust to living in the bush and to having for neighbors people who might have been her servants in England. When their fortunes improved, the Moodies moved to Belleville.

Mrs. Moodie wrote poetry and fiction with a didactic purpose, most of it of little contemporary interest. Her two best-known books, *Roughing It in the Bush* (1852) and *Life in the Clearings* (1853), tell the story of her experiences as a settler in Upper Canada. Her sketches of the characters she encountered break out of the stilted diction and formalism that mar her other writings. *Roughing It* has become a minor Canadian classic. Michael Peterman sums up her literary ambitions and political allegiance: "She was imaginatively anchored to social and literary ideas she had learned in England and which she came . . . to idealize even more because of distance."[20]

Moodie herself appears as a character in works by other writers, including *At My Heart's Core* by Robertson Davies, *Small Ceremonies* by

Carol Shields, and *Susanna* by Elizabeth Hopkins. Atwood rewrites
Moodie's story, emphasizing the aspects that she finds most compelling:
the settler's conflicted doubleness, her love-hate relationship with her
new country, her confrontation with the terrifying but numinous possibilities of the natural world.

In *The Journals* Atwood writes a critique of the conventional stereotypes of the pioneer as conqueror of nature. Instead, these poems
inscribe a character who is thwarted by the land. Atwood explains that
her volume "explores the tensions between straight line [of civilization]
and curve" of nature (*SV,* 124). She analyzes Moodie's double vision:
"Mrs. Moodie's determination to preserve her Wordsworthian faith col-
lides with the difficulty she has in doing so when Nature fails time and
time again to come through for her. The result is a markedly double-
minded attitude towards Canada. . . . Two emotions—faith in the
Divine Mother and a feeling of hopeless imprisonment—follow each
other on the page without break or explanation. . . . Moodie copes with
the contradiction by dividing Nature itself in two, reserving the splen-
did adjectives and the Divine-Mother attributes for the half that she
approves of and failing to account for the hostile activities of the other
half" (*SV,* 51).

Atwood's afterword argues that Moodie's doubleness persists in contemporary Canadians: "We are all immigrants to this place even if we
were born here: the country is too big for anyone to inhabit completely,
and in the parts unknown to us we move in fear, exiles and invaders.
This country is something that must be chosen—it is so easy to leave—
and if we do choose it we are still choosing a violent duality" (62). Sherrill Grace finds in the phrase "violent duality" a key to Atwood's texts
and chooses it as the title for her study of Atwood.

The book starts with a surprising poem:

> I take this picture of myself
> and with my sewing scissors
> cut out the face.

Now it is more accurate:

> Where my eyes were,
> every-
> thing appears

This poem highlights the book's central themes of perception, of civilization versus the bush, and of the narrator's complicated relationship to her new world. Imagery of vision, language, and transformation elucidates the immigrant's struggle to come to terms with an alien environment where the boundaries between plant and animal, civilization and wilderness, human and animal are permeable. She needs "wolf's eyes" to understand her new environment. Judith McCombs argues persuasively that Moodie herself ultimately becomes a wendigo, a creature allied with the darker aspects of nature.[21]

Moodie records her alienation from the new land as a problem of language. She herself is the foreign language ("Disembarking at Quebec"). But learning the bush language proves difficult because it is not a human one; it is the language of wolves, bears, trees, the land itself. Contrasts between civilization (with its straightness, order, and imagined certainty) and bush (wild, disordered, jagged, and unpredictable) heighten the tentativeness of the settlers' position as the poems contrast alienation and adjustment, order and disorder, often in terms of language.

Journal I 1832–1840

This section of the book depicts Moodie's life from her arrival in Canada through her short stay on a farm near Cobourg and then on a farm in a more remote area. "Disembarking" depicts the immigrant's alienation from the new country. The accouterments of civilization she brings with her, her knitting, a book, a shawl, insulate her from the bush and combine with her lack of conviction to keep her from fitting in. In the poem's terms she is unheard and invisible in this country. She herself has become "a word / in a foreign language." In "The Wereman" Moodie imagines that her husband changes shape when he is out of her sight. He may change her also through his altered perception, "the fox eye, the owl eye." In "Further Arrivals" she explains that the immigrant's journey is an interior one as well. When she looks in the mirror she finds herself becoming like the land, her fingers like twigs; but the shape is alien to her. The paradox of Moodie's complex relationship to Canada is summed up in "The Two Fires": "each refuge fails / us; each danger / becomes a haven" (23). Danger becomes refuge; light turns into dark, order into trap. In "Departure from the Bush" she realizes she has not yet learned the lessons the land has to teach her.

Journal II 1840–1871

This journal covers the period when Moodie lived in Belleville and wrote her two books about life in Canada. It starts with "Death of a Young Son by Drowning," a poem about the loss of her hopes for the future. Her dead son, through his burial in the ground, becomes her link to this alien place. The nine poems that comprise this journal describe the arrival of newcomers, deaths of children, frightening dreams, and human acts of violence. "The Immigrants" contemplates the newcomers sympathetically and foresees the difficulties they will face. The last poem, "The Double Voice," juxtaposes Moodie's attempts to find nature uplifting against her knowledge "that men sweat." This section emphasizes Moodie's characteristic doubleness.

Journal III 1871–1969

Atwood writes: "Most of Journal III was written after I had come across a little-known photograph of Susanna Moodie as a mad-looking and very elderly lady. The poems take her through an estranged old age, into death and beyond. After her death she can hear the twentieth century above her, bulldozing away her past, but she refuses to be ploughed under completely" (63–64). This section extends Moodie's life up to the present time, turning her into a crone, identified with the land, the pioneer past. In "Later in Belleville: Career" she has time and money for more luxuries, but she is wistful, finding that the genteel refinements she had missed so much before mean less to her now than when she lacked them.

To be at home in the bush, Moodie must accept its disorder and contradictions. Like the drowned speaker of "This Is a Photograph of Me," she eventually attains power from her posthumous connection to the land. After death she is more certain of her relationship to the land. Riding a bus in modern Toronto she asserts defiantly, "this is my kingdom still," and reminds us that the landscape still exerts power over us: "this is the center of a forest / your place is empty" ("A Bus Along St. Clair: December," 61). The transformation is complete: Moodie has become a crusty crone, the spirit of the land she inhabited so uneasily.

In the same year that *The Journals of Susanna Moodie* was published, Atwood published *Procedures for Underground,* continuing to develop ideas of transformation, pioneer life, mythic rites, and the encounters between humans and animals.

Procedures for Underground (1970)

This book continues Atwood's preoccupations with transformation, the tensions between self and landscape, humans and animals. As its title suggests, its focus is on the shadow world, the world reflected in water, the world on the other side of the picture, "the country beneath / the earth" (24). There are more affirmative possibilities here, more positive relationships, inscribed in the poet's gift of transforming and memorializing events, in the evolving ice age couple who are learning to make fire, in the speaker who brings food to her partner, in the tributes to the protagonist's parents and sister, and in the recognition that terrifying ritual descents may have successful, even if problematic, outcomes.

Yet even while she focuses on ritual, myth, and numinous experience, Atwood's vision also becomes increasingly political. Two poems interject the antiwar theme (first broached in *AC*). "Three Desk Objects" expresses predicaments voiced by many poets during the Vietnam War as they believe even ordinary objects now seem to be complicit in war's destructiveness. Similarly, "Projected Slide of an Unknown Soldier" recaptures the terror of war in a photographic slide of a soldier's horror-stricken face.

The title poem, based on a Bella Coola legend, describes the journey of the seer, the wise person, or the artist, the one who journeys underground, or into her own depths, and comes back with a wisdom that is awesome and fearsome for the traveler as well as for those who have not made the journey. The matter-of-fact, "how-to" title belies the poem's message of terror and danger: "For this gift, as for all gifts, you must / suffer" (25). In "Fishing for Eel Totems," another poem of shamanic vision, the speaker gains magic knowledge of the fish language from eating the eel. Again, as in *The Circle Game* and *The Journals of Susanna Moodie,* some of the personae here speak from underground ("We Don't Like Reminders") or under water ("Interview with a Tourist"). This book is replete with doublings and mysteries, with dreams, and with talismanic animals. "Dream: Bluejay or Archeopteryx" and "Delayed Message" speak of numinous beings rising from the water, while "Buffalo in Compound: Alberta" links the ordinary zoo buffalo to a horned god. In contrast to these totemic animals, "Dreams of the Animals" articulates Atwood's perception that civilization is disrupting the lives of animals. While the wild animals dream lyrically of other animals, the iguana in the pet shop dreams of the sawdust in its cage.

"Highest Altitude," "A Morning," and "A Soul, Geologically" continue familiar themes of journey through dangerous terrain and of the
connection between self and other, self and landscape. Human connection finds a place here in "Carrying Food Home in Winter" and in the
poems of family. Throughout Atwood's work, political overtones color
the getting, preparing, and eating of food. "Carrying Food Home in
Winter" is a love poem that celebrates the act of nourishing another as a
means of connection. The food is transformed into human bodies, as
eating, cooking, and caring for each other become acts of love.

A new persona appears here, the poet, the author. Several poems
address the connection between artists and their subjects. "Eden Is a
Zoo" describes a crayon drawing of the speaker's parents. The artist
then controls the parents in her picture and imagines that they are
trapped there: "Are they content? / Do they want to get out?" (6) The
concluding poem, "Dancing Practice," depicts an imperfect practice ses-
sion and contrasts it with the idealized version "transformed" by the
artist's vision: "(because / I say it)" (79). Peter Stevens finds in this statement a triumphal affirmation of "the prerogatives of poetry in a threatening, tense world."[22] And yet there is also a tongue-in-cheek quality to
these affirmations of the poet's power. There are two other poems of this
type, and they are also ambiguous in tone.

"Younger Sister, Going Swimming" places the poet in parentheses as
she watches her younger sister about whom she writes her poem. The
juxtaposition of poet with the subject of the poem, and the ironic parentheses raise familiar Atwoodian questions of the relationship of story and
teller. "Woman Skating" is a strikingly visual picture of the narrator's
mother at an outdoor ice-skating rink. It ends with a gesture toward
memory, or the construct of poetry that preserves the moment in memory. "Dancing Practice" brings the book full circle, returning to the
theme articulated in "Eden Is a Zoo," celebrating (perhaps whimsically)
or questioning the poet's power to transform, contain, create, or control
an imagined world.

The world of *Procedures for Underground* is a richer one, with a larger
group of characters, a wider range of themes, and more affirmative possibilities, than *The Circle Game*. In contrast, the next book, *Power Politics*,
shrinks into a claustrophobic, obsessive, enclosed urban world, where
the two central figures spar with each other for control. The poet's
power is somewhat suspect here, for it becomes again a distancing strategy.

Power Politics (1971)

Power Politics is a sequence of poems exploring the situation of "The Circle Game," the complex and intricate power struggles of heterosexual relationships. The presentation here is an early contribution to an evolving feminist analysis of social issues, for the concept of heterosexual relationships as political was a new one, first articulated by Kate Millett in her groundbreaking book *Sexual Politics,* published in 1970. In fact, when Atwood's book appeared, interviewer Margaret Kaminski expressed surprise that a book called *Power Politics* dealt with heterosexual relationships rather than, for example, women in unions. Atwood explains that while there are defined rules and strategies for "objectified, external encounters" such as labor unions and for fighting wars, personal relationships are often difficult because they are fraught with emotion and lack clear rules.[23]

Power Politics marks a dramatic shift in Atwood's poetry. In contrast to her preceding books, this volume is an urban one, set chiefly indoors, in restaurants, houses, movie theaters, places where two people take center stage. Yet although the setting is different from previous books, and the plot focuses on two central characters, familiar Atwood concerns recur. The voice is one we recognize: the speaker's ironic distance, her self-conscious observation of herself and her partner, her use of the present tense, her witty allusiveness, and her bemused stance of victim-storyteller. Familiar paradoxes recur: the speaker is both victim and creator of her story. The lovers torment each other, but they remain locked in the embrace/struggle: Speaking in the persona of a movie-goer, she asserts, "I paid my money, I / want to see what happens . . . I'm / finally an addict" (3). The book is a witty, acerbic, and inventive monologue addressed to the speaker's partner. By turns she questions, cajoles, describes, and attempts to classify and categorize him by comparing him to a diverse series of beings and phenomena including a wooden general, a comic book superhero, "a strange biological phenomenon," Jesus Christ, "a marooned starfish," a stone, a soldier, a hostile nation, Frankenstein's creature, melted gold, "the sun in reverse," a bird, a fishhook. Alternately serious and comic in its examination of the embattled terrain of heterosexual relationships, the book juxtaposes imagery and symbolism ranging widely from the Christian religious iconography of the crucifixion, to popular legends and folktales such as Dracula and Bluebeard, to the mystic philosophy of the tarot, to the rhetoric of war, to comic books, and to Hollywood films.

The book's cover design by William Kimber, based on a watercolor by Atwood, converts the tarot's Hanged Man icon into a bandaged woman hanging upside down from the outstretched arm of an armored knight. Bound together, the bandaged woman and the man encased in armor are both locked up, enclosed, rigid, immobilized. Thus the cover points to the paralyzing effect of traditional gender-role stereotypes of heroic rescuing male and fragile dependent woman.

Just as the "knight in shining armor" carries a host of connotations, there are a range of qualities associated with the Hanged Man of the tarot, including stagnation and frustration, loss of touch with reality, psychic abilities, sacrifice, victim consciousness, total trust in and surrender to a higher force or being, initiation, and transition from one state into another.[24] Arthur Edward Waite interprets the hanged man as signifying "deep entrancement, not suffering, . . . life in suspension, . . . great awakening."[25] Moreover, according to Waite, "[I]t is a card of profound significance, but all the significance is veiled" (116). Atwood exploits many of these possibilities—including the veiled significance—both seriously and comically.

The epigraph to this book is "you fit into me," a widely anthologized poem that signals the subject of the volume, the power struggles in romantic relationships between men and women. It begins:

> you fit into me
> like a hook into an eye
>
> (1)

Minimalist, unpunctuated, deceptively simple, the poem lures us in, placing the reader ("you") squarely in the poem with an image suggesting at one level romantic and sexual fulfillment (in these days of Velcro fasteners, we need to remember the hook and eye that has been a traditional fastener for women's clothing) and at another level something more sinister. We may imagine a love poem will follow. The ordinariness of a familiar pairing such as the hooks and eyes that fasten clothing evokes an ordered, comfortable, domesticated world. The first couplet consists of a short first line of direct statement and a longer second line that is a simile expanding the meaning of the first line. This leads us to expect that a similar pattern will recur, that ideas will be developed, and that a series of similes will continue to elaborate the initial concept. But the expanding rhythm collapses in the truncated second pair of lines.

Simultaneously, the comfortable image breaks open, and the poet inserts alternative meanings of "hook" and "eye" to reveal a viscerally painful and destructive relationship.

> a fish hook
>
> an open eye

And somehow, the poem has turned on its reader, for the "you" that the poem addresses has become the perpetrator of violence. The situation the poem describes is ongoing in the present: there is no end punctuation, no closure, no mitigation. Moreover, there is no alternative perspective, no omniscient author to explain or offer context. This poem is vintage Atwood in its sly deflation of romantic plot possibilities; its insistence on the power struggle within sexual relationships; its rhetorical control, ambiguity, wordplay, and dramatic reversal. The poem may be read as a searing indictment of a particular relationship or of the whole arena of sexual politics, or as an archly playful deconstruction of contemporary Western romantic love conventions and of readers' expectations for love poetry. Atwood apparently intended the poem to be humorous. She is somewhat bemused that whereas audiences laugh at poems that mock women written by male poets, they are shocked and horrified by her epigram.[26]

The book holds up for examination the overwrought expectations, the superheated obsessions of romantic ideology, and the stereotypes of appropriate sex-role behavior, female compliance, and male assertiveness. Romantic relationships in Atwood's work are often toxic and addictive. One of her many female protagonists, for instance, Marian McAlpin, Rennie Wilford, or Joan Foster, could be the speaker of these poems, wryly observing and demonizing her lover as she flees from his camera or his hostile gaze. The poems are love poems full of pain, separation, and reconciliation. The pair feed on their illusions and desires, magnifying and exaggerating the partner's traits as their moods change. For example, in "They eat out" the woman plunges a fork into his heart and he changes into a glowing figure wearing a superhero's costume. The other diners are awed or bored: "they cannot decide if you are a new weapon / or only a new advertisement" (5). Is he a superhero or ridiculous? Or both? These poems remind us that conventional romance ideologies contribute to inflated fantasies that the beloved cannot fulfill; the resulting heights of joy and depths of agony are produced by the lover's imagination.

The speaker admits her complicity in their embattled relationship. Indeed, she wonders: "why did I create you?" (47) She has been distancing herself and analyzing their actions like a scientist: "I approach this love / like a biologist / pulling on my rubber / gloves & white labcoat" (10). Her analytic stance and her resistance to touch are symptoms of emotional withholding that often appear in the Atwood canon. Moreover, she is collecting their experiences for her own artistic purposes: "Please die I said / so I can write about it" (10).

McCombs draws convincing parallels between this book and Mary Shelley's narrative of Frankenstein. In both books the first part describes the creation and rejection of the creature, the central part speaks of the creature's travels in the world, and the conclusion describes the creature's destruction of his creator. In her view, the central section of *Power Politics,* with its poems about war, reflects global horrors, the "atomic nightmare given life" (McCombs 1981, 50). In "at first I was given centuries," Atwood's narrator ruminates in a darkly humorous vein on the increasing destructiveness and speed of wars. Her meditation "We hear nothing these days / from the ones in power" shows how power and brute force act to silence communication. These lines prefigure *The Handmaid's Tale* and many of the poems in *True Stories* that continue the inquiry into institutionalized power and governmental oppression.

Developing the parallel with Shelley's novel further, we note that just as Frankenstein feels guilt and remorse for his creation, the narrator of *Power Politics* regrets her creation, remarking "it was my fault but you helped" (55). Nevertheless, she has set the plot in motion and it is moving inexorably to its own denouement. The victim storyteller's recognition of her complicity in creating the stories she inhabits is a subtle but significant shift in Atwood's work. From this recognition, the victim may conceivably become aware of her power and the possibility of making other choices in her life and in her plot. Awareness of her responsibility may help the narrator to take steps to move from what Atwood describes in *Survival* as victim position one (unawareness of one's victimization) or two (I am a victim but that is inevitable, a law of nature or society) toward position three (anger at victimization) or even four (creative nonvictimhood). And the speakers of the next volume, *You Are Happy,* move to the nonvictim position.

The narrator of *Power Politics* is both creator and victim of the stories she tells. As Dennis Cooley's rhetorical analysis demonstrates, she wields great power through her control of language.[27] Rather than shrinking submissively, she is exaggeratedly present, assertive. Cooley argues that

at first her questions are rhetorical, almost phrased as attacks as she
pushes the man away, but by the end of the book they are more likely to
be requests for information as she seems to acknowledge his pain and to
offer future possibility. Whereas Cooley sees the speaker as changing,
becoming more pliant and accepting of her lover, I read the book as a
continuing struggle, with lapses in the hostilities, requests for truces,
and resumption of the battle. The concluding poem is ominous: the
lover is traveling toward the narrator "carrying a new death / which is
mine and no-one else's." Yet he is walking "towards firm ground and
safety" (56). If the lover is bringing her death (literal or metaphorical),
then where is the firm ground? Whose is the safety? Does his safety
result from his killing her?

   Power Politics, like the previous books of poetry, is spoken by one central voice, the victim-storyteller. Like the other books, it is tightly knit
thematically and stylistically as well as narratively. Indeed, *Power Politics*
may be read as one long poem, a series of variations, ranging from comic
to tragic, on the theme of heterosexual relationships. In later books,
starting with *You Are Happy,* there is a greater range of voices, and the
storytellers become more aware of their responsibility for the stories
they tell. *You Are Happy* features the voices of mythic beings, Circe and
Ulysses, and marginalized creatures whose voices Atwood translates for
us, such as a pig, worms, and the head of a decapitated hen. The central
speakers of *You Are Happy,* the enchantress Circe and the contemporary
woman, choose the role of nonvictim for themselves as they explore the
possibilities of heterosexual love and the implications of stories and storytelling.

You Are Happy (1974)

You Are Happy is one of Atwood's most lyrical sequences, published the
year after she was separated from James Polk and moved to Alliston,
Ontario, with Graeme Gibson. Focusing on heterosexual love, on myth,
and on the paradoxes of stories and storytelling, this book contrasts with
the more cynical and Gothic *Power Politics* in which both characters take
turns as victim. In the three-year interval between these two books,
Atwood continued to explore the problem of victimization. In *Survival*
she argues that people may choose to be "creative non-victims"; at the
conclusion of *Surfacing* the narrator decides not to think of herself as a
powerless victim. Similarly, the central speakers in *You Are Happy,* the

priestess/goddess/enchantress Circe and the contemporary women, are the equals of their male companions and reject the victim role.

You Are Happy is composed of four sections, each with its own voice(s) telling stories. The first and last sections are set in the present, while the two central sections are set in a mythic past. The first section, "You Are Happy," describes an ending relationship, and the last, "There Is Only One of Everything," describes a growing one. The two central sections tell the Homeric legend of the hero Odysseus and the enchantress Circe from the point of view of characters who are silent in the original Greek version: "Songs of the Transformed" are the songs sung by Odysseus's sailors whom Circe has transformed into animals, and "Circe/Mud Poems" tells Circe's story.

The first section describes a relationship that is ending. Language has failed the couple. Poems with such titles as "Useless," "Memory," "Chaos Poem," and "Repent" hint at the unhappiness and loss. "November" alludes to the year's end, as the speaker prepares to heed the advice of "Mournful November" to pare down, strip away the past, cut her losses:

> Kill what you can't save
> what you can't eat throw out
> what you can't throw out bury
> What you can't bury give away
>
> (17)

Even "Spring," which might suggest rebirth, emphasizes the ending that must come before rebirth can take place. The speaker confesses that an "apocalypse [is] coiled in [her] tongue" as she searches for the word "finished" (23). Centered and set off on two lines, the repeated iteration of "finished" accentuates the finality and gives the impression of an echo, the lingering memory of a word after the fact.

Akin to the echo is reflection, and, not surprisingly, mirrors, a recurring Atwood motif, figure in this story of failed love as well. Mirrors in Atwood stand for a range of aesthetic ideas connected with stasis and movement and for psychological issues such as the search for identity, narcissistic self-absorption, entrapment, and stasis. In *A Room of One's Own,* Virginia Woolf wrote that women are expected to be mirrors for men, reflecting them back in images larger than life. The narrator in "Tricks with Mirrors" at first assumes such a role, reflecting her partner while commenting ironically that "Mirrors / are the perfect lovers" (24).

But the poem itself is a trick with a mirror, for the mirror speaks and reminds him "there is more," urging him to "think about the frame," the larger context, the world beyond his narcissistic wish for reflection.

In the book's second section, "Songs of the Transformed," 10 creatures that are usually marginalized and silent, even unnoticed—a pig, a bull, a rat, a crow, worms, an owl, the Siren, a fox, a hen's head, and a corpse—sing their songs, articulating their wryly humorous or somewhat sinister stories. The pigs, drawn from the legend of Odysseus, whose warrior companions were transformed into swine by the sorceress Circe, tell their stories here along with other creatures. Some of them, such as the rat or the owl, exact revenge on the humans for past wrongs. The worms are silently plotting rebellion: "When we say Attack / you will hear nothing / at first" (35). The corpse warns that it brings "news of the country / I am trapped in" (43). The crow is a would-be politician, the hen's head a philosopher.

The Circe/Mud poems recount the relationship of the hero and enchantress from her point of view. Circe is a goddess, daughter of Helios, the sun, and Perse, a sea nymph, a daughter of Ocean. Thus her origin connects her to the worlds of air and water. According to Christine Downing, Circe is an aspect of Aphrodite, the Greek goddess whose provenances include a consciousness grounded in relationship and feeling and a recognition of transience.[28]

Atwood explains that the first Circe poems she wrote acted "as a priming agent," prompting her to complete the sequence (Sandler 1990, 50). She comments that "everybody needs [a mythology]. It's just a question of getting one that is livable and not destructive to you" (Kaminski, 32).

The mythology of Circe is a potent one, with a long and varied history. Atwood's use of it emphasizes the woman's voice, a sexual relationship of equals, and the idea of story. As Judith Yarnall explains, Circe is a descendent of the all-powerful goddess of a matrilineal society, the giver of both life and death.[29] Circe represents the powers of transformation, sensuality, and fertility: the pigs associated with the Mother Goddess are sacred symbols of fertility and growth. Predating the Homeric legend, Circe represents a religion that values women and generativity. By the Homeric period, women's power was being challenged by a patriarchal system represented by the heroic warrior Odysseus. In the Homeric rendition of the encounter of Circe and Odysseus, according to Yarnall, "the most profound transformation that takes place in this myth is the turning of male-female hostility into union and trust" (21). In the centuries since Homer, as patriarchal cultures placed greater value on logic and conquest, the story of Circe took on a darker coloring, and she was seen as a witch, a femme fatale, a monster. But Atwood returns to the Homeric version, of a meeting of equals. Yarnall writes, "In one regard her perceptions are closer to Homer's than those of any intervening interpreter of the myth: she focuses on the issue of trust between a man and a woman and on the relationship of trust to sexuality" (187).

Atwood finds a livable mythology in the story of Circe. Her 24-poem sequence retells Circe's version of a mutual love, an equal partnership of a man and a woman. The Circe of this sequence knows her power and is definitely not a victim. A priestess and a prophet rather than a goddess, she is forthright, direct, sharp-tongued, passionate. It is easy to be sympathetic to her, and consequently critics have welcomed her appearance in Atwood's poetry.

Circe describes her search for real men, not the mythologized heroes "who can fly / with the aid of wax and feathers." Instead, she hopes to discover "the ones who have escaped from these / mythologies with barely their lives" (47). Because Odysseus is human, with a "flawed body," Circe recognizes him as a suitable mate. Yet she finds his heroic ambitions ridiculous and teases him: "There must be more for you to do / than permit yourself to be shoved / by the wind from coast / to coast to coast" (51). She disclaims responsibility for the transformation of Odysseus's men. Indeed, according to some traditions, the men simply turned into the beasts that represent their deepest natures.

Although the relationship between the two lovers is a contentious one, they are equal partners. Yet like most contemporary heterosexual relationships, theirs is shadowed by romantic fantasies of the passive, sexually receptive woman and the heroic, sexually active male partner. Circe retells a story she has heard of a headless "mud woman" that two boys sculpted and used for sexual purposes. Again, as in the silent reflecting mirror, the perfect lover is the silent one, the all-accepting one. Circe thinks that Odysseus might prefer such a mud woman. More, she asks herself, "is this what I would like to be? It would be so simple" (61). Their connection goes through a series of changes; they are hostile, they relent, they struggle against each other and then come to trust each other. She generously offers him food and tells him the names of her trees and plants (names, of course, have magical qualities; to know the name of something is to have power over it). Jane Lilienfeld traces the progress of the love affair and finds that in these poems "Atwood uses women's anger [at the imbalances of sexual politics] to create new

possibilities for love, for Circe is forced to imagine a new world in which
love might consist of equality and compassion. . . . At the end of the
cycle, the imagined island wherein a new kind of love is possible establishes the space . . . [where] ordinary mortals" may experience similar
love.[30]

Circe, the sorceress, has power within her own sphere, and she has
the gift of prophecy. She warns Odysseus that his saga will inevitably
continue without her. He begins to distance himself from her, preparing
to leave her enchanted island and return to his wife, Penelope. Knowing
the future, she recognizes that she too is the subject of a story, and its
rules are inescapable. She confronts Odysseus with her knowledge that
he plans to return home as foretold in the story. Yet she hopes that there
might be another story with another outcome, on a second island. This
is a place she knows nothing about, so she is free to fantasize a different
future for them in the lyrical conclusion to this section. "There are two
islands" recapitulates and transforms many of the symbols—such as
snow, November, and birds—that stood for loss in the earlier poems. In
this November poem there are still apples on the trees.

Atwood's version of the Circe story points to a central thematic concern with the power of story. Here the twentieth-century writer parts
company with the Homeric narrator, for Atwood's Circe is self-con-
sciously aware of herself as a character with a predetermined role in the
story. This recognition links her to a series of poems in this volume
(including the songs of the owl and the Siren and "Gothic Letter on a
Hot Night") that explicate Atwood's paradox of the story and its teller.

The owl and the Siren of the book's second section both seem to exist
as vehicles for telling their stories repeatedly. The owl has only one song,
that of death. Similarly, the Siren reveals her song, a potent one that
lures men to their deaths. She complains that she is tired of "looking
picturesque and mythical" and promises to reveal her irresistible song in
exchange for escape from her island. Her song is the traditional
woman's song of dependence, a "cry for help." Compelled to repeat her
"boring" song, she must remain on the island; she cannot escape her
story. She is just as much a victim of her song as the feckless sailors she
lures to their destruction.

"Gothic Letter on a Hot Night" spells out a related paradox of the
storyteller. The poem is a framed narrative, a nested story narrated by a
speaker facing a writing block. The narrator tells the story of a woman,
an unidentified "she" (is this the "I" of the first stanza, or another
woman?) who has told stories of loss and destruction and lacks stories

Northern Gothic: The Early Poems, 1961–1975

now, but would like to have them again. The stories she has lived or told appear to have a life of their own, to create the destruction that forms their subject. What is the author's responsibility for the stories she tells? Does she record them? Imagine or create them? Or, in a paradoxical reversal of agent and object, is she the subject of a story that is writing her? These questions recur throughout the Atwood canon, as story-telling becomes an ambiguously inflected imperative for the protagonists.

In the book's fourth section, "There Is Only One of Everything," Atwood continues to explore heterosexual love. As indicated by their titles, some of these poems reflect the positive tone of the Circe section, suggesting that love may contain sacral values: "First Prayer," "Four Auguries," "Book of Ancestors." As Jane Lilienfeld notes, many of the themes and images (such as birds, an owl, a mirror) that appeared earlier in this volume appear again, often with more positive connotations. She suggests that the love story in the book's concluding section may be Circe's fantasy. The woman here is not a victim, for she defends her right to her anger and asserts her needs: *"Be alive,* my hands plead with you" (87). Touch as a means of emotional connection is important here as it so often is in Atwood's work.

"There Is Only One of Everything" is a love poem that recognizes the transience of love and accepts change and the passage of time even while it finds value in the immediacy of the present. This poem is a twin to Circe's address to Odysseus, "Your flawed body," in which the enchantress comes to her love of the man through recognition of the scars that mark his history and render him human, individual, and real because he is flawed.

"Late August" is a poem of harvest, abundance, and lush richness of plums and apples, akin to the lush November of Circe's "There Are Two Islands." The book's culminating poem, "Book of Ancestors," moves from ancient times to the present as it knits together the themes and image patterns that comprise this volume. Part one imagines an ancient ritual of human sacrifice as it might have been experienced by the victim as an ecstasy of self-abandonment and release. In part two the contemporary speaker and her partner view temple frescoes of sacrifice and think that the gods are irrelevant or dead. Part three takes place indoors in the present as the couple achieve a moment of harmony by opening themselves to each other and assuming the risks of relationship. Although the season is winter, the mood is more positive than in the "Mournful November" of earlier poems in this volume, for here the snow is luminous and a warm fire burns in the fireplace. The man lies on the floor in the "ancient pose" of sacrifice, but this time he is "intact," and she observes that in his opening to her, becoming vulnerable, they are at last able "to take / that risk, to offer life and remain / alive, open yourself like this and become whole" (96).

Two years after the publication of *You Are Happy* Atwood compiled her *Selected Poems,* representing her poetry from *The Circle Game* through *You Are Happy.* Such a compilation recognizes an author's considerable achievement. *Selected Poems* includes all but one of the poems from *The Journals of Susanna Moodie* and selections from the other books. In 1982, she edited the *Oxford Book of Canadian Verse in English,* an update of the A. J. M. Smith anthology published in 1960. From her own work, she chose two poems from *Selected Poems,* "Death of a young son by drowning" (*JSM*) and "There Is Only One of Everything" (*YAH*). From her later collection, *Selected Poems II,* she chose four poems: "Marrying the Hangman" (*THP*), "You Begin" (*THP*), "Notes Towards a Poem That Can Never Be Written" (*TS*), and "Variation on the Word *Sleep*" (*TS*).

Chapter Three
"Home Ground, Foreign Territory": Atwood's Early Novels

The protagonists of Atwood's first three novels (which Atwood explains constitute a group) tell Gothic tales of dispossession and perilous journey as they negotiate the dangerous terrain of contemporary North American society. In giving them voices Atwood expands the possibilities for women's stories beyond the confining narrative conventions that have traditionally kept women in plots centering on romance and lack of agency. In contrast, her plots include detective thrillers and political satire as well as comedies of manners. These three women—Marian McAlpin of *The Edible Woman* (1969), the nameless heroine of *Surfacing* (1972), and Joan Foster of *Lady Oracle* (1976)—seek to establish their careers and to explore their romantic options.

Marian McAlpin finds that her courtship story conflicts with the conventional romance plot. Consequently, she must invent her own form to inscribe her narrative. Because the language in which to tell her story is not available to her, she enacts her resistance to the conventional story with her body by refusing to eat. The narrator of *Surfacing* has invented a cover story to hide—even from herself—a past she prefers to deny. But in falsifying her memories she becomes emotionally estranged, trapped in the story she made up. Through undertaking a spirit quest she revises her story so as to accept responsibility for her past and thus opens up the possibility of change. Joan Foster is a professional storyteller. But she fictionalizes her own story as well so that her life comes to resemble her Gothic novels. Because their companions often fail to listen to their voices, the three heroines articulate their needs through symbolic gestures as they seek to break free of social or personal constraints. Marian McAlpin becomes anorexic but regains her appetite by consuming a symbolic cake. The nameless narrator of *Surfacing* recovers from emotional numbness through her quest and ritual immersion. Joan Foster fakes suicide to escape from a series of entrapping relationships and continues to tell her tales.

As a storyteller Atwood claims the role of trickster, and in these novels she simultaneously tells stories and comments metafictively on the narrative process. As narrators of their stories, her protagonists often become versions of the trickster. Marian McAlpin, an earnest young woman whose life spins out of her control, seems to be a naive innocent aided by the trickster Duncan. The nameless narrator of *Surfacing* has become trapped in the story she fabricates, the story of her past that she has rewritten as a defense against her guilt because of an abortion. Joan Foster is Atwood's first self-conscious trickster figure, a woman who delights in spinning stories but finds herself caught in the plots she fabricates. Later characters will take on the trickster role to varying degrees.

Atwood's many-faceted novels depict a range of recurring thematic and rhetorical concerns, including mother-daughter relationships, city and wilderness, rationality and irrationality, art and reality, ambiguous lovers and fathers, women's friendships, the artist's quest, the voyeuristic gaze, and the complexities of storytelling and interpretation. The novels balance serious purpose and humor as they invoke irony and wit to critique social institutions and to interrogate and parody the literary conventions that shape them.

The novels here highlight some of the ambiguities and paradoxes of storytelling. Each of the narratives unfolds from a protagonist's superheated imagination. Their stories critique limiting social conventions, but at the same time they reveal the narrator's complicity in the stories they write for themselves, thus raising questions about their tales. For example, is Marian's fiancé, Peter Wollander, a dull but harmless man? Or is he the demon lover she imagines him to be? Because we see the story through her eyes we cannot know if, as she fears, he is trying to destroy her or if Duncan's comment that she is trying to destroy him (perhaps by demonizing him) has validity. In the case of *Surfacing* and *Lady Oracle* the protagonists have created fictions about themselves that once shielded them from painful situations but now limit their lives. But when they recognize their fictions, will they change their stories and lead fuller lives? The stories avoid closure and remain open-ended, reminding us that storytelling is the stuff of human life; consequently it is, like life itself, complex and multifaceted.

The Edible Woman (1969)

A comedy of manners, Atwood's first published novel showcases her gift for caricature as it takes a darkly comic look at the conventions of romantic fiction, of advertising, and of courtship and marriage. Atwood often uses the conventions of a particular genre to inscribe her story and at the same time to tweak or parody those conventions. *The Edible Woman* critiques and parodies the conventional romance plot, a mainstay of the Western literary tradition, in which young lovers meet, overcome obstacles, and marry. In contrast, this is the story of a recent college graduate, Marian McAlpin, who resists marriage as she struggles to find her place in society. The book draws from other literary ancestors as well, including such fictions as the Gingerbread Boy, *Alice in Wonderland,* and the myth of Persephone.

Atwood composed the first version of the novel from May through August of 1965 on examination booklets while she was a temporary instructor at the University of British Columbia. In part, the novel grew out of her experiences in graduate school and a brief stint at a market-research company (1963–1964). Atwood herself even makes a cameo appearance in the novel as a student dressed in black who attends a party. She explained to an interviewer, Valerie Miner, that the book "expresses [her] own early fear of marriage" (189–90), a fear she overcame sufficiently to marry James Polk in 1967.[1] Submitting the book to the publisher McClelland and Stewart in October 1965, she wrote, "Hope you enjoy *The Edible Woman.* You will rejoice to know that it has a plot and some characters, both of which elements were lacking in previous novel" (TF 92.2). Her previous novel, "Up in the Air So Blue," remains unpublished.

Confusingly, in the original edition (and some subsequent editions) the heroine's surname is spelled both MacAlpin and McAlpin. Perhaps this variation is appropriate in a book about a young woman's identity confusion. I use the latter spelling here. Another confusion vexed the book: the publisher misplaced the submitted manuscript for a year, an accident more likely to happen to the works of an unknown writer. After Atwood's first volume of poetry, *The Circle Game,* won the prestigious Governor General's Award, McClelland and Stewart, apparently with some embarrassment, agreed to publish the novel. Atwood revised the typescript, and the book appeared in 1969.

Critics take a range of stands on the novel.[2] Coral Ann Howells observes that it is "subversive rather than confrontational" and "engages obliquely with social problems" (Howells, 39). As D. J. Dooley notes, "[T]he novel deals chiefly with behavioral symptoms . . . and with the absence rather than the presence of moral choice." Robin Skelton finds the book Swiftian, well written, witty, shrewd, and interesting, yet wishes that the characters were more fully developed. Calling the book a farce rather than a satire, Jane Rule observes, "It is the puff pastry it claims to be—a treat of wit and invention." J. Brooks Bouson analyzes the novel's "refusal to consent to femininity," explaining that "through the dialogized female voices in the novel, Atwood both presents and undercuts the conservative messages given to Marian by the mid-1960s culture" (Bouson, 17). W. J. Keith's introduction is a lively and helpful reader's guide. Several critics explore the novel's pervasive food imagery. Especially useful are the discussions by T. D. MacLulich and Sharon Rose Wilson, who read the novel by the light of Lévi-Strauss; the Gingerbread Boy (MacLulich); and a range of fairy tales, nursery rhymes, and food motifs such as Peter, Peter Pumpkin Eater, the Robber Bridegroom, and Fitcher's Feathered Bird (Wilson, 83). David Harkness and Glenys Stow investigate Atwood's references to Lewis Carroll's novel of a young woman wandering in a world of strange creatures and magically transformative foods, *Alice in Wonderland*.

What are we to make of the title *The Edible Woman*? Does it signal a serious book? A comedy? A study of cannibalism? A collection of recipes? Is there something disturbingly (or deliciously) erotic about it? Its epigraph refers to a recipe for puff pastry, a time-consuming and complicated confection, from the popular cookbook *The Joy of Cooking*. And intriguingly, Atwood writes that an interest in symbolic cannibalism and "a confectioner's display window full of marzipan pigs" provided the inspiration for the concluding scene (*SW*, 369), a comic denouement in which the narrator bakes a cake in the shape of a woman and offers it to her fiancé. Clearly, food as metaphor and symbol will be important here, and in fact the motif recurs throughout the Atwood canon, where the getting, preparing, and eating of food correlates with power.

The novel introduces themes of male and female roles that resonate in subsequent work. Atwood is a keen social observer and satirist; however, her work is provocative and playful rather than propagandistic. Her books raise feminist and other political issues, but their voices are always plural and dialogic, questioning more than they answer and often interrogating feminism as well as other social ideologies and practices.

Atwood's exploration here is related to an emerging social critique broached by Betty Friedan in her 1963 polemic, *The Feminine Mystique,* a precursor of the second wave of feminism. In that same year, another darkly comic protofeminist novel, Sylvia Plath's posthumous *The Bell Jar,* appeared. Like *The Edible Woman* it elucidates the tensions of a young woman struggling to build a career and a romantic relationship. Interestingly, Plath uses food imagery in a crucial scene as a metaphor of contemporary society's indigestible values. Both Plath and Atwood portray heroines struggling to maintain their identities in a conservative social climate that perceives women as decorative objects and consumers, or even items to be consumed, rather than as acting subjects or producers of art. Confused and uncertain, they doubt their own sanity. They rely on actions and symbols rather than language to express their problems: Plath's Esther Greenwood attempts suicide; Marian McAlpin stops eating, runs from her fiancé, and bakes a woman-shaped cake to enact her dilemma.

Marian is the first of Atwood's self-conscious, introspective first-person narrators, a woman facing the contradictory and divisive expectations of twentieth-century North American middle-class culture. She is an educated, sensitive outsider whose story critiques the culture that has marginalized her. Although her job is to "manipulate words," she is not an author; she struggles with issues of authority, and she lacks the discourse to explore or articulate her discomfort with her domineering fiancé and her dead-end job.

Marian prides herself on her common sense, but her veneer of practicality crumbles as she invests the rituals of dating with Gothic terror. Like the protagonist of *Alice in Wonderland* she appears to be an innocent young woman caught in a strangely distorted world. She cowers in corners; weeps unexpectedly; hides under a couch; identifies with animals killed for food or sport; and views her fiancé, Peter Wollander, as a hunter, a threat. She thus takes on the role of Persephone, pursued by a deathlike suitor (and indeed, she descends into a maze symbolic of the underworld). Courtship literally becomes a chase when she runs away and finds Peter's pursuit of her disturbingly analogous to his rabbit hunt. She experiences the Gothic heroine's fear as she shrinks from his attempt to "capture" her image in a photograph. This emphasis on the threatening aspects of the specular, the gaze, is a recurring thematic strand in Atwood's poetry and fiction.

Marian's job at the market-research company Seymour Surveys is to "manipulate words" (109), translating psychological jargon such as "In

what percentile would you place the visual impact value?" (12) into col-
loquial language for consumer surveys. Her department consists of older
women with unappealing names, Mrs. Withers, Mrs. Bogue, and Mrs.
Grot, and three younger women, the "office virgins." Because Marian
doesn't fit either category—and her mother is absent from the novel—
she has no positive female role models or support systems and experiences herself as powerless, drifting, passive. She describes the office
structure as like an ice cream sandwich, with the male executives at the
top, the mechanical equipment at the bottom, and her department "the
gooey layer in the middle" (12).

The culinary description of her office echoes the food motif initiated
in the book's title. And at the crux of the food imagery lies the heroine's
awareness that women in contemporary Western society are perceived as
consumable commodities. Imagery of eggs and seeds abounds, suggesting female reproduction, a central issue in the novel. Marian's two
friends, Clara and Ainsley, are absorbed in preparations for childbearing.
Ainsley decides to have a baby and begins a campaign to find the father
for her child. Clara, who has two small children and is pregnant with her
third, is frequently described in egg imagery. Indeed, she seems to Marian like an ant queen, an egg producer, and Clara wishes she could hatch
her babies like eggs. The eggs Marian cooks often take on the characteristics of living creatures. Worse, the morning after she becomes engaged
to the upwardly mobile young lawyer, Peter, she cannot eat her egg,
thinking, "It's alive."

Conflicted and anxious, she finds it increasingly difficult to eat.
Watching Peter cut his steak, she imagines the living cow and finds her
steak inedible (153). She stops eating meat, then vegetables, and eventually she does not wish to disturb even the mold growing on the food
in the refrigerator.

The boundaries between humans and other animals are ominously
permeable to Marian, emphasizing the novel's Gothic motif of transformation and portending a loss of control. The women at Seymour Surveys are like "toads" (10), or "a Sargasso Sea of femininity . . . liquid,
amorphous" (171–72)—spreading, formless, huge, ugly. Clara's babies
are like leeches or octopuses (25), barnacles or limpets (30); unborn,
they are parasites or diseases (galls, elephantiasis of the navel, a huge
bunion) (113). Newborn infants are like shriveled prunes (133). Duncan, an ambiguous figure, in part Marian's spirit guide, is an aged child,
a turtle in its shell (92). Marian finds bodies and their processes messy,
unpleasant, uncontrollable.

Clara's body expands with her pregnancy like an ant queen, a pumpkin, a "boa constrictor that swallowed a watermelon" (25) and shrinks back to size after her child is born (114). Like Clara, and like Alice in Wonderland, other characters change shape, becoming formless or grotesque. Marian sees her reflection as "small and oval" in Peter's eyes (80); she dreams her feet dissolve like jelly (38); her head feels like a scooped cantaloupe after Peter has proposed to her (80); her clothes are strewn around the room like an exploded female scarecrow (80); her voice becomes "soft and flannelly" (87); her head is truncated in a spoon reflection (148). She worries about "middle age spread" (91). On her visit to the beauty parlor she becomes an edible confection herself as the hairdresser treats her head "like a cake: something to be carefully iced and ornamented" (217).

In contrast to the unpredictable, messy, changeable bodies of real people, billboard and advertising images are clean and beautiful. The Moose Beer ad portrays plaid-jacketed sportsmen neat and clean as they scoop trout or stand on the immaculate deer they have just killed. Advertisements promulgate sex-role stereotypes, urging men to aim for the sportsman image and pressuring women to live up to a glamorous doll-like image. Aiming for just such an idealized image in preparation for Peter's party, Marian acquires dramatic makeup, a new hairdo, a girdle, and a red dress. She views her appointment at the beauty salon as a kind of surgical operation in which she is reconstructed into an unrecognizably glamorous creation. During the process "her whole body feels curiously paralyzed" (218). Seeing this version of Marian, Duncan comments that the party is a masquerade. He thus calls attention to the concept of femininity as masquerade, an idea that would become prominent in feminist analysis. Women are supposed to become decorative objects, feminine and passive. Because Marian is uncomfortable with this role, both Ainsley and Peter accuse her of "rejecting her femininity" (77). In refusing to eat and in rejecting Peter, is she rejecting her femininity? Or is she rebelling against the indigestible image of femininity "fed" to women in American culture?

The novel pays a great deal of attention to clothing worn by both men and women, because the masquerade of gender is an important signal in courtship, a process that the novel infuses with ominous overtones of sexual predation, cannibalism, and murder. Lucy, one of the "office virgins" at Seymour Surveys, dresses like a fishing lure, although the men she hopes to attract aren't biting (110). When Ainsley tries to seduce Marian's friend Len, dressing in pink checked gingham to appear innocent, Marian thinks of her as a pitcher plant awaiting an insect (72). Masculinity is a masquerade as well. Peter dresses carefully and enjoys clothes for their semiotic value as signs of status. Marian sees him as "nicely packaged," wearing clothes that are like interchangeable identities: his red plaid "hunter's" jacket, his "tweedy casual jacket . . . and the series of his other phases from late summer through fall" (239). In contrast, Duncan shuns conventional images of masculinity and treats clothing primarily as fabric. Rather than allowing clothing to transform him, he acts on clothes. To soothe his anxiety he irons obsessively, and we often see him in the laundromat.

Peter values his bachelorhood and avoids marriage until Marian runs away from him; then he responds according to the traditional courtship formula: he chases her and proposes. But our view of Peter as the hunter and pursuer, the rescuer and the attacker, is shaped by Marian's Gothic fantasies. She hopes for a lover who will rescue her from a boring job and raise her social status, yet she fears that he will dominate or destroy her. In her fantasies, she conflates him with the plaid-jacketed hunter in the Moose Beer ad and with a serial killer (153). Her fear arises both from romantic fantasy and from awareness of the real dangers men pose for women (116–17). Once they become engaged, she accepts the culture's romantic ideology: she yields the role of decision maker to Peter and assumes an exaggeratedly compliant stance, falling into the very stereotype of self-abnegating femininity she dreads. Peter makes decisions for them, starting with ordering from the menu at restaurants. She stops eating and speaking for herself; in fact, her narrative changes from first person to third person.

With Peter, Marian enacts a comic version of the typical courtship rituals of flight and pursuit. His yuppie social status and his eagerness to capture Marian on film suggest the aspects of marriage that Marian resists: rigidity, conventionality, loss of self. His name, which means "rock," has a range of associations, such as the male sexual organ or the misogynistic husband of the "Peter, Peter, Pumpkin Eater" rhyme. Marian continually meets him on his territory—in his home, an upscale restaurant, or his car. It is only in the final scene when she confronts him with the symbolic cake-woman that she takes control and stages an encounter on her own territory, at her apartment.

Like other Atwood texts, *The Edible Woman* counterpoises a realist fiction against an ambiguous subtext of quest, renewal, rebirth, and redemption. The unworldly Duncan (whose name links him with the Duncan Hines brand of packaged cake mixes) represents the mythic dimension. A student of literature, he is a foil to the practical careerist Peter. He seems both old and childlike, appearing and disappearing unexpectedly and claiming that he is a changeling: "I'm not human at all, I come from the underground" (142). He leads Marian into Gothic realms associated with the underworld, mystery, and self-exploration: the Royal Ontario Museum mummy exhibit and the maze where he leaves her to find her way back to downtown Toronto. Like Peter, Duncan is both potential rescuer and possible victimizer, saving Marian from an unsuitable marriage but posing danger as well, for he is certainly an inappropriate match for her. Duncan is in part an alter ego of Marian's, a Jungian animus who surfaces from her unconscious to compel her to realize her own unacknowledged attributes. D. J. Dooley observes that Duncan " is quite aware that he is playing a role, whereas [the others] are falling into roles without knowing it" (Dooley, 142). Dell Texmo argues that "the clear-sighted Duncan, who sees through her masquerade and forces her to question it, . . . helps Marian iron herself out just as he has ironed her laundry for her."[3]

Interpretation is an ongoing issue in Atwood's novels. In this case the protagonist is uncertain if she is interpreting events accurately and worries that she may be going crazy because her feelings of discomfort at her engagement to Peter run counter to conventional beliefs of romantic bliss. She tries to accept the stereotypical assessment of Peter as a suitable mate, although she fears that he is trying to destroy her. When she asks Duncan for advice, his enigmatic response compounds her confusion.

The book depicts a battle of the sexes. Its characters are all either victims or aggressors; Marian perceives herself to be a victim while Peter and Ainsley pursue their prey. No neutral position seems possible, except for Duncan, who parodies the courtship conventions. Attempting to resolve her confusion, Marian bakes a cake in the shape of a woman and offers it to Peter as an alternative to herself. Peter refuses to eat the cake and leaves quickly. As soon as he goes, Marian's appetite returns. She begins to eat again, deciding that "after all [it] was only a cake" (285). Duncan observes, "[Y]ou're back to so-called reality, you're a consumer," as he finishes the cake and pronounces it "delicious" (293). Catherine McLay writes that the cake-baking scene is a feast, a celebration of freedom and rebirth as Marian releases herself from identification with the victim.[4] As Coral Ann Howells notes, the gesture of cake baking is a feminine one; Atwood uses the idea of woman's place in the kitchen to both enact and critique the ideology of woman's place (Howells, 53–54). Similarly, the novel borrows the romance comedy plot to deconstruct the typical romance story in which the hero rescues the heroine from marrying the wrong man. In this novel, however, neither man is right, and Marian avoids marriage.

Does Marian change in the course of the novel? Atwood's conclusion leaves the answer unclear. In interviews she offers two interpretations of the ending.[5] She tells Graeme Gibson that "Marian is acting. . . . Up until that point she has been evading, avoiding, running away." (In a later interview with Linda Sandler, Atwood has a less positive interpretation, commenting that Marian ends where she began: "I[I]t's more pessimistic than *Surfacing*. . . . *The Edible Woman* is a circle and *Surfacing* is a spiral" (Sandler 1977, 14).

If Marian has gained understanding, it is limited. Her insights are few; she is still not sure "who is trying to destroy whom?" The ending is a comic moment rather than an epiphany, leaving the protagonist and the reader ready to pursue the quest further. Having liberated herself from social expectations and from an inappropriate marriage, she now has the potential to re-create herself.

The Edible Woman is an urban book, set in the deathlike gray world of a Canadian city (Toronto, although it is not named in the novel), and this may to some extent shape the limited vision of its conclusion. The next book, *Surfacing,* moves from the gray city to a green island as the protagonist's quest unfolds. Atwood has said that her first three books comprise a unit. *Surfacing* and the third book, *Lady Oracle,* revisit the questions of courtship, romantic fantasies, and sexual politics.

Surfacing (1972)

Surfacing, Atwood's second published novel, appeared after the author had already won acclaim and awards for six volumes of poetry. It continues to develop signature themes such as the quest journey and the contrast between city and nature. Thematic and stylistic similarities between Atwood's poetry and her fiction are especially pronounced. The book's terse, pared-down language and structure echo the spare concentration of her poems, while its themes of journey, of dive and descent, and of the relationship between people and landscape resonate in the early poems as well. Atwood points out that criticism of this novel tended to run along national lines. Canadian critics looked at her nationalism; American critics focused on her feminism.[6]

Useful studies of this novel include George Woodcock's monograph and essays by Judith McCombs (1982), Sherrill Grace, and Robert

Cluett.[7] Grace reads the novel as a version of the Demeter story and finds two quests, the quest for the narrator's father and a second, or "muted," quest for her mother. She explains that the while the quest for the father is a traditional journey through space, quest for the mother is "a journey into time and 'wild space,' . . . [that] gains impetus and power until it carries the speaker into the very center of illumination from which she is reborn" (Grace 1988, 43–44). Cluett finds that Atwood's "drastically inhibited" deployment of stylistic resources parallels the protagonist's retreat from urban civilization with its "ornate 'civilized' values" (Cluett, 87).

Surfacing describes the unnamed first person narrator's search for her father and mother and for her place in the world. The book explores many connotations of surface: a noun meaning the top layer or boundary or superficial outward appearance; a verb meaning both to form the surface of and "to rise to the surface, to emerge after concealment." The narrator's companions, Joe, Anna, and David, focus on outward appearance and adhere to superficial values as they film a collage of unconnected "random samples" or apply makeup to create a pleasing surface. Her friend David is "a pastiche, layers of political handbills, pages from magazines . . . verbs and nouns glued on to him and shredding away, the original surface littered with fragments and tatters" (182). The superficial "Americans" represent the excesses of consumerism; the narrator considers them plastic-covered, wearing the proper look for their surroundings.

I read this novel primarily as a woman's quest and secondarily as a quest for cultural identity, describing Canada's struggle to come to terms with its past; to understand the proper uses of power; to mediate hegemonic United States influences; and to reconcile a series of dichotomies, including French and English language and culture as well as city and wilderness. The narrator's failed affair may suggest Canada's historic relationship with England. Acknowledgment of her abortion may indicate acceptance of responsibility for the violence of Canadian history. Wilderness (the bush), the world of nature, is an important source of values, although retreat to the past may be a tempting but untenable position. Joe, Anna, and David represent possible future directions. David is dangerously violent and sexist; Anna has capitulated to the oppressor. Joe is "only half formed" (235) and therefore holds promise.

The personal quest story tells how the unnamed narrator uncovers the secret of a past she falsified to herself. Through the device of her fabricated memories, the novel raises the question of women's relationship to authorship and authority. Through her journey she reimagines her past, travels from the gray world of the city to the green world of nature, and connects to sources of personal power through a hallucinatory ritual similar to the Native American spirit quest. Nevertheless, we will do well to remember that Atwood remains a trickster, and there are clearly elements of parody and self-mockery here (Woodcock, 26).

As the protagonist moves from a corrupt and alienating city to her family's island cabin, her journey mirrors the Demeter-Persephone myth, a tale of death and rebirth, of the separation and reunion of mother and daughter. As a young woman she experiences the "hell" of an illicit affair and an abortion, much as Persephone experiences the trauma of rape and descent into the kingdom of Hades. On the narrator's return to the island, she reconnects symbolically with her mother. And if the corrupt urban world is Hades, then the island is Eden, and indeed the novel is rich in biblical as well as mythical allusions, as when the hanged heron symbolizes Christ (167). But this paradise has been neglected; it is full of mosquitoes, weeds, and tourists who hunt and fish, leaving their garbage behind.

Fittingly for a quest story, there are many maps, pictures, pictographs, photos, reflections, and mirrors that provide clues the narrator must probe as her journey propels her from city to wilderness, from surface to depth, from cabin into myth and magic. Early in the novel the narrator declares that she is on her "home ground, foreign territory" (8). This paradoxical juxtaposition of home and foreign territory is a stylistic device that provides a clue to the narrator's central conflicts and the book's thematic structure. Her quest raises questions of nationalism, postcolonialism, environmentalism, and gender that the novel explores in complex, ambiguous ways. Prompted by news that her father has disappeared, she begins a journey that is both outward and inward to find a subject position, an identity, and to discover her home. Robert Cluett points out that most of the novel's adverbial elements are locative ("on top," "beside," "behind") rather than temporal ("when," "after" [75–76]). Interestingly, Atwood's original title for the book was "Where Is Here?", a question borrowed from Northrop Frye's formulation of the Canadian search for identity (Frye, 1965).

Indeed, the novel's first sentence describes the speaker's uneasy relationship to place: "I can't believe I'm on this road again" (3). The narrator and three companions are traveling from Toronto, her present home, to the island cabin, her childhood summer home. As a traveler she is in between places, unfixed. The literal journey parallels her spiritual journey, a quest for meaning that leads her to reexamine her past and to probe beneath the surface of daily life.

As in the "home ground, foreign territory" example, the narrator's stylistic fragmentation derives from her alienation and signals her disordered perspective, a cognition that registers information but does not organize it. She strings together independent clauses with almost no coordinating or subordinating linkage. Consequently, all observations have equal weight, and causality is seldom indicated. Much of the novel is description of place, yet her sense of displacement is profound: "Nothing is the same, I don't know the way any more. I slide my tongue around the ice cream, trying to concentrate on it, they put seaweed in it now, but I'm starting to shake, why is the road different, he shouldn't have allowed them to do it, I want to turn around and go back to the city" (9–10). Because she lacks a coherent sense of self, she takes in information but does not integrate it into her experience. The stylistic discontinuities reflect her emotional fragmentation and displacement.

Her awareness of place is linked to boundary issues. For example, abortions raise issues of boundaries, for the boundary between woman and embryo is complex. Politically, the narrator deplores the Americans crossing the border, invading the Canadian landscape, littering and spreading disease, greed, violence, destruction. Geographically, boundary issues are salient. Judith McCombs describes the novel's land- and waterscape and its consequences: "Literally, this *is* a place of flow and change: there are no certain boundaries between earth and water, water and air. . . . If one insists that this land offer human order and fixed boundaries, as the father did with his belief in logic and rational order, then winter can drive one crazy. . . . but if one sees this landscape as sacred, numinous or Christian, then one sees it without fear or loathing, but with worship" (McCombs 1982, 113). The novel's conclusion rests on the tension between bush and city.

Wilderness and city: the tensions between these two antithetical places animate the novel as the narrator finds that the urban South is invading, destroying, and victimizing the wild North. The South is the United States (and its Canadian counterpart, urban, industrialized consumer society), home of the plaid-shirted tourists who invade the Northern bush, hunting, fishing, killing, destroying. The North represents the endangered natural world of lakes, trees, animals, and a threatened native culture. In the same year that *Surfacing* appeared in print, Atwood published *Survival,* which argues that Canadian literature articulates a pattern of victimization and concludes that Canadians are themselves the victims of British and American imperialism. As a representative Canadian and a woman, the narrator of *Surfacing* believes that she is the quintessential victim. She identifies with the logged woods, the hanged heron, the frog used as bait in fishing, victimized by human greed and selfishness.

Because she is at ease in the woods, she observes the natural world in sensuous detail, describing the dying white birches, the rotting heron, the stunted vegetables in the garden. In contrast, her discomfort with people distorts her perception. Her focus alternates between detailed close-ups and distant views. We see the bristles on David's face as he starts to grow a beard, we see that Anna's face looks dry and puckered without her makeup, but we never learn the color of their eyes, nor anyone's height or body shape. Among her friends the narrator feels like a foreigner. She sees them in fragments rather than as wholes as she struggles to make sense of what she perceives, reading the world as if it is a foreign language she must decipher. Her fragmentation derives from disconnectedness; for her, emotional distance provides safety. Thus, we learn more physical details about the minor characters such as the grocery store clerk than about the people she is close to, even the man she lives with. Similarly, we learn the first names of the people she is with, but not the names of her closest relations: her father, mother, brother. Most significantly, we never learn her name.

The names of the narrator's friends carry biblical overtones, but the present-day characters are pale shadows of their biblical forebears. The name Anna derives from the Hebrew Hannah, "graceful one," best known for her passionate longing for a child (1 Samuel, chapter 1). Anna is childless, worried about her makeup. While David shares his namesake's adulterous proclivities, he conspicuously lacks his virtues. Whereas King David was a warrior, a musician, and a poet, this David's battles are waged against his wife, while his art, the film *Random Samples,* is a collage of unrelated images. The narrator's lover, Joe, like the biblical Joseph, speaks little and reveals little about himself, yet he has an important role. Joe remains loyal to the narrator and represents redemptive possibilities, possibly fathering her child. Perhaps the narrator must remain nameless until she discovers who she really is. The characters lack surnames, partly to indicate how little the narrator knows them, and partly because they are archetypes: the shadowy lover, the unhappily married couple.

Another series of archetypes, birth, death, and rebirth, produces a cluster of important image patterns in the novel. In his perceptive reader's guide, George Woodcock discusses these patterns, commenting that the embryo (submerged in amniotic fluid in the womb) and the submersion-surfacing image pattern are interrelated, for birth "is a kind of surfacing" (40).

In the last section of the book the narrator undertakes a vision quest, following her father's pictograph maps to a cliff now submerged underwater. Here she dives three times, symbolically purifying herself, reconnecting with her unconscious, dying and being reborn. On the third dive, she perceives a shape that she invests with meaning and takes to be her father's dead body. The shape reminds her of the abortion she has misremembered. Symbolically reborn through her dive, she is now able to emerge from the deathlike hell into which her guilt for a failed affair and abortion cast her. Feeling charged with new energy, she seeks to purge her life of the corrupt creations of civilization and to live according to a more primitive, purer law.

When the others are ready to leave, she throws the *Random Samples* film canisters into the water, destroying their superficial production, and runs away to the woods to pursue her ritual spirit quest. In a hallucinatory state she experiences visions of her father and her mother, seeing them as magical, powerful totems. After several days the manic intensity lessens, and she goes back to the cabin, realizing that to live in this world she must make compromises with society. She surveys herself in the mirror, to take stock of her new knowledge and to determine how to live with this insight. She now plans to return to the complex, inharmonious world of society, resolving to avoid being either victim or victimizer. To accomplish this she must mediate between her vision and the urban world. She reflects that she will need to make choices, to select the most valid means of living in civilization. At this juncture, Joe comes back looking for her. Because she considers him safe, she may return with him, although she realizes the future may be difficult.

The novel is enigmatic and its conclusion leaves open questions. Does the novel valorize women's kinship with nature and identify women with preverbal, prerational mental states? Such a position would see the narrator's retreat into the woods as a positive statement, and indeed some critics have made that argument. Has the heroine achieved clear insight? Is a return to the destructive urban world desirable? Remembering Atwood's duplicity, it is useful to consider many possibilities. Coral Ann Howells observes that the narrator's quest is "markedly incomplete . . . surfacing is a gerund (a noun made out of a verb), indicating process and activity rather than a completed action" (Howells,

32). On the other hand, Richard Lane argues that "the narrator . . . [decides] not to be controlled completely by either side of the binary structure [body/nature/myth or culture/society]. Thus she chooses the natural-mythical rebirth . . . as a way of re-negotiating her position *in* society, *in* language and *in* the realm of competing interpretations."[8] Or perhaps Atwood is caricaturing the quest. Robert Lecker argues convincingly that "the nature of the rebirth and the affirmation of self-discovery remain ambivalent. What Atwood really seems to be saying is that the mythical pattern of separation, initiation, and return must itself be seen as a sham in a culture where rituals have lost their potency."[9]

The book ends in a moment of stasis, balance. The lake and woods are poised in an equilibrium against Joe, who represents the city and who may be either a rescuer or an intruder. Is return to a violent consumerist society with a rather dull man a good alternative? Is Joe a worthy companion? In the narrator's eyes, Joe "isn't anything, he is only half formed . . . balancing on the dock which is neither land nor water, . . . head thrown back and eyes scanning" (235). The dock "which is neither land nor water" reminds us of the paradoxes of folk riddles (for example, the hero must be neither clothed nor naked, arriving neither by night nor by day). In folktales and mythology the spaces between the boundaries, are sites of magic and energy. Throughout the novel, Atwood embeds reminders of a mythic, spiritual vision counterpoised to the ugliness and cruelty of the urban world: Anna reads palms, the narrator illustrates a book of fairy tales and undertakes a vision quest similar to that of the Native American spirit quest. The conclusion continues this pattern with its riddling paradoxes and a possible allusion to the tarot cards.

The language of the concluding paragraph suggests the fool in the Waite-Rider tarot deck, who is depicted at the edge of a cliff, head thrown back, and eyes scanning. The fool represents the optimist, hope, expectation, choice, futurity, the fairy-tale hero, the youngest child. He is the beginning and the end, the paradox of zero, which may be either nothing or complete in itself. Joe, the "half formed," who has possibly impregnated her, may be the mediator to bring her back to civilization. As a potter, an artist/creator, he is connected to earth. His return for her may indicate that he has passed the test traditionally imposed on the hero. Interestingly, both in the early drafts of the novel and in Atwood's screenplay based on the novel, Joe is a more appealing person than in the published novel; he talks more and expresses more concern for the narrator. In fact, in the screenplay, the narrator climbs into the boat to return to the city with him.

Surely the open-ended, ambiguous published version is more fitting. In many ways this conclusion is the prototypical Atwood ending. The protagonist tells and revises her quest story, but its significance and outcome are enigmatic. She is now poised at the moment of decision, while her future remains unclear. She embodies the dilemma of a contemporary North American woman struggling to find a meaningful way to live in a complex society. Joan Foster in *Lady Oracle* enacts a similar quest.

Lady Oracle (1976)

The narrator of Atwood's *Lady Oracle,* Joan Foster, also known as Louisa K. Delacourt, is a flamboyant red-haired woman who returns from suicide dramatically to continue a turbulent, adventurous life authoring Gothic novels and engaging in romantic affairs. Joan repeatedly reenacts her central plot—her seductive pretense of dependence on men who appear to be rescuers but become threats to her safety. The novel both parodies and exploits the features of the Gothic tradition, in the process raising questions about writing, identity, the distinctions between serious art and escape fiction, the author's control of her text, the place of the writer in society, the interconnections and confusions of literature and life, and the functions of literature.

Lady Oracle revisits earlier themes in a comic mode, as a young woman struggles to tell her story and to negotiate the mazes of courtship and career. Whereas Marian McAlpin stops eating to reject society's standards of femininity, Joan Foster overeats for the same purpose. Similarly, Atwood comically rewrites a plot device from *Surfacing,* the narrator's symbolic descent and surfacing. Joan stages her own feigned death by drowning to escape the complications of her life. The book also pokes fun at literary publishing and reviewing and at popular taste, for Joan Foster is both pilloried and lionized by critics and patronized by publishers for the wrong reasons, and she becomes a cult figure after she has supposedly drowned. The novel also caricatures aspects of popular art (the Royal Porcupine, a flamboyant artist, exhibits frozen road kill), Canadian nationalism (Arthur and his friends edit a nationalist magazine, *Resurgence*), and popular Gothic romance.

Gothic narratives blend fantasy and realism as they address the anxieties produced by a bourgeois family structure that locks women in the home to keep them innocent and powerless.[10] As I suggest elsewhere, Gothic narratives "depict womb-like structures such as the castle or the tower, allude to mysterious family secrets, and emphasize women's sexual vulnerability. . . . Mothers and the values traditionally associated with motherhood—caring, nurturing, empathy—are dramatically lacking in these novels. Consequently, the Gothic tale re-presents a motherless (and often fatherless) young woman, unprotected, facing the dangers of patriarchal society. It is . . . a story of a woman's education and development." Through their adventures Gothic heroines often resolve their conflicts, come to terms with their mothers or with a maternal principle, and learn to interpret more accurately the situations in which they find themselves. At the same time the Gothic novel emphasizes "multiple levels of narration, . . . modes of discourse, . . . tensions between fantasy and reality."[11]

Because the Gothic mode reveals anxieties about the changing place of women in families, it may be that times of changing social roles lead to the production of Gothic fiction. Atwood wrote her first three novels in a time of feminist political activism that saw a flowering of Gothic novels by women, including Doris Lessing's *The Four-Gated City,* 1969, and *The Summer Before the Dark,* 1973; Susan Fromberg Schaeffer's *Falling,* 1973; and Sheila Ballantyne's *Norma Jean the Termite Queen,* 1975. These ironic, darkly humorous novels conclude ambiguously, with their protagonists poised to encounter new possibilities but the outcome uncertain. In 1974 Ellen Moers coined the term "female Gothic," identifying it as a genre that explores the relations between parent (especially mother) and child. Atwood comments that "the Gothic novel [is] very much a woman's form. Why is there such a wide readership for books that essentially say, 'Your husband is trying to kill you'?"[12] Margery Fee explains, "[T]he primary terror at the heart of the female Gothic tradition is the terror of male rejection or violence . . . Another part of the terror is . . . the loss of identity" (Fee, 63). And it is to counteract that terrifying loss of identity that Gothic heroines spin out their stories, for through storytelling they attempt to assert and define their selfhood. Coral Ann Howells observes: "*Lady Oracle* is a story about storytelling, . . . for Joan offers us multiple narratives figuring and refiguring herself through different narrative conventions" (Howells, 66).

Gothic novels frequently include supernatural allusions, and Atwood continues this tradition here with references to Greek goddesses, astral travel, spiritism, automatic writing, and the labyrinth/maze that leads to the underworld. Her working papers for this novel include research material on the Delphic oracle, the Cumaen Sibyl, Diana of Ephesus, and the Homeric hymn to Apollo. Characteristically, Atwood uses supernatural allusions here both to suggest and to undercut possibilities of transformation and spiritual renewal. For example, Joan's mother sitting in front of her three-sided mirror suggests, both seriously and ironically, the triple goddess. In fact, her mother, her Aunt Lou, and Joan together may be a version of the triple goddess: maiden, mother, and crone or wise woman.

Discussing *Lady Oracle* with J. R. (Tim) Struthers, Atwood calls the novel an "anti-Gothic" and explains that she is "examining the perils of Gothic thinking" that casts people in stereotypes such as "the dark, experienced man, who is possibly evil and possibly good, the rescuer, the mad wife, and so on. . . . [But because] real people don't fit these two-dimensional roles, you can either discard the roles and try to deal with the real person or discard the real person."[13]

Molly Hite sees Joan's problem as a function of society's power structure that gives men a disproportionate power in heterosexual relationships so that they become both the rescuers and the destroyers. Several other critics cite Joan's relationship to her mother as the central conflict.[14] Roberta Rubenstein lays the blame for Joan's problems on her inability to separate from her mother adequately, thus perpetuating a pattern of trying to resist her mother's control. Margery Fee argues that "Joan is so angry at her mother that she cannot express it, or even admit it. In order to protect herself, then, she has to transform her mother into a monster who deserves such hatred and anger. So Joan projects her own monstrous impulses onto her mother, and later onto her various lovers" (Fee, 65). As Roberta Sciff-Zamaro theorizes, "Her mother, who is a projection of Joan herself, will continue to be a monster until Joan will be able not to destroy her, but rather to free her mother."

The novel itself is a series of stories within the framework of Joan's story as told to a newspaper reporter. Atwood wanted to write a novel that was "all tangents," in contrast to her pared-down previous novel, *Surfacing* (Rosenberg, 112). And indeed, the Gothic, a subgenre of the romance, is characterized by excess, disorder: it features high drama, exaggeration, repetition of events, and doubling and fragmentation of characters. As we have seen, *Surfacing* was bare, restrained in language and plot, limited to two weeks of present time (with flashbacks). In contrast, *Lady Oracle* resembles the baroque mirror, scrolled and festooned, that Joan sees as the shape of her life. Thus Atwood is exploring the limits of a long-standing rhetorical tradition of the romance, balancing the tensions between expansion and control, between spinning out a plot and reaching narrative closure. Her heroine, Joan, is the epitome of excess, using expansion as a means to resist the domination of others (Hite, 139–41, 157). Physically, she eats excessively to resist her mother's attempts to mold her into a svelte young debutante. Financially, she remains free by spinning out the stock plots of the romance novels that earn her living.

Like the costume Gothic novels Joan authors, this is a tale of an unprotected and vulnerable young woman facing the dangers of patriarchal society, living by her wits and saving herself repeatedly from the controlling designs of her mother and of the men who both rescue and threaten her. The book begins with Joan sitting on the balcony of her rented apartment in Terremoto, fantasizing about the possible approach of a "sinuous and dark" figure (8), thus illustrating how her fondness for romantic fantasies informs her life as well as her novels. And indeed, as in her recent past in Toronto when an unidentified person leaves dead animals and threatening notes on her doorstep, her life increasingly resembles the "costume Gothic" fiction she writes. To escape this mysterious pursuer Joan plots her own supposed death, faking an accidental drowning by falling off a sailboat on Lake Ontario. (It later turns out that a witness to the boating incident accuses Joan's sailing companions of murdering her.)

The novel alternates between the present time and flashbacks, starting with her unhappy childhood as a fat girl in a cold and loveless family. Marriage thwarts her mother's desires for romance because Joan's father is absent from home during World War II, returning a cold and unemotional man with a secret past. Locked in her castle like the typical Gothic heroine, powerless to use her abundant ambition and energy in the world outside her home, Joan's mother focuses on perfecting her daughter. But Joan resists, by overeating and flaunting her obesity.

The plots of Joan's novels reenact her family plot, retelling the story of an innocent young woman at the mercy of a beautiful but cold woman (her rival/her mother), and a cold, distant father/husband. Just as her mother hoped for rescue through romance, Joan, along with her heroines, always wants to be rescued by love. Just as Joan's father proved duplicitous, so are the men in her life: her first lover, Paul; her husband, Arthur; her lover, Chuck Brewer, the Royal Porcupine; the scheming journalist, Fraser Buchanan. Joan repeatedly finds that she must rescue herself.

In contrast to Joan's manipulative and cold biological mother, her Aunt Lou is the good mother, the fairy godmother, a model of benevolent female power and comfortable sexuality. She recognizes Joan's worth, encourages her imagination, and gives her the gifts that gain her independence: money, approval, and recognition of her imaginative powers. Another gift is her description of Automatic Writing, a process of writing while staring into a candle reflected in a mirror. Years later Joan's experiments with this technique culminate in a book of poetry called *Lady Oracle*. Aunt Lou herself is oracular, offering seemingly simple, practical advice that Joan later finds ambiguous. When Aunt Lou dies, she leaves Joan money she uses to escape the escalating conflict with her mother and move to London.

Aunt Lou shares Joan's love of escape fantasy and introduces her to sentimental romance films. They cry over movies such as *The Red Shoes*, in which Moira Shearer must choose between a career as a ballerina and marriage. Sharon Rose Wilson remarks that although dancing with a partner is an acceptable activity, a part of the courtship ritual, dancing alone, performing, is socially unacceptable. Thus the film's heroine is punished for desiring independent achievement. Similarly, attempting to have both marriage and a career, Joan conceals her Gothic romance authorship from her husband, fearing he will think it trivial. She believes he will appreciate her more recondite volume of poetry, but he proves jealous of her literary success.

Joan invents her life just as she invents her fictions. She hides her past as a fat child from her husband, she takes her Aunt Lou's name for her pen name, and indeed, Louisa K. Delacourt becomes more than a pseudonym; it becomes an alter ego. The book spins out a series of dramatic plots—Joan's role as a mothball in a childhood dance recital, her later involvement with the leftists and their bomb plot, a series of affairs, her Gothic romances, her unexpected fame as a cult poetess. Although all her lovers have names suggesting royalty—a Count, Arthur, and the Royal Porcupine—none turn out to be the prince she hopes to find. Ironically, although she gives voice to the hopes and desires of her protagonists and of the silent ordinary women who read her novels, she silences herself, for she obliterates her past and assumes the role of inept airhead to hide from Arthur her identity as a successful writer.

Does Joan succeed in discarding her "Gothic thinking" to recognize the complexity of her friends and family? The first stirrings of such a shift in her attitude occur when she feels sympathy after her mother's death: "Nobody did appreciate her, even though she'd done the right thing, she had devoted her life to us, she had made her family her career as she had been told to do" (200). Later, she has a dream or vision of her mother standing on the terrace, stretching out her arms in invitation.

Joan realizes that "she'd never really let go of me because I had never let her go. . . . She needed her freedom also; she had been my reflection too long . . . I would never be able to make her happy. Or anyone else. Maybe it was time for me to stop trying" (363). Shortly after this recognition, Joan finds that she cannot complete her current romance novel, *Stalked by Love,* according to the expected formula. She decides to quit writing Gothic novels and to write science fiction instead. (Does this mean that she is looking toward the future rather than the past? That her stories will be less romantic? That she will write speculative fiction rather than escape stories? Or is science fiction another form of escape literature?) Moreover, she acknowledges that her fantasies all become traps and that she has been running away her whole life. Nevertheless, she prepares to escape yet again. She dances barefoot giddily on the terrace but steps on the broken glass littering the porch and cuts her feet in an ironic enactment of the story of *The Red Shoes.*

The book ends at the same balcony where it begins. A mysterious man climbs up and knocks at her door. In traditional romance fiction, when the heroine hears someone on the balcony and asserts "I knew who it would be," the villain or rescuer appears and the book ends in tragedy or comedy. In Atwood's novel, the ending is deferred, for the man on the balcony is neither killer nor rescuer (or, given the disturbing tendency of men in the novel, he may be both). He is the newspaper reporter investigating the story of her drowning. Joan first hits him with a Cinzano bottle, then begins a friendship with him and tells him her story. And she avers, "I didn't tell any lies. Well, not very many" (378). Because the entire novel may be his version of her story, the novel raises the question of the woman author's control of her text, or indeed of any woman's authority over her own story. Has the journalist gained control of Joan's narrative, or has she retained control, shaping the story to suit her own purposes? This question of textual authority will reappear in *The Handmaid's Tale.*

Joan claims that she will return to Toronto to clear the friends who have been accused of pushing her overboard in her staged drowning. Yet she delays and visits the reporter, of whom she is starting to speak in romantic ways. She believes that he knows her better than anyone else, because she has told her whole story to him; she believes that he has seen a part of her that no one else has seen when she beans him with the bottle. Atwood explains, "She's gotten as far as saying, 'I am who I am—take it or leave it.' . . . She feels better with [him] . . . than with anybody else [because] . . . the new relationship will be on some kind of honest basis" (Struthers, 66). But the conclusion leaves unanswered questions. Will there be a "new relationship"? Will Joan return to Toronto? Which parts of the narrative are true and which are lies? Who was responsible for the threatening notes? And on and on.

In *Lady Oracle* Atwood writes a fiction of a Gothic novelist continuing to spin out the Gothic narrative of her life. The reader is left with the loose ends that Joan believes are her stock in trade when she confesses that she will never "be a very tidy person" (380).

And Atwood the storyteller continues to spin out her narratives. Her next novel, *Life Before Man,* traces its lineage to another genre, the nineteenth-century realist novel, in particular George Eliot's novel *Middlemarch*. Focusing on central issues of heterosexual relationships and of career and marriage, *Life Before Man* has a more schematic structure as it retells a love triangle from the points of view of the three central characters.

Chapter Four

Lost Worlds: Three Novels

In the next three novels, *Life Before Man* (1979), *Bodily Harm* (1981), and *The Handmaid's Tale* (1985), which Atwood links as a group, the canvas is larger, the settings and characters more fully realized, and the narrative strategies more complex. As in the earlier novels, the narrators are Gothic heroines, literally or figuratively imprisoned, telling their stories in order to understand their situations and to survive. They are educated middle-class women whose stories raise questions of narrative authority and interpretation. Again, Atwood "expands the brackets" of traditional fictional forms such as the detective thriller and the dystopia as the novels explore and rewrite women's relationship to the traditional male adventure-romance plot.

Each of these novels has a larger cast of characters than the previous ones, and complex social issues are more salient. *Life Before Man* addresses issues of science such as evolution, extinction, and pollution; moreover, it questions the scientific worldview. *Bodily Harm* deals with the psychological ramifications of illness and health, governmental and sexual politics, imperialism, drug dealing, global economics, and journalistic responsibility. *The Handmaid's Tale* explores ideas of governmental politics, totalitarianism, and the individual's responsibility to protest or struggle against repressive governments. The novels continue to incorporate or to comment on evolving feminist social and political critiques, including pornography, the gaze, and the masquerade of gender.

Again, the novels juxtapose the green world of nature and the gray world of the city. Nature, particularly in its cyclic recurrence, may represent a source of spiritual strength counterpointed against a deadening urban environment (*LBM*); however, nature has been tainted by human corruption. Gardens in these novels are fallen Edens: there is no fresh fruit on St. Antoine (*BH*); the tulips in Serena Joy's garden remind the protagonist of the red blood visible on the bodies of Gilead's executed victims hanging publicly like slabs of meat (*HT*).

The time frames become more complex. Whereas Atwood's first novel (*EW*) takes place almost entirely in the narrative present, her subsequent novels are built of layered timescapes, as the narrators remember their pasts and fantasize about the future. *Life Before Man* has the longest time span in the narrative present of all Atwood's novels (just under two years); most of the other novels take place in a few weeks, or even days, with the largest portions devoted to memory or fantasy. The cyclic time of myth is a subtext counterpointing the linear time of urban twentieth-century Western culture in *Life Before Man*. Rennie's stories (*BH*) intercut time frames from her childhood in Griswold, her young adult life in Toronto, and her trip to the Caribbean in the narrative present. Offred's memories of "the time before" Gilead (*HT*) are a subversive destabilization of official history, for the despotic rulers of Gilead want to obliterate such a past.[1]

Women's friendships become increasingly important in the later novels. Starting with Virginia Woolf's statement that "Chloe liked Olivia" (*A Room of One's Own*), feminists have theorized female friendships. Woolf argues that women's portraits in fiction have often been too simple because they portray women only in relation to men, not in relation to each other, and thus lack depth. In Atwood's previous novels women's relationships with each other were tenuous. In this triad women's friendships become more important and more valued. The women in *Life Before Man* are rivals rather than friends, but in the conclusion Lesje wishes to forgive Elizabeth. Rennie recovers from her emotional paralysis through her connection with Lora (*BH*), and Offred has important relationships with both Ofglen and Moira (*HT*). Moreover, each protagonist experiences a symbolic reconciliation with her mother.

In *Bodily Harm* and *The Handmaid's Tale,* the protagonist's role of storyteller, witness, and reporter reaches its apex as the protagonists find voices with which to inscribe their tales of the human spirit struggling to survive in an imperfect world.

Life Before Man (1979)

Atwood's fourth novel, *Life Before Man,* narrated from the point of view of three central characters (including, for the first time in the Atwood canon, a man), has a more complex structure than previous Atwood texts. In contrast to the elaborate Gothic fantasy of *Lady Oracle,* its plot in the narrative present is a minimalist tale of overlapping love triangles as the marriage of Elizabeth and Nate Schoenhof disintegrates and the relationship of Nate and Lesje Green develops. Other familiar themes of narrative indeterminacy; of realist text and mythic subtext; of rationality and irrationality; of life, death, and rebirth; and of the gray world of the city and the green world of nature appear. Just as Atwood's fictions often "expand the brackets" of the genres that shape them, this novel uses realism to interrogate it. As in other Atwood texts, the narrative is layered: a realist surface grounded in historic, linear time overlays an ambiguous mythic subtext. Moreover, its relatively equal weighting of three narrators indicates the multiplicity of interpretation.

The narrative devices of realism—attention to detail, an emphasis on time as duration and succession, and the presentation of inner mono-logue as a revelation of the experiences and feelings of individual charac-ters—work here to parody and to undermine the realist conventions. Counterpointed against these conventions, the novel insinuates, through seasonal and natural allusions, a covert subtext, a mythic story of cyclical death and rebirth, that may portend a more optimistic vision.

The title's many meanings indicate that the novel invites multiple interpretations. For the paleontologist Lesje Green, life before man refers to the time of the dinosaurs; for Elizabeth it may mean that life takes precedence over heterosexual relationships; and for Nate it may suggest that we have not yet evolved into our full expression of human civility. Other meanings include the length of life stretching out before humans, or the imperative of a life force that may have to disregard humans.

Atwood explains that this is the first of a unit of three novels[2] and that it is written in homage to George Eliot's *Middlemarch:* "It's about life as lived by the middle. . . . It's the middle of Toronto, it's somewhat the middle of the twentieth century, the people are middle-aged."[3] Coral Ann Howells observes that both *Middlemarch* and *Life Before Man* "con-struct a fabric of multiple discourses through dynamic images of lives in process" and both argue against scientific determinism (Howells, 91). Many critics find *Life Before Man* bleak, pessimistic, and repetitious, a dry rendition of the dreary lives of three Torontonians. Atwood addresses this critique in an interview with Adele Freedman: "Depres-sion or pessimism are relative to what you think is really out there in the world. If you think the world is Disneyland, my book is depressing; if you think it's Buchenwald, it's Anne of Green Gables."[4]

Although this book is Margaret Atwood's least-discussed novel, there are useful studies of it.[5] Bouson argues that the novel critiques "socially constructed myths of romantic love" (Bouson, 90). Wilson reads the imagery of dismemberment and alienation and finds a pattern like that of L. Frank Baum's *The Wizard of Oz*: each character lacks important parts and repairs the loss through a quest journey (Wilson, 175–85). One indication of the novel's complexity is reflected in the disagreements about what kind of a fiction it is: a comedy of manners (Goetsch, 137–49), a realist fiction (Atwood[6]), a "transitional text" (Kolodny[7]), or a romance (Carrington, 229; Wilson, 165–97).

The novel is written in the present tense in dated blocks of text (from 29 October 1976 through 18 August 1978) that detail the thoughts and actions of three central characters who comprise a love triangle: Elizabeth Schoenhof, an exhibit planner at the Royal Ontario Museum; her husband, Nate Schoenhof, by turns a lawyer and a toy maker; and Lesje Green, a paleontologist at the museum. Atwood explains, "I wanted a triangular structure. From the point of view of A, B and C were wrong. From the point of view of B, C and A were wrong [and so on]. I wanted a nice little triangle" (Hancock, 269).

The book starts slowly, with part I taking 55 pages to cover three days. A major plot event, the romantic connection of Lesje and Nate, does not get under way until we are almost halfway through the book. Well into the book, Lesje exclaims in frustration: "Nothing has happened yet." Some readers share Lesje's frustration; critics have remarked on the sameness of events and the lack of differentiation of characters. Cathy N. Davidson and Arnold E. Davidson argue that "no obvious change in significance would be effected" if the events of the novel were rearranged ("Prospects and Retrospects in *Life Before Man*," 205–21). Sherrill Grace comments that the book seems to argue that "history, public and private, is pointless."[8]

In fact, a marriage breaks up, a romance starts, there are two attempted rapes, and a great deal of action occurs offstage (in fantasy and in memory): one suicide, one attempted suicide, and three deaths. But the rhythm of the novel slows and obscures the action, layering it with contemplation and memory. And instead of focusing on the dramatic events, the novel emphasizes the characters' thoughts as they carry out the routines of life. Atwood is intentionally downplaying drama to accomplish another purpose, a playful, ironic subversion of the conventions of realist narrative. Gayle Greene and Carol Beran recognize Atwood's achievement. Carol Beran observes that *Life Before Man* "subverts traditional plotting. Atwood marginalizes the rites of passage—births, deaths, marriages, sexual initiations—that often form the climactic moments of novels by having them take place off-stage, generally before or after the time period covered in the novel" (14). Gayle Greene argues that Atwood "has actually accomplished what [Virginia] Woolf and other modernists strive for: she has freed the narrative from plot so that she can focus on the inner events that are the real adventures" (Greene, 67). Thus the minimal plot undermines the narrative tradition that depends on representing external action and conflict.

Just as the plot is minimized, the setting is confined, claustrophobic. The tacky hotel room, Elizabeth's bedroom, Nate's workroom, Auntie Muriel's living room, Chris's small apartment, Lesje's small apartments and office—all are confined indoor spaces. The Royal Ontario Museum is small and enclosed, in contrast to the wild space once occupied by living dinosaurs. Through the use of the museum setting, the book stresses the idea of the past, of history, and emphasizes the role of the observer, but more important it signifies Atwood's recurring critique of Western science and its rational, linear worldview. As John Berger explains, institutions such as zoos came into being to evoke a lost connection with animals at the time that humans lost the immediacy of their relationship to the natural world.[9] Natural-history museums commodify the natural world and turn it into spectacle by wrenching animal remains from their natural locations for display.

Similarly, the novel's narrative structure turns the characters into spectacle, or scientific subject. Employing the unusual narrative device of dated segments of text, the novel reveals the characters' thoughts and emotions not from within as in first-person narration, but from the perspective of a distanced observer. Sherrill Grace calls these dated narrative blocks a "collection of field notes that attempts to sum up the species it purports to describe" (Grace 1980–81, 168). And note that Lesje, the scientist, is also a bemused observer, a cataloguer who often finds living people more difficult to understand than the bones she labels. Motifs of seeing and being seen continue this emphasis on the observer's gaze (see, for example, the two epigraphs and pages 5, 9, 10, 31, 59, 144, and 291–92).

The focus on observation links the scientific worldview to the conventions of narrative realism, and indeed, the novel arose in the eighteenth century in conjunction with the scientific revolution. The realist genre makes claims to objectivity and scientific validity. Linda Nochlin explains that Realist artists tried to imitate scientific attitudes in art by "impartiality, impassivity, scrupulous objectivity, rejection of a priori metaphysical or epistemological prejudice, the confining of the artist to the accurate observation and notation of empirical phenomena and the descriptions of how, and not why, things happen."[10] Realists emphasize the temporal fragment as the basic unit of perceived experience. *Life Before Man* is just such a collection of temporal fragments describing the thoughts and behaviors of its characters.

The novel's focus on the shallow, boring lives of the characters reveals the limits of living according to clock time rather than event time or seasonal time. Words and phrases calling attention to time echo like a metronome throughout the novel. For example, 10 sentences describing the abortive rendezvous of Nate and Lesje in a tacky hotel room contain 10 references to time and sequence. The characters continually look at their watches, observe the sequence and duration of events, worry about the passage of time, remember their pasts, and ponder the future. Their quotidian reality, twentieth-century human time, is measured by clocks and calendars and limited by the inevitability of death.

As a foil to the linear time frame, the narrative alludes to a seasonal, cyclical rhythm. One series of dates establishes the rhythms of the historical/political world (11 November, Remembrance Day; 15 November 1976, the election victory of Parti Quebecois; 9 July, Elizabeth's birthday). As is typical of Atwood's gift for parody and black humor, some of the dates are used for their darkly comic effects. For example, two violent sexual encounters occur in the entries for 16 February 1977, just after Valentine's Day, a holiday usually associated with romantic love. Further, at Christmas, the celebration of spirituality and birth, we have instead Martha's mock suicide. The timing of these events calls attention to the characters' lack of love and spirituality.

Yet the temporal structure of the novel insinuates the theme of spiritual possibility, as the novel foregrounds the seasons and the tone shifts from autumnal despair and death to summer's fertility and fruition. Part I is elegiac. The novel begins in backward-looking despair as Elizabeth mourns her dead lover, Chris Beecham, at Halloween, traditionally a time to pay homage to the spirits of one's beloved dead. Parts II and III occur in winter, from November 1976 through February 1977, a time of stagnation, although the connection between Nate and Lesje has a tentative beginning. Part IV takes place in spring and early summer, from March through July 1977. In keeping with the spring motif of growth and fertility, this section is built around growing sexual desire, and seduction. The mood shifts from loss to hopefulness as the romance of Nate and Lesje continues. Images of fertility and sterility characterize Lesje's thoughts on 29 April, the day before May Day. On 22 June, the summer solstice, she is confused about her supposed triumph over her rival Elizabeth (276). Part V takes approximately a whole year, from 3 September 1977 through 18 August 1978, and ends with tentative optimism.

Each of the characters is connected with a season. Chris, for example, is identified with summer. His surname, Beecham suggests the green world of growth, while his first name indicates his godlike quality. A nature deity, red-haired and passionate, he first appears in the novel on a burning August afternoon in 1975, to flaunt his affair with Elizabeth. But in October 1976, as Elizabeth spurns him and the year approaches its end, he kills himself, symbolically enacting the death of the fertility god who dies at harvest time so that new life may grow in the following season. In contrast to the declining Chris, the burgeoning Lesje is identified with spring, with bones and the earth, and she will take Elizabeth's place to continue the cycle of generation.

In contrast to the novel's claustrophobic urban setting, the characters fantasize about open, natural spaces with more leisurely temporal structures. Elizabeth visits a planetarium and thinks about the stars and the intervals of astronomic time. Lesje's signature fantasy is of prehistoric dinosaurs. Nate imagines tropical islands and exotic native people diving for sponges. Each of these spatial fantasies presupposes a more open, larger natural world and an organic, cyclical time where the lives and deaths of individual humans are perceived as part of the rhythm of nature. Images of the green world attain weight and symbolic power by their repetition, their psychological value, and their contrast with the constricted, urban lives of the protagonists.

In contrast to its elegiac start, the novel ends with a muted possibility of celebration (although it is characteristically ambiguous). Gayle Greene points out that while the characters were initially static and locked into stagnant relationships, they each "end with the capacity to imagine better things and to make new connections" (82). The novel's concluding sections evoke a time of fruition presented in images of harvest, fertility, pregnancy, renewed desire, and utopian yearnings. Each character experiences a connection to the green world and finds at least a temporary resolution of concerns. Lesje (whose surname is Green) may be pregnant. Further, she is no longer afraid of Elizabeth and is prepared to make peace with her. Nate thinks of making love with Lesje outdoors. Elizabeth is unexpectedly moved by pictures of Chinese peasants harvesting glowing purple eggplants. She plans a front porch picnic for her daughters, finding herself newly able to experience deep emotion and to affirm her connection to the green world.

Just as *Lady Oracle* employs Gothic and romantic conventions for parody and caricature, *Life Before Man* uses realism to undercut it. Three of the novel's strategies in particular—the exaggerated references to temporality, the minimal plot, and the dated narrative blocks that suggest objective scientific observers—work to reveal the shortcomings of the realist conventions. In counterpoint with this deterministic and constricted perception, the novel interpolates a cyclic view of time that opens up mythic possibilities of renewal.

In contrast, *Bodily Harm* is an intricately plotted novel in the detective thriller genre that presents a tale of a woman writer unraveling a plot of romance and political intrigue as she awakens from emotional paralysis.

Bodily Harm (1981)

Bodily Harm tells the story of Renata (Rennie) Wilford, a "lifestyles" journalist recovering from a mastectomy who flees Toronto for a working vacation on a Caribbean island and finds herself in the midst of a political revolution. Its Caribbean setting seems a radical departure for Atwood. Yet its female protagonist relating her story, its subversion of literary conventions, its focus on sexual and governmental politics (and avoidance of political solutions), its complex interweaving of realism and fantasy, its ambiguously interpolated mythic and biblical subtexts, and its enigmatic conclusion are familiar Atwood themes. The book has been widely reviewed and continues to receive critical attention, which Lorna Irvine summarizes in her thoughtful and provocative monograph, *Collecting Clues*. Of particular interest are a debate between Jennifer Strauss and Helen Tiffin on the novel's politics, and Roberta Rubenstein's analysis of the Pandora myth in the novel.[11]

An overtly political novel, *Bodily Harm* is informed by discussions of postcolonialism and by evolving 1970s feminist discourses, particularly on pornography and on the politics of women's bodies, as formulated by French feminists such as Helene Cixous and Luce Irigaray. Retelling the stories of Rennie and of Lora, a woman Rennie meets in the Caribbean, the novel examines sexual and class politics in the context of misogyny and violence ranging from erotic scopophilia (pleasure in looking, as signaled by the John Berger epigraph: "A woman's presence . . . defines what can and cannot be done to her") to governmental intrigue and political revolution. The novel reflects Atwood's political interests. In the year it was published she addressed a world meeting of Amnesty International in Toronto and published *True Stories,* a book of poems with strong thematic links to *Bodily Harm* that deals in part with political oppression and torture (see especially "Notes Toward a Poem That Can Never be Written").

Illness, a new theme for Atwood, figures prominently in the novel. In fact, Atwood considered using for epigraphs quotations about the complexities of surgery, "which is at once murderous, powerful, healing and full of love" from physician Richard Seltzer's books *Confessions of a Knife* and *Mortal Lessons.* One of *Bodily Harm*'s dedicatees is Jennifer Rankin, an Australian poet who died of breast cancer (the others are Graeme Gibson and his sons). In the novel, Rennie's illness becomes a metaphor for the disorder of the body politic.

Atwood again sets a woman's narrative into the context of traditional fictional conventions, in this case the typically male-centered detective thriller. According to Grace Epstein, in the thriller, a heroic male validates his sexual prowess by seducing beautiful women, but the core of the plot is his demonstration of his heroism in contest with other men.[12] Epstein argues: "Atwood's female protagonist struggles to gain control of her life and her body and to write a narrative that aptly reflects . . . her experience as a woman" (80). *Bodily Harm* interpolates feminist questions about the way society reads women's bodies in the thriller, thereby problematizing the narrative. Marilyn Patton demonstrates how Atwood exploits the form of the detective thriller to parody and critique the genre: "While maintaining some thriller characteristics, the very fragmented, non-linear form of the novel makes demands on the reader which render impossible either the climax or the instant gratification available in the usual linear, climactic thriller. Additionally, the operation of multiple levels of the plot . . . is an attempt to force the reader to . . . recognize that the thriller style itself may be dangerous, insofar as it condones simplistic approaches to, for example, international politics and male-female relationships" (Patton, 163).

The narrative juxtaposes the present with stories from different times in the past. It begins with Rennie's statement "This is how I got here" (11), but in fact we can't really be sure where "here" is. The confusion of time and place reflects Rennie's psychological perplexity. Assessing the narrative confusion, Lorna Irvine points to the novel's use of a detective board game, Clue, and explains that the reader must untangle the clues to resolve the story. Irvine sets out several problematic aspects, such as the confusion of time and space in the novel, the frequent references to Rennie's states of passivity, and the pervasive hospital and illness imagery. The first four parts of the novel each end with Rennie in bed (the first three times alone, the fourth with Paul) or being drunk or drugged. Irvine's intriguing theory is that the entire story is Rennie's drug-induced dream while she is undergoing surgery (Irvine, 96–99).

Several critics have noted that hand imagery is important in the novel. Sharon Rose Wilson reads the novel as grounded in (among many other intertexts) the fairy tales "The Girl without Hands" and "The Robber Bridegroom," which tell of the rebirth and transformation of a young woman married to death. Rennie remembers her grandmother's disorientation and fear that she has misplaced her hands. In the conclusion touching becomes a way for Rennie to experience herself as fully alive and connected to others.

Is Rennie Wilford lucky? On the novel's second page a policeman tells her she is lucky because he scared away an intruder who broke into her apartment. Although they rescue her from physical violence, the police imply that she has invited the intrusion. Repeatedly in the novel men rescue her, yet the rescuers soon pose threats. In the book's conclusion she is in jail, caught in the middle of a revolution in a small Caribbean island, in need of rescue from abusive law-enforcement authorities, witness to her cellmate's terrible beating. Nevertheless, she believes herself to be lucky. The word lucky resonates through the text.

In her hometown of Griswold, Ontario, a place Rennie describes as boringly middle-class and uptight, people believe that "good luck was unlucky . . . [because] everything evened out in the end: if you had too much good luck one day, you'd have bad the next" (72). After Rennie's mastectomy the nurse and physician tell her she is lucky; however, she continues to feel vulnerable and threatened and wonders "why doesn't she feel lucky?" (22) On the Caribbean island a deaf-mute tries to shake Rennie's hand to bring her good luck, but she misunderstands his intent and runs away. The mysterious American expatriate, Paul, who rescues her by interpreting the situation, explains her reaction as "Alien reaction paranoia. . . . Because you don't know what's dangerous and what isn't, everything seems dangerous" (76). Paradoxically, in the book's conclusion, having learned what is dangerous, Rennie will feel lucky for the first time.

Rennie's mastectomy initiates the metaphor of disease, of both the physical and the social bodies, that structures the novel. She begins to have fantasies of her body as rotting, disintegrating, and she feels disembodied, disconnected from her body. Significantly, it is a wound in her breast, a site of her sexual identity, that initiates Rennie's crisis. Frightened by her illness, she toughens the shell she has already built around herself to hide her vulnerability. When her withdrawal prompts her lover, Jake, to leave, she feels lost and empty; indeed, the book begins with his absence.

Jake is a package designer who enjoyed "packaging" her, dressing her in sexy underwear. The metaphor of packaging recurs through the book to signify confusions of outside and inside, surface and depth. Rennie appears whole, but she feels maimed; a travel brochure touts the islands' beauty but ignores poverty and political corruption; men who appear to be rescuers are also destroyers; a box that purportedly holds medicine actually contains a gun. Rennie faces these contradictions as she tries to interpret the unsettling events she encounters. Rennie has been a "packager" herself, writing about "lifestyles" and starting fashion fads.

Crime and violence are rampant both in Toronto, where Rennie lives, and in the Caribbean country to which she travels for a working vacation. The book starts when Rennie returns to her apartment after Jake has moved out. She learns that an intruder broke into her apartment and left a coiled rope on her bed as a sign of harmful intent, an ominous linking of sex and violence. The fact that one of the titles Atwood considered for this novel was "Rope Quartet" signals the centrality of this incident. After the intruder has entered her bedroom, Rennie feels violated and worries about "faceless strangers." She wonders—what is at the end of the rope? "A hand, then an arm . . . and finally a face" (41). She thinks of this man as "an ambassador, from some place she didn't want to know any more about" (41). But the other men in Rennie's life (Paul, Daniel, Dr. Minnow, and even Jake) are also dangerous, "ambassadors" from places she would prefer not to know about.

Rennie's relationships with these men carry overtones of violence. Jake enjoys playing sexual power games, decorating their apartment with erotic, sadomasochistic pictures, and climbing in through the window and pretending to be a rapist. Just as Jake enacts the role of the demon lover, the dark side of the romantic lover, so too is Daniel Luoma, the surgeon who performs the mastectomy, also an ambivalent figure. Signifying the ambiguity of the medical profession, Daniel is the man who simultaneously invades Rennie's body and saves her life. Paul, the handsome stranger that Rennie meets on St. Antoine, is perhaps the most ambivalent, a potential rescuer or destroyer. He is implicated in drug dealing, gun running, and political intrigue. His involvement in this range of activities points to the dangerous links between drugs, power, violence, and romantic fantasy. Coral Ann Howells argues that Rennie tries to implicate the men she meets in her romantic fantasies, to turn them into rescuers (Howells, 116). They all reject this role, and Rennie finds herself in prison, at the mercy of the very authorities who ought to be protecting her.

In the novel's terms, the danger men pose to women starts in scopophilia and escalates through pornography to rape and murder. Rennie researches the topic of pornography for a magazine article and is nauseated by the gynephobic violence she discovers. Coral Ann Howells explains that "Atwood uses the rhetoric of pornography to explore the connections between the discourses of sexuality on the one hand and discourses of political power on the other" (Howells, 119).

Feeling disoriented and vulnerable after her mastectomy and Jake's departure, Rennie convinces the editor of *Visor* magazine to give her a travel feature assignment in the Caribbean nation composed of the twin islands, St. Antoine and Ste. Agathe. She finds that the islands fester with social ills; political corruption, poverty, and violence are rampant. She tries to ignore the evidence of this corruption and seems surprisingly naive for a reporter. For example, she agrees to pick up a box of medicine from the customs office at the airport, then finds that the box is surprisingly heavy and "too big to fit into the trunk" of a taxi (121). Yet although she feels duped, she does not investigate the contents or inquire. Rennie's willful blindness to the political and social problems is in part a caricature of Canada, wishing to be helpful but removed from and oblivious to the real conditions of third-world countries.

Rennie has rejected the role of investigative journalist for that of "lifestyle reporter," a commentator on fashion trends. Confronted with the gap between the travel story she planned to write and the facts of the islands' poverty and corruption, she at first becomes silent. When she ultimately does decide to tell their stories, she will need a different language, the language of the reporter or "subversive" (301). Thus, when Dr. Minnow, a veterinarian who is running for Prime Minister in the local election, asks her to write about the political events on St. Antoine, she refuses, explaining that she's interested only in what people wear and what they eat. He responds, referring pointedly to the significance of such apparently trivial matters: "What the people eat, what they wear, this is what I want you to write about" (136). And indeed, Atwood reveals the connection between food and political power in most of her novels, explaining the relationship in her address "Amnesty International," delivered in 1981, the year *Bodily Harm* was published: "By 'politics'. . . I mean who is entitled to do what to whom, with impunity; who profits by it; and who therefore eats what" (*SW,* 394).

Many of the problems of this small country are caused by the hunger of larger capitalist countries for its food and resources. Tourists drive up the price of sugar. Paul remarks that no one wants St. Antoine to grow

anything but bananas (46). The main resource St. Antoine supplies is
not food, but a dangerous inedible substitute for real nourishment: the
island has become a distribution center processing Colombian drugs for
shipment to the United States. The CIA is implicated and so are most of
the island's ruling cadre. Paul himself is "the connection." Drugs have
implications for Rennie as well. She is often depicted smoking marijuana
or drinking alcohol, pastimes that suggest both her desire to rebel
against a straitlaced upbringing and her general lack of purpose and
direction. Moreover, her use of drugs is linked to a different addiction:
her addiction to love.

Drug dealing is the evil hiding within this fallen Caribbean Eden, a
place that is beautiful on the surface but rotting and corrupt under-
neath. The coiled rope on Rennie's bed and the many other rope images
remind us of the snake. The novel develops the failed Eden metaphor in
imagery of politics, religion, and ecology. For example, there are many
gardens and brightly colored flowers, but there is no fresh fruit at the
hotel where Rennie stays, and imagery of rotting food is prevalent.

Names in the novel have biblical and religious overtones, frequently
used ironically. For example, the islands are named after the saints
Agatha and Anthony. Saint Agatha was a third-century Sicilian martyr
who was killed by having her breasts amputated. Although Saint Peter
healed her, she died in prison. (Notably, the novel does not reveal
whether Rennie actually leaves prison or only imagines that she does.)
The first Saint Anthony is the patron saint of lost things, and the later
St. Anthony of Padua is the patron saint of the poor. Dr. Minnow suggests the fish that symbolizes the work of the Catholic church. As a veterinarian and a political reformer he is the would-be healer, a Christlike
figure who is killed for his political involvement. Lorna Irvine notes that
he "connects also with the Fisher King," the wounded ruler who is
unable to nourish his people (Irvine, 104). Jake comes from Jacob, the
supplanter, the brother who tricks his twin, Esau, and his father. The
biblical Jacob wins his father's blessing in his brother's place by "packaging" himself falsely, placing the skin of a goat on his arms so that he
will feel hairy like Esau to his blind father's touch.

Lora stands for crown of laurel leaves, the ancient emblem of victory.
Irvine points out the unusual spelling here and suggests it may connote
"oral," referring to the stories that she and Rennie exchange (41). The
word "lore" is linked as well. Repeatedly raped and brutally beaten, Lora
is far from victorious. Her terrible suffering becomes the means by
which Rennie attains her victory of sympathetic self-forgetfulness and

"massive involvement" in the life of another human. Reaching out to the wounded Lora, Rennie attempts to save her life, and in the process she herself is reborn.

After Lora's brutal beating, Rennie grasps her hand and attempts to "bring her back to life . . . gritting her teeth with the effort. . . . this is a gift, this is the hardest thing she's ever done. . . . Surely, if she can only try hard enough, something will move and live again, something will get born" (299). It is not clear if Lora is alive. Her face bloodied and beaten to a pulp, Lora is now a "faceless stranger," the face at the end of the hand and arm. Through her efforts to rescue Lora, Rennie experiences herself as reborn, thus actualizing her name, Renata. Bouson comments that the narrative here "offer[s] two competing versions of reality [as it] replaces the image of the dehumanizing hand that beats and mutilates with that of the healing hand that rescues" (Bouson, 130). Similarly, the narrative offers competing versions of the fates of Lora and Rennie.

Thinking about herself, Rennie worries: "She will never be rescued," then continues, "She has already been rescued. She is not exempt. Instead she is lucky, suddenly, finally, she's overflowing with luck" (301). In the novel's paradoxical conclusion, Rennie, imprisoned in a politically unstable country, at her most vulnerable and helpless, feels herself to be lucky. Interestingly, Atwood called this book her "most affirmative, because you can only measure affirmation in terms of what it's set against. Having hope for the human race in India is a really different thing from having hope for the human race in Texas."[13]

Rennie has come into awareness of human interdependence, of the linkages of the personal and the political, of the cancerous physical body and the corrupt and rotten body politic; consequently, she is now willing to risk herself to help another person. Moreover, she decides to renew her dedication to investigative reporting and therefore believes herself to be a "subversive" (301).

Diana Brydon questions the value of Rennie's transformation; she finds that the novel moves away from historical consciousness to individual consciousness, a quasi-religious rebirth. "*Bodily Harm* appears suspicious of [political action], preferring a personal transformation and the reporter's authority to describe events as she sees them to any kind of interactive dialogue."[14] Indeed, Atwood is often suspicious of political solutions; accordingly, her protagonists become witnesses rather than activists.

The novel reaches its climax at a writer's moment of commitment, of dedication to her vocation. Rennie's transformation is complete when she determines to become an investigative reporter, to write what she sees, declaring that "she is a subversive. . . . A reporter" (300–1). And perhaps *Bodily Harm* is the subversive story that Rennie writes after she returns to Canada. Rennie's act of touching Lora and her commitment to becoming a political writer mark her acceptance of journalistic and human responsibility and her attempts to find ways of connecting. Similarly, in Atwood's next novel, *The Handmaid's Tale,* the protagonist chooses storytelling as her means of political action.

The Handmaid's Tale (1985)

Begun in England in 1984—the year that gave a name to one of this novel's literary ancestors, George Orwell's classic dystopia—*The Handmaid's Tale* inscribes a terrifying vision of a near-future dystopian world, the totalitarian nation of Gilead, where women are denied literacy and compelled to serve as domestic or sexual servants. A complex and many-layered political satire, the novel joins a long tradition of dystopian fictions that point out dangerous social tendencies in hopes that readers will act to forestall the outcomes they depict. At the same time it also looks wryly at recurring Atwood themes such as women's friendship; mother-daughter relations; other literary genres such as the comedy of manners, the Gothic, and the romance; conventions of storytelling, narration, authorial authority, and interpretation; and language itself. The title emphasizes the idea of story and reminds us that we are reading the story from the victim's perspective. The narrator, Offred, continues the storytelling tradition of Joan Foster and Rennie Wilford. Her tale, a science-fiction costume Gothic, may be Joan Foster's new novel. Or perhaps the narrator is a reporter revealing the daily life of Gilead, following Dr. Minnow's mandate to report "what people wear, what they eat."

The novel garnered many awards, including the Governor General's Award for Fiction in 1986, as well as the Arthur C. Clarke Science Fiction Award and the Toronto Arts Award. Atwood's first book to attain best-seller status in the United States, it remains her most frequently studied and written-about text. Most larger studies of Atwood include chapters on *The Handmaid's Tale,* and two useful monographs explicate and contextualize it.[15]

The Handmaid's Tale is the first novel of Atwood's to be produced as a full-length feature film in the United States. Its dramatic plot elements—sexual oppression, love, and betrayal set in the context of political revolution—make it highly cinegraphic. Yet the film was relatively unsuccessful at the box office. Indeed, many features of the novel do not translate well into film. As Atwood observes, movies must be about action, and a great deal of the novel takes place while the narrator heroine is sitting or lying in bed alone. In the film some aspects of the novel were lost: the ambiguity about the fate of Offred's husband, Luke, and Offred's monologues. Since Offred knows Luke is dead, her affair with Nick is less conflict ridden. The film omits her memories of her mother, her wordplay, and her self-conscious questioning of her motives and actions; it changes the focus from her inner life to her actions so as to emphasize the romance plot.[16]

The novel purports to be a narrative recorded on audiocassette tapes after the fact by the protagonist, the handmaid Offred, one of the group of young women with viable ovaries who has been taken from her own home, "re-educated" at the Red (reeducation) Center and assigned for reproductive purposes to a high-ranking Commander in order to ameliorate the declining population of Gilead. Offred's tale "braid[s] . . . three time lines: the time before Gilead, the Red Center memories, and [her] time in Commander Fred's household" and recounts in meticulous detail the daily life of a handmaid in a repressive totalitarian country (Thompson, 55). As Thompson observes, Offred has an "ongoing love affair with the written word," and she is anxious "to tell her story as accurately as possible" (59). Accordingly, she frequently revises passages to get them more correct, or tries out multiple versions when she does not know the outcome (in the case of her friend Moira's story or Luke's fate). Yet she realizes that "all I can hope for is a reconstruction" (*HT,* 340). Moreover, the story we read has been transcribed, edited, and ordered by an archivist, Professor James Darcy Pieixoto of Cambridge University, who discovers the tapes in an attic; thus it is filtered through the perspective of a reader from another culture. This renarrating and rewriting of the story leads Michele Lacombe to call it a palimpsest (a layer of text written over an erased text).[17]

As in other Atwood novels, the multilayering of texts brings into question the conventions of storytelling, literary criticism, and interpretation. To what extent does the author of this tale or of any text have authority over her own written words? The question of textual authority has been of particular importance to women, for historically men have been the critics, editors, and publishers. I call Offred a Scheherazade figure and describe the novel as an exploration of storytelling, "a provocative inquiry into the origins and meanings of narrative. . . . It begins— with the handmaid's narrative—exploring silence and speech, oppression and resistance. The novel ends—with a male scholar's narrative—questioning the limits of narrative and interpretation. The subtexts of both narratives are . . . meditations on storytelling and meaning. Both face the storyteller's paradox: they are eager to communicate, but anxious about the limits of communication; they find language simultaneously empowering and constraining. . . As [Offred] retells her story, she questions the limits of narration, of memory, of language itself."[18]

Indicating immediately its layering of discourses, the novel starts with three epigraphs—a Sufi proverb, a quotation from Jonathan Swift's "Modest Proposal," and Genesis 30:1–3. These quotations, drawn from the domains of literature, political satire, and religion, point to a wide scope of political and spiritual issues, indicate a seriousness of purpose, and signal to the reader that several strata of meaning and language will be superimposed on each other and played against each other to produce ironic effects.

Among the questions critics debate are these: Is the novel feminist? What is its genre? The two questions are related, because every genre sets up assumptions that shape the reader's relation to the text. This novel has been called dystopian science fiction, satire, romance, palimpsest, political allegory, and epistolary narrative. I believe that the novel is predominantly a satire, a genre that, like dystopian fiction, addresses an exaggerated version of present evils to readers who have some power to act. What are the targets of satire here? One target is patriarchal politics. Another is right-wing religious fundamentalism, an ideology that was politically active and particularly visible in the United States during the 1980s. Serena Joy, the Commander's wife, is a version of Phyllis Schlafly, a lawyer and public speaker who actively crusaded against the Equal Rights Amendment. But Atwood's satire cuts many ways, chaffing not only the conservative right wing but also militant feminists like Offred's outspoken mother, who participates in burning of pornographic texts, and ordinary women like Offred who remain marginalized and passive.

Another genre that figures importantly here and throughout the Atwood canon is the female Gothic, a narrative of a motherless young woman finding her way in an oppressive patriarchal society. Replete with political and sexual intrigue and numerous closed or secret rooms (the dormitory at the Re-education Center, the Commander's office, the handmaid's room, Nick's room, the doctor's examining room, Jezebel's, and the room in Maine where the narrator presumably records her story), the novel narrates the tale of an unprotected young woman seeking to understand a confusing society and to escape from male oppression. Additionally, as we shall see, the novel employs the Gothic motif of hiding and revealing.

Is the tale feminist? It addresses questions of concern to feminists such as reproductive rights, the male gaze, sexual politics, and women's access—as readers, speakers, and writers—to public discourse and other sources of power and status. Epigraphs that Atwood considered for the novel include a quote from a feminist theoretician, Germaine Greer, about the pressures on women to bear children and a quote from Paulette Jiles about women's belief that they are Scheherazades who need to tell their stories to save themselves. Scholars have argued both for and against a feminist interpretation of the novel.[19] For example, Madonne Miner reads the novel as nonfeminist, arguing that in choosing a romance plot for herself, Offred refuses the options of political action. Viewing the novel as political allegory, Sandra Tomc counters Miner and suggests that the romance plot becomes another satirical strategy for Atwood to extricate Offred (Canada) from her entrapment at the hands of Gilead (the United States).

In its emphasis on the gaze as oppressive, the novel borrows from feminist film theory that elucidates a male gaze objectifying women. The gaze is important in the three novels of this group. In *Life Before Man* the style itself suggests a distanced observer recording the behaviors and thoughts of the characters. Rennie in *Bodily Harm* is a reporter, an observer, but she is closely watched by a series of men, including her lover, an intruder, and the prison authorities. *The Handmaid's Tale* is most explicit in its yoking of violence and the gaze. The women of Gilead are color coded to strip them of their individual identities and to mark their social status and relationships to men: in a parodic version of nuns' habits the handmaids wear red robes and white wimples, the wives blue dresses, and the Marthas (the servants) green. The Eyes, the spy network of Gilead, enforce discipline through surveillance. Searchlights illuminate the nights; the handmaids must show their passes at checkpoints on the street when they go marketing. Stephanie Barbé Hammer is particularly insightful in her explication of the gaze as a means of enforcing social discipline.[20] The government, aware that "the best and most cost-effective way to control women . . . was through women themselves," appoints the Aunts—older, infertile women—to supervise and monitor the handmaids (*HT*, 390). Aunt Lydia warns the handmaids she is reeducating that "to be seen is to be penetrated" (38). Aunt Helena was a supervisor of Weight Watchers in the time before. In that role, she served to control women's appetites for food so that their bodies would remain slim and acceptable to social standards. In Gilead, she controls women's appetites for freedom and knowledge, slimming down their minds and behaviors to be acceptable to Gilead's social standards.

The emphasis on the gaze is related to the Gothic theme of uncovering secrets. Accordingly, there are many instances of hiding and revealing. The handmaid's names are obliterated as they assume the names of their Commanders (Of-fred, Of-charles, Of-warren). Thus, the narrator's name (probably June) is hidden but revealed as a possibility to the inquisitive reader. The Mayday underground is secret, but Ofglen reveals its existence to Offred. Bodies of "criminals," publicly visible but with pillowcases covering their faces, hang from the red brick wall (that Atwood informs us was formerly the wall of Harvard Yard). Costumes are another means of hiding and revealing. As we have seen, the handmaids as individuals are hidden while their red robes and white wimples indicate their status. Offred's friend Moira wears the stolen clothing of an Aunt from the Red Center as a disguise when she attempts to escape. When the Commander smuggles Offred into the nightclub/brothel Jezebel's, he disguises her doubly by dressing her in a tawdry costume and covering her in his wife's blue cloak. Here, as in *The Edible Woman,* Atwood presents the concept that femininity, indeed gender itself, depends on masquerade.

Similarly, language and women's relation to it is salient in the novel. Women are forbidden to read. The shops they are allowed to frequent, poorly stocked groceries and produce stores, display signs with pictorial icons. The Bible is unlocked only when the Commander reads it prior to the monthly "ceremony" of sexual intercourse. Aunt Lydia tells the handmaids that "knowledge is temptation" and "pen is envy." Surprisingly, at Offred's first secret rendezvous with the Commander, he invites her to play Scrabble with him, an unexpected violation of the taboo. The words they place on the board are clever combinations of high-scoring letters as well as amusing puns referring to sexuality and language: larynx, zygote, limp, gorge, rhythm. Because language is forbidden, the game is eroticized. Indeed, even the tiles seem deliciously sensuous; Offred imagines eating them like candy. Joseph Andriano considers the novel itself a game of Scrabble, built on power plays revolving around use of language.[21]

Reading is illegal, but even conversation is treasonous. Stock phrases and rituals of greeting are permitted, but discussion is a punishable offense. Because she is most often alone in her tiny, sparsely furnished room (Atwood may be alluding ironically here to Virginia Woolf's observation that, in order to write, a woman requires a room of one's own), Offred spends a great deal of time thinking, and her reflections on language are an important ingredient of the novel. She often engages in puns and wordplay, pondering the origins of words such as Mayday and habit. Because their significance is determined by context, these words often function as indications of the distance between the "time before" and the time of Gilead. For example, the contemporary mayday, an international distress signal derived from the French *m'aider* (help me), is the name of the Gilead underground.

Yet despite the constraints on socializing and conversing, even within the patriarchal world of Gilead, a fragile, invisible women's community manages to exist. Although they are confined to their homes, the women develop networks of support and information. Offred comments that the English language lacks a word for women's friendship comparable to "fraternize," which acknowledges a brotherhood of men; if there were such a word, it would have to be "sororize" (15). In spite of the grim situation in Gilead, she makes meaningful connections with two other women, Moira, her friend from "the time before," and the handmaid Ofglen. Thompson observes that Offred's longest relationship is with Moira. Here and in the later books, friendship between women becomes increasingly important in Atwood's work.

The novel explores another women's connection, the mother-daughter bond, for in this complicated version of the myth of Demeter and Persephone, Offred is both the daughter searching for her lost mother and the mother hoping to recover her lost daughter. During the time she is imprisoned in her Commander's house, the land of Gilead suffers a plague of sterility, just as Demeter's mourning for her daughter brings sterility to the earth. Of course, every mother is also a daughter herself: another thread of Offred's narrative remembers her mother and refigures their relationship. Her birth mother, an ardent feminist and therefore a political enemy of Gilead, has been exiled to the toxic-waste colonies.

Offred comes to think more sympathetically about her mother as she narrates her tale. She realizes her mother's strengths and limitations and comes to accept her (154–57, 234). Moreover, in telling her story she puts into practice her mother's insistence on telling women's history, and recording her tale becomes a means of political action of which her mother would approve. In a sense, she has become her mother. The portrait of Offred's mother is drawn with tongue in cheek: she verges on caricature of the earnest feminist whose life is shaped by her politics and excludes emotion. Nevertheless, Offred muses, "No mother is ever, completely, a child's idea of what a mother should be, and I suppose it works the other way around as well. But despite everything, we didn't do badly by one another, we did as well as most. I wish she were here, so I could tell her I finally know this" (234).

In contrast, Serena Joy, her Commander's wife, is ambiguously positioned as stepmother/rival. Each of the two mothers was politically active in connection with women's issues (although their interpretations of what women want are diametrically opposed), and each has been silenced by the Gileadean regime. Offred's feminist birth mother spoke out against pornography and on behalf of women's reproductive choices. Serena Joy was an antifeminist, an advocate of women's subservient role. Nevertheless, she too has been silenced and unhappily finds herself enacting the role she endorsed. With the power that remains to her, she has become Offred's enemy, coconspirator, and rival in a bizarre triangle set up by the patriarchy.

When Offred first meets Serena Joy, she wants "to turn her into an older sister, a motherly figure, someone who would understand and protect me" (21), but she realizes even at their first meeting that this is impossible. Nevertheless, she comes to feel compassion for her pseudostepmother (208). Serena Joy, eager for a child, forms an alliance of convenience to get Offred pregnant with the aid of the chauffeur, Nick (because the Commander is probably sterile). And in spite of the danger to all, Offred continues to carry on an affair with him.

Interestingly, the word "nick" contains many punning meanings: notch or incision; a notch used to keep score; the critical moment, as in "the nick of time"; to unite or couple (used of breeding stocks); to catch, take unawares, nab, or steal. On the other hand, Old Nick is the devil. Nick is a shadowy figure, a screen onto which the protagonist projects her desires for love, for sexuality, and, most especially, for children. He arrives in the nick of time, to couple with her and to steal her from Gilead. He is an instrument of a romance plot that some critics argue undermines the novel's subversive potential.

The extent to which the affair is liberatory is a matter of critical debate. As I noted, Madonne Miner argues that the romance plot casts Offred in a passive role. And indeed, Offred borrows the clichéd language and passive stance of popular romantic fiction to describe the liaison. I believe the issue is more complicated. Her affair and narrative may be her ultimate acts of political engagement. For example, history shows us that political revolution does not necessarily produce an egalitarian society. As Adrienne Rich has written, revolution has often been a revolving door, substituting one order of privileged males for another, rather than a transformation that brings about a systemic change. A sexist political order preceded Gilead and a similar one follows it, as evidenced by the power relationships and the sexist pronouncements of Pieixoto portrayed in the "Historical Notes." Moreover, through her desire for Nick, Offred rejects Gilead's repressive culture to assert her sexuality and her personhood. Ironically, she escapes through the very means by which Gilead sought to entrap her: through the actions of her body, especially her fertile womb. Indeed, Offred's narration of her tale may be the most subversive act possible for her. Her recorded story may have been intended for political outreach by the Gilead underground. Ironically, because the act of narration itself is subversive, Offred's story—the tale of an ordinary woman rather than a heroic rebel— becomes heroically rebellious.

As in other Atwood novels, the ending is enigmatic. In the last chapter Offred steps into the black van escorted by two Eyes, with Nick's promise that he has staged a rescue, a Mayday. Yet her fate is unclear. Professor Pieixoto is unable to determine what happened to her. And her story is retold to us through his point of view. "Atwood has written an open-ended text, (play)fully conscious of the possibilities of deconstruction, reconstruction, and reinterpretation. By . . . inserting gaps in the text, by punning and playing with words, and by suggesting multiple versions, she engages in metafictional commentary on the storytelling process. . . . As Offred's /Atwood's stories are reread and reinterpreted, the ending is postponed, rewritten" (Stein 1991/92, 278).

Storytelling and interpretation continue to be central themes in Atwood's next three novels, *Cat's Eye, The Robber Bride,* and *Alias Grace.* As they tell their stories, the protagonists reclaim their silenced voices to question and unsettle both social and fictional conventions. For, as we shall see, women's stories challenge our assumptions about autobiography and history.

Chapter Five

Victims, Tricksters, and Scheherazades: The Later Novels

The next three novels, *Cat's Eye* (1988), *The Robber Bride* (1993), and *Alias Grace* (1996), told with Atwoodian humor, irony, social realism, and satire, revisit familiar themes: Gothic quests, female friendship, victims, doubles and doubling, memory, myth, and storytelling. The stories are told and retold through multiple narrators, media, or versions, yet gaps always remain. Thus questions of identity and interpretation arise.

Storytelling, with its links to memory, history, and the past, is central. *Cat's Eye* starts with Atwood's eloquent formulation of time as a nonlinear dimension. The novel's present action takes place in a few days, while most of the book is the protagonist's memory of her girlhood. *The Robber Bride* deals with the construction of history. Antonia (Tony) Fremont, a military historian, observes that history is written backward, by the victors. Grace Marks and Simon Jordan alternate the narration of *Alias Grace,* with their stories moving between the present and the past.

Women's friendship is more prominent here than in previous novels. *Cat's Eye* focuses on girls' compelling, often painful friendships and rivalries. *The Robber Bride* counterpoints the stories of women's sexual rivalries with their developing friendships. Grace Marks remembers her intimate friendship with Mary Whitney, and the novel hints that she may have internalized Mary's personality as an alter ego (*AG*).

The protagonists are victims, tricksters, and Scheherazades. The narrator of *Cat's Eye*, Elaine Risley, comes to terms with her past through her autobiographical narrative and paintings. In *The Robber Bride* all of the characters are storytellers. Each friend takes a turn narrating the story of her life, especially her betrayal by Zenia, a master storyteller, a spinner of plots, a trickster whose tales may teach difficult lessons. In fact, Zenia may be a fabrication, a story herself. And after she has disappeared, the three other protagonists cement their friendship by sharing stories, mainly about her. The protagonist of *Alias Grace,* based on a historical woman imprisoned for murder, is the quintessential Atwood Scheherazade, a beautiful and inventive woman who spins her story to a man in hopes that he will rescue her.

Storytelling raises the question of the author's control over her text. Telling a story gives the teller a measure of power; however, once the story is told, the teller loses control, giving up her power to the reader or listener. This issue is problematized, as we have seen, in *The Handmaid's Tale,* where Offred's story is reassembled and edited by a scholar from a later period (*HT*). Atwood continues to explore this theme. Elaine Risley finds the interpretations of her paintings by critics and reviewers hilarious (*CE*). Zenia, who continually invents new stories, teaches that stories have multiple interpretations, some entrapping and others liberating (*RB*). There are multiple versions of Grace's story, including both stream of consciousness and selective narration (*AG*).

Cat's Eye (1988)

Cat's Eye tells and retells—humorously and poignantly, through her narrative and through her paintings, in the present and in memory—the fictionalized autobiography of a successful 50-year-old artist, Elaine Risley. Atwood's most autobiographical novel, it recounts the narrator's psychological retrospective that parallels the retrospective of her paintings in a small Toronto feminist art gallery, Sub-Versions. The novel's complex and multiple structure evokes the complex multiplicities of identity, time, perception, and narrative. Each section of the story, named after one of Elaine's paintings, moves between present and past. Her paintings are sophisticated, multifaceted, and often parodic responses to masterpieces of the Anglo-European aesthetic canon and to Elaine's experiences growing up in post–World War II Toronto.

At the time the book appeared in print Atwood was approaching 50, with her *Selected Poems II,* published in 1987, a poet's equivalent of the artist's retrospective exhibit. Parallels between Atwood's and Elaine's lives are readily apparent: the childhood divided between cities and the bush, the scientist older brother, the entomologist father, the career as an artist. Elaine's story examines the making of an artist, and it depicts her enjoyment of and frustrations with the trappings of her career: the misguided or patronizing interviewers, the facile labels, the reviewers' fashionable jargon. But Atwood insists, "This is a work of fiction.

Although its form is that of an autobiography, it is not one." Just as Atwood's other novels explore and question the generic conventions that shape them, *Cat's Eye* uses the conventions of autobiography to explore the possibilities and limits of autobiography, and of women's autobiography in particular.

In *Cat's Eye* Atwood inscribes a richly sensuous picture of childhood in postwar Toronto and a painfully honest portrayal of the rivalries and cruelty of young girls. She explains, "I sometimes get interested in stories because I notice a sort of blank—why hasn't anyone written about this? *Can* it be written about? Do I dare to write it? *Cat's Eye* was risky business, in a way—wouldn't I be trashed for writing about little *girls,* how trivial? Or wouldn't I be trashed for saying they weren't all sugar and spice? . . . But also I wanted a literary home for all those vanished *things* from my own childhood—the marbles, the Eaton's catalogues. . . . The textures. Part of fiction writing I think is a celebration of the physical world we know—and when you're writing about the past, it's a physical world that's vanished. So the impulse is partly elegiac."[1] Surely, some of these elegiac, celebratory impulses motivate Elaine's paintings as well.

Through its artist protagonist, the novel makes both social and aesthetic statements. Elaine resists the stereotype that women can't be successful artists and risks the self-assertive role of painter. Aesthetically, the centrality of the artist foregrounds questions of perception, artistic production, canonicity, interpretation, and authority. The novel investigates perception through its central images of surveillance (the objectifying gaze) and of the cat's-eye marble that shapes Elaine's vision. The objectifying gaze is shown to be destructive and distancing, whether wielded by men or by women. Nevertheless, the artist may employ her gaze to paint pictures and thereby construct an identity as artist and tell her story.

Several intertexts appear in the novel, including theories of time and cosmology, Shakespeare's *King Lear,* feminist art theory, the conventions of autobiography, and two fairy tales that use frozen perception to symbolize emotional paralysis: the Grimms' "Rapunzel" and Hans Christian Andersen's "The Snow Queen."

Two temporal sequences structure the novel. In the narrative present Elaine describes her visit from her home in Vancouver to Toronto for the opening of her retrospective. In the memory sequence, Elaine retells her girlhood in Toronto, especially her vexed friendships with Carol Campbell, Grace Smeath, and Cordelia (whose surname we do not learn); her time in art school; and her first and second marriages. Her brother, Stephen, tells Elaine that "if we knew enough we could walk through walls . . . and travel [backward] through time" (233). And indeed, Elaine's memories of her childhood are a kind of time travel into her past. As Eleonora Rao explains, Elaine's "return to Toronto occurs not only in space but also in time. . . [Consequently] the novel challenges the dualism of subjective and objective time, as it shows how the structure of chronological time proves to be an inadequate basis upon which to conceptualize and narrate past time" (Rao, 107).

Cat's Eye starts with Elaine meditating on time as dimension: "Time is not a line but a dimension, like the dimensions of space. I began then to think of time as having a shape, something you could see, like a series of liquid transparencies, one laid on top of another. You don't look back along time but down through it, like water. Sometimes this comes to the surface, sometimes that, sometimes nothing. Nothing goes away" (3). Appropriately, the novel's temporal structure produces a textured depth very like shifting layered transparencies. Atwood's acknowledgment of physicists and cosmologists Stephen Hawking, Paul Davies, Carl Sagan, and John Gribbin provides clues to the functions of time here. Rao explains that as "these [cosmological] theories increase in sophistication and complexity, . . . our interpretive models . . . become [more fragile]. The universe is regarded as the product of randomness; identity becomes a shifting construct" (Rao, 115). Accordingly, the novel evokes the instability of memory and narrative and the susceptibility of all subjects (including persons, texts, and paintings) to interpretation. This instability characterizes autobiography as well, despite its claims to factuality.

Autobiography blurs the boundaries between fiction and fact. The autobiographer selects incidents to shape a story in accord with both her perceptions and social conventions. According to Jill Ker Conway, autobiographical stories reproduce traditional fictional plots: "For men [in Western society], the overarching pattern for life comes from adaptations of the story of the epic hero in classical antiquity. Life is an odyssey, a journey through many trials and tests."[2] For women, however, the plot derives from a different tradition, "from the secularized romance, the life plot linking the erotic quest for the ideal mate with property and social mobility. . . . The female heroine is a creature of pure emotion and little intellect, who exists to become the perfect mate for the self-creating hero. Her life history ends when she encounters him, because her existence thereafter is subsumed within his" (Conway, 13–14). Conway argues that this form has created a template for self-presentation that persists into our contemporary period and keeps women from acknowledging either their active agency in producing desired outcomes or their wishes for power, achievement, and adventure. Atwood disrupts this odyssey/romance dichotomy to produce a fictional autobiography that resists traditional patterns. Thus, her female protagonist breaks with the convention that a woman's life history revolves around finding and winning a mate; Elaine seldom speaks about her spouses and focuses on her girlhood and her career rather than on courtship and romantic encounters. Yet Elaine's story is a far cry from the goal-oriented odyssey of the male life story; instead, rather than describing herself acting as a purposeful agent striving toward a goal, she views her life as a series of events that happen to her and denies her own agency in achieving her goals. For example, her decision to become a painter seems accidental: "[I]n the middle of the Botany examination it comes to me, like a sudden epileptic fit, that I'm not going to be a biologist, as I have thought. I am going to be a painter" (270). (And here, it is fascinating to note that Atwood once described her own decision to be a poet in similar fashion: "A large invisible thumb descended from the sky and pressed down on the top of my head. A poem formed" ["Why I Write," 44]).

Several critics discuss the ways this novel engages autobiographical conventions.[3] Nathalie Cooke suggests that Atwood might have chosen the autobiographical form to cause us to question our assumptions about autobiographical fiction, to "eliminate the problem of closure" (since the autobiographer does not know how her life/story will end) and thus allow for the ambiguous endings that Atwood favors, and to compel us to rethink our schemes for literary categorization. Coral Ann Howells and Jessie Givner ground their discussions in Paul De Man's essay "Autobiography as De-Facement" to analyze Atwood's disruption of the distinctions between autobiography and fiction. De Man writes that "autobiography deprives and disfigures to the precise extent that it restores" (81).

Givner finds that Elaine's narrative and paintings participate in this disruption by their use of figuring and disfiguring, facing and defacing. For example, Elaine sees her face on a poster defaced with a mustache and a "graceful goatee to match" (20). She takes this as a sign that she has achieved "a face that attracts mustaches. A public face, a face worth defacing" (20). The face/deface imagery links Elaine to her friend, enemy, and alter ego, the young Cordelia, who draws mustaches on the pictures of women in the Eaton catalogues that the friends cut out and paste into scrapbooks. The adult Elaine titles her painting of Cordelia "Half a Face," and her other paintings also play with the idea of whole and half faces, mirrors and reflections. Similarly her paintings sometimes "deface" canonical artistic masterpieces by using their subject matter to insinuate her own parodic meanings.

Intertwined with the theme of facing and defacing, the novel introduces typical Atwood motifs of mirrors, twinning, and doubling. For example, Elaine and Cordelia, who mirror each other, read a horror comic about a girl who enters her sister's body through a mirror. Similarly, Elaine has two daughters resulting from two marriages. Elaine's paintings contain mirrors, reflecting glass, and the globes that become "her signature." She paints triptychs, multiple versions, to indicate "shifts in perspective," the multiplicity of identity and subjectivity (Howells, 155, 158). Perhaps most significant, Elaine's commemorative visit to the ravine at the novel's conclusion mirrors her childhood trauma.

Elaine's childhood is happy until she is eight. Then a dramatic change occurs in her life; her family settles in a permanent home in Toronto. Before this move, the Risley family had lived during winters in cities and during summers in tents or cabins in the bush, where her father conducted entomological research. Until the move to Toronto, Elaine and her brother are comrades and equals. She expects that having a permanent home and finding girlfriends would be pleasant; however, she discovers that because she moved so frequently and didn't attend schools, she doesn't know the codes that govern girls' friendships and thus becomes the butt of their teasing. Alice Palumbo points out that the novel elucidates the development of suburbs: the conflict between the girls is grounded in "the jockeying for social advantage and position of the suburban world" of the rising middle class in postwar Canada.[4] As a girl in Toronto, Elaine is by turns befriended, ostracized, scolded, and "improved" by the trio of Cordelia, Grace Smeath, and Carol Campbell. Because Mrs. Smeath considers Elaine a "heathen," she condones their scapegoating. The harassment confuses Elaine, causing her to withdraw, to shut down emotionally.

Sharon Rose Wilson and Judith McCombs find parallels for Elaine's emotional paralysis and later release in the novel's intertextual material, two fairy tales about young people with frozen vision: "The Snow Queen" and "Rapunzel." In both tales a powerful older woman subjugates the innocent youth: Dame Goethel locks Rapunzel in a tower, and the Snow Queen casts her spell over the young Kay, freezing his vision,

rendering all objects flat and distant. In each story the oppressed youth
regains freedom by learning sympathy, human feeling, and connection.

In Atwood's version, as in the two fairy tales, vision or perception is
central and complex. The critical gaze of Elaine's friends and Grace's
mother, Mrs. Smeath, threatens her fragile self-concept. In response, she
develops a defensive "cat's eye" view of the world, a distanced, distorted,
frozen perception derived from looking through her favorite marble
(151). Yet she later uses her visual skill, her perception, to create herself
as an artist and to produce paintings that avenge herself on her childhood antagonists and that establish and further her career as a painter.

The other girls, led by Cordelia, terrify her by constantly watching
her for misbehavior. Feminist art and film scholars have theorized a male
gaze that objectifies women. But the harsh and punitive gaze of her girlfriends is also damaging to Elaine and leaves her feeling uncertain and
terrified. For example, Cordelia brings a small mirror to school and tells
Elaine with disgust: "Look at yourself! Just look!" Terrorized by
Cordelia's disgust, Elaine feels "as if my face, all by itself, has been up to
something, has gone too far" (168). As a result of their critical gaze, she
becomes self-conscious and insecure, constantly expecting new torments. Their most dramatic torment occurs in a scene reminiscent of
Atwood's early poems: a protagonist undertakes an icebound journey
that is both dangerous and potentially liberating. One day as they walk
home from school Cordelia tosses Elaine's hat from a bridge onto the
ice-coated creek in a ravine below. Climbing down to retrieve her hat,
Elaine breaks through the thin ice, gets chilled, and lies as if paralyzed.
She overcomes her paralysis through a hallucinatory vision of a magical
cloaked woman (the Virgin Mary) who releases her with the talismanic
words, "You can go home now. . . . It will be all right" (201). The event
liberates her both from the ravine and from her vassalage to the three
friends. After the experience she finds she has grown distant, frozen:
that she has "something hard in me, crystalline, a kernel of glass" (206).
She loses interest in the other girls, and consequently their power over
her diminishes. Ultimately the roles of Elaine and Cordelia are reversed,
for Elaine gains power and purpose in her life while Cordelia has difficulty coping. In the book's conclusion, Elaine revisits the ravine and
rewrites her memory of her childhood trauma.

As the two scenes in the ravine indicate, Cordelia and Elaine are inti-
mately linked. Although Cordelia torments Elaine, the two have a deep
connection that allows for moments of genuine pleasure. Cordelia later
reveals that she hated the other girls at school and considered Elaine her

best friend. (By including Cordelia's memory, Atwood adds another voice, with a different story of their shared past.) Indeed, Cordelia scapegoats Elaine because of their similarities: she projects her self-loathing. Elaine and Cordelia share an ironic perception of the world. Both are unconventional and creative, Cordelia as an actor and Elaine as an artist. Both attempt suicide. Indeed, we may question whether Cordelia is a separate individual; on one level she is an aspect of Elaine, representing her wilder, darker side, her own self-denigration, her doubts and uncertainties. Elaine thinks, "We are like the twins in old fables, each of whom has been given half a key" (434). Moreover, in the conclusion, when Elaine makes peace with the Cordelia of her childhood, she recognizes that her fears "are not my own emotions any more. They are Cordelia's; as they always were" (443).

Cordelia, of course, reminds us of the abused, disinherited third daughter in Shakespeare's *King Lear*, the stubborn, defiant, but loyal daughter who answered "nothing" when her father asked for her affirmations of love. "Nothing" resounds through the book: especially "nothing" figures in Cordelia's inquisitions into Elaine's supposed misbehaviors. Elaine usually has nothing to say for herself when Cordelia questions her. But as she emerges from Cordelia's oppression, she turns the tables, responding to Cordelia's "What do you think of me?" with the retort "nothing."[5] Although the feckless Cordelia does not complete college, Elaine succeeds, and she takes courses in art school, continuing to produce art.

As it addresses art history and Elaine's paintings, the novel introduces feminist art criticism. In the 1970s feminist art historians and critics began to analyze the traditions of European art and its iconography of the female body. Elaine observes that paintings of women are like paintings of fruit, flowers, or meat; all are objectified subjects. She finds that her relationships with male artists, especially her teacher and her first husband, are unsuccessful because they objectify her, try to turn her into someone else, or fail to see her. But as a painter Elaine creates her own images of women based on her experience, although derived in part from conventions of the Anglo-European artistic tradition. Her paintings reflect her complicated responses: she is a woman painting female nudes, a woman gazing at the female body in ways that are different from and yet have affinities with the ways in which male artists have gazed.

In her painting "Torontodalisque: Homage to Ingres," Elaine conflates images from her personal history with those of Western art history.

On a personal level the paintings of Mrs. Smeath are Elaine's revenge. In social and aesthetic terms, these paintings comment on both bourgeois Toronto and the romanticized, eroticized exoticism of Ingres's odalisque. In place of Ingres's pale, turbaned nude woman stretched out alluringly on a couch, Elaine's Mrs. Smeath reclines in her apron and hat, while her rubber plant and crocheted afghan stand in contrast to the exotic setting and the sexual innuendo of the drapery and the fan in the original paintings.[6]

Another painting that comments on the Western art tradition is "Falling Women." In the Victorian tradition, men fall heroically in battle, but a woman "falls" from respectability when she acts sexually.[7] Elaine portrays literally falling women rather than metaphorical fallen women. In contrast, Elaine paints a falling man, her brother, who was killed by hijackers, carrying a child's wooden sword like those he used to play with. Charna from the Sub-Versions Gallery interprets this painting ("One Wing") as Elaine's comment on the "juvenile nature of war" (430).

Issues of increasing interest to Atwood are those of interpretation and of authors' control over their products. For example, Offred's story in *The Handmaid's Tale* has been edited and rearranged by a male scholar from a different culture. In Elaine Risley's case, journalists, reviewers, and critics impose their interpretations on her paintings. For example, right after her mother died, she painted a series of six panels of her mother cooking, a double triptych in mixed media called "Pressure Cooker." She finds the politically motivated interpretations of her painting "hilarious." For "some people thought it was about the Earth Goddess. . . . Other people thought it was about female slavery, others that it was a stereotyping of women in negative and trivial domestic roles" (161). It was, in fact, her attempt to remember her mother: "I suppose I wanted to bring her back to life" (161).

As she walks through the gallery on opening night, Elaine comes to see Mrs. Smeath with more compassion. She recognizes the pain that she painted in Mrs. Smeath's eyes and acknowledges that her former foe is after all a "displaced person," just as she herself is (and even Cordelia). Elaine now retrospectively extends her sympathy to the wounded women, Cordelia, Grace, and Mrs. Smeath, and thereby liberates herself. Returning to the bridge over the ravine that marks the site of past abuse, Elaine sees a vision of Cordelia and forgives her tormentor using the words that had given her release before: "It's all right. You can go home now." At this point, Elaine remarks that the "snow in my eyes withdraws like smoke" (443); her perception thaws, just as the characters in "Rapunzel" and "The Snow Queen" are liberated from their frozen perceptions. When she can see Cordelia with eyes of love and forgiveness, then the frozen chip that keeps her distant and aloof melts. Her compassion extends to include two older women sitting near her on a plane en route home to Vancouver. She reflects that what she misses is not the past, but the possibility of such a friendship with Cordelia in the future: "two old women giggling over their tea" (446).

Yet it should not surprise us that Atwood's resolution here is ambiguous. Bouson points out that Elaine has many revenge fantasies toward Cordelia that we must balance against her reconciliation (Bouson, 181). Appropriately, the book gathers together its central themes but ends with an image of uncertainty in which Elaine connects perception with cosmology, seeing by the light of stars "which are not eternal as was once thought, which are not where we think they are. If they were sounds, they would be echoes. . . . Echoes of light. . . . It's old light, and there's not much of it. But it's enough to see by" (CE, 446).

Atwood's next novel, The Robber Bride, continues to explore women's friendships. Three middle-aged women tell their stories and cement their friendship as they celebrate their triumph over a fascinating and mysterious antagonist, Zenia, who might be an older incarnation of the fascinating and mysterious antagonist Cordelia.

The Robber Bride (1993)

Atwood writes of the femme fatale at the center of The Robber Bride, "The treacherous vamp is as old as Delilah, of course. . . . In recent years we've been in the habit of labeling such potent, destructive, leather-bar figures 'male fantasy,' but aren't they, from some angles, female fantasies as well? The beautiful strong-minded woman who can topple men with one sultry glance scowls out at us from every fashion magazine we open. The presumed audience for these mermaids and sirens is not male. Zenia may be a shadow cast by men, but she's a shadow cast by women as well" (TF, 169.3). Atwood contrasts the villainess with Hamlet's unfortunate sweetheart Ophelia, the pallid, pure woman, the quintessential victim. And indeed, Zenia is Ophelia's mirror image. She is the woman who seduces men, who manipulates women, who leads a life of danger and adventure. Yet in the conclusion she is discovered just as Ophelia is, drowned amid foliage.

A complex and many-layered book, The Robber Bride revisits familiar Atwood themes. Set in a meticulously described Toronto during the

period from the 1960s through 1991, the novel explores and problematizes questions of identity, good and evil, heterosexual relationships,
friendship, war, history, and victimization, but above all of storytelling.
Atwood explains that the book's trickster figure, Zenia, a mysterious
and alluring woman who spins a series of plausible but conflicting stories about herself, is akin to the novelist, a creator of illusion, of lies that
contain "another kind of truth" (TF 169.3). In fact, each of the four protagonists is a storyteller who re-creates and renames herself in response
to childhood trauma. Atwood's novels frequently involve doubles and
doubling; this novel has four central figures and plays multiple variations on its central themes.

The novel is an intricately patterned series of frames within frames,
stories within stories. The outermost frame (the first chapter, "Onset,"
and the last chapter, "Outcome") is narrated by the military historian
Antonia (Tony) Fremont, who reflects on the indeterminacy of history
and searches for the meaning of her own history. The next frame consists
of two sections (each called "The Toxique") that describe lunches Tony
shares with her friends Roz and Charis. At the novel's center within that
double frame are the stories the three friends tell about their lives and
about how Zenia betrayed them. "Black Enamel" is Tony's story,
"Weasel Nights" is Charis's, and "The Robber Bride" is Roz's. And
interspersed in their stories are snippets of Zenia's multiple conflicting
narratives.

Although *The Robber Bride* is on the surface a story of women battling
about men, it may be read more cogently as the story of an evolving
friendship between three women who band together in the face of their
mutual enemy, Zenia, perhaps the flashiest femme fatale since Becky
Sharp, the villainess of Thackeray's *Vanity Fair*. Although Atwood's
works often portray the tensions of sexual politics and heterosexual relationships, women's friendships become increasingly important, and *The
Robber Bride* develops them in a lighter, comic vein. The book starts with
Zenia returning from the dead to threaten the three protagonists—
Tony, Charis, and Roz—with further losses, and it ends as the three
women join together ceremonially to bury Zenia and to cement their
friendship by telling stories about her.

The Robber Bride is a woman-centered book that, as the title indicates,
transforms the traditional Robber Bridegroom tale (an Atwood favorite)
of the murderous husband into a woman's story. In the folktale, a young
woman saves herself from death at the hands of her prospective husband
by telling the story that reveals he is a wife murderer. The novel's three

protagonists console themselves and help each other by telling stories about the mate-stealing exploits of Zenia, the Robber Bride. Relationships with husbands and lovers are important to the three protagonists; however, they learn that romantic stereotypes have been toxic and that where heterosexual relationships have failed, female friendship has been a source of strength.

The Robber Bride copyright is held by O. W. Toad. While Atwood often uses this anagram for her name, it is especially noteworthy here, for it signals the importance of wordplay in the novel. Tony Fremont thinks of words forward and backward, calls herself Tnomerf Ynot, and plays with palindromes such as "raw sexes war" (401). Her code serves to disrupt meaning, to point to the slipperiness of labels, and to empower her through control of language. As a child writing dirty words backward on the window, she gloats: "They are Tnomerf Ynot words. They make her feel powerful" (138). When she renames her husband, she transforms him from Stew, meaning food; an article of consumption; or mental agitation, worry, fret, to West, meaning a direction, a place, the Western world. Indeed, Tony notes that technically his code name should be Wets, but she cheats a little, thus asserting her power over the code she uses.

Tony's code is one of many reversals in the novel. Just as she reverses language, the novel problematizes labels and questions prevailing systems of gender, class, power, and status. As Tony points out, war is a reversal in which both sides take turns "trying to avoid being the victims" (21). Roz's son, Larry, dates a series of "bimbos" to cover up his homosexuality. Roz's twin daughters reverse fairy tales, making all the characters women. And Zenia has become the "robber bride," replacing the bridegroom of the folktale.

Tony narrates the novel's first frame section, "Onset," which carries connotations of assault or onslaught in contrast to the more benign "start" or "beginning." In this section Tony raises questions of meaning, interpretation, and explanation, observing that "history is a construct" and the historian determines meaning by choosing the thread to follow (4). Moreover, history is written backward, after the fact, by the victors. She chooses October 23, 1990, as her starting point for the novel, setting her own tale of friendship and betrayal in the context of global strife: "The Soviet bloc is crumbling, the old maps are dissolving. . . . There's trouble in the Gulf, the real estate market is crashing, and a large hole has developed in the ozone layer. . . . Tony has lunch at the Toxique with her two friends Roz and Charis, . . . and Zenia returns from the dead" (4). Thus linked to global phenomena, Zenia becomes a physical force.

Paired with the "Onset" is the brief concluding "Outcome" section. The story's plot has been resolved: Zenia who has once risen from the dead is now dead again, and this section describes the scattering of her ashes in Lake Ontario. But what does the story mean? Has Tony learned anything? This section starts as Tony ponders the story of Zenia and the meaning of history. She wonders: "Do the stories of history really teach anything at all?" More, "was [Zenia] in any way like us. . . . Are we in any way like her?" (466). The critics' answer to this question is a resounding "yes," Zenia is a shadow self, a mirror of the darker side, the hidden fears and anxieties of each character. Her power over them derives from her awareness of these fears. Each character recognizes both her fear of what Zenia represents and her wish to be like Zenia: powerful, beautiful, daring, outrageous, sexy.

Within the novel's outermost frame—Tony's prologue ("Onset") and her quest for the meaning of history ("Outcome")—lies another two-part frame, the two lunches at the Toxique, where the friends meet. On the first occasion, Zenia returns from the dead. On the second, Charis has a vision that Zenia is dead. "Toxic" suggests the destructive nature of Zenia, but even more so the three protagonists' unfortunate romantic relationships. Additionally, the letters of Toxique are an anagram for Quixote, the hero of a melodramatic quest, and the trio are on a kind of melodramatic quest for Zenia. Because the women perceive Zenia to be their enemy, they invest a great deal of energy in hating, fearing, and planning to attack her. But through encountering her, they achieve self-knowledge and build a stronger bond with each other. For she is the trickster who teaches (and tricks herself as well). Or she may be simultaneously a real person and a projection of the three others.

At the book's center the stories of the three friends are told in the present tense, from the point of view of each woman. Each tells a tale of an unhappy childhood in a family disrupted by war. Each has renamed and re-created herself in an attempt to heal her childhood scars. Antonia becomes Tony or Tnomerf Ynot, the warrior queen, to overcome the pain of her mother's abandonment and her father's alcoholism; Karen becomes Charis to avoid the pain of sexual molestation by her uncle; Roz Grunwald becomes Rosalind Greenwood in correlation with the rise and fall of her Jewish family's fortunes.

Zenia manipulates the women and exploits their friendship to steal their lovers: Charis's lover, Billy, Roz's husband, Mitch, and Tony's husband, West. She is the supreme storyteller, but she is the only woman who does not tell her own story here. When she is alive she is like a goddess: her hair is black and alive like Medusa's (433); she is associated with imagery of the moon, of light and dark. When she is supposedly dead, she returns to life again. When she is cremated for the (seemingly) second time, the jar containing her ashes cracks as it is being thrown into the water. She cannot be contained in her narrative, or in her body. She is the unknown, yet she is the focal point of all the others' stories. Even after her final death, they continue to tell stories about her. Coral Ann Howells notes that "they need her, or their stories about her, in order to define themselves, for the 'good' women are shown to be as dependent on the 'Other Woman' as she is on them" (Howells, 83). She is, like Joan Foster, the author heroine of *Lady Oracle,* a woman of excess, of multiple heterosexual relationships, a woman whose life is built around stories. Joan also fakes a suicide, fabricates a series of different identities, and has affairs with unusual men. Atwood comments that "Zenia is, among other things, an illusionist. She tells stories so plausible that each of her listeners believes her; their belief comes in part from the structure of their own inner lives, from their wish and need to be taken in. But isn't this the goal of every novelist—to deceive? Doesn't every novelist play Zenia to every reader's willing dupe?" (TF, 169.3). Indeed, Atwood drew a cartoon Christmas card in which an interviewer asks, "Which of the characters in *The Robber Bride* is really you?" and she responds, much to his chagrin and puzzlement, that she is Zenia.

If Zenia is multiple and puzzling, so are the others. Accordingly, critics offer a range of explanations.[8] Linda Hutcheon suggests that the four women are "a revisiting (and overcoming?) of Atwood's 'four basic victim positions' and their attendant emotional states of denial (Roz), resignation (Charis), dynamic anger (Tony) and creative refusal (Zenia, of course)." As J. Brooks Bouson observes, Zenia "appropriates the speech of the female victim in order to manipulate and assert power over others" (Bouson, 150). Sarah Appleton Aguiar suggests that Tony represents the past, Charis the future, and Roz the present.

The three women are also three aspects of the personality: Tony the mind, Charis the spirit, and Roz the body. Tony teaches war history and writes books about war. Charis is concerned with spirituality, healthful living, meditation, tarot cards, and yoga. Roz owns her own business, publishes a successful magazine, and develops a line of cosmetics. She is interested in appearances, advising the oblivious Tony on clothing and home decorating.

Another possibility is that the three protagonists are aspects of the triple goddess—the maiden, the mother, and the crone—a theme Atwood has used repeatedly. Together, the three symbolically form one powerful woman. Concerned with spirituality and right living, Charis typifies the maiden aspect. Just as the maiden Kore changed her name to Persephone after Hades raped her, Charis abandoned her birth name of Karen after her uncle sexually molested her. Charis repeatedly crosses the water by ferry from the corruption of urban Toronto to the peace and serenity of her home on the island, where she presides over an organic garden. Roz is Demeter. Mother of twin daughters, Paula and Erin, and a son, Larry, she is the practical one, immersed in the quotidian world. She is the one who calculates the bill at the restaurant, who arranges Zenia's funeral. Tony, the wise woman with large owl-like glasses, is associated both with the crone Hecate and with Athena, the Greek goddess of wisdom and of war. (Note that her mother is named Anthea, an anagram for Athena.) Tony's military-history lectures use the metaphors of women's crafts such as weaving and knitting to elucidate the details of battles. It is from Tony's perspective that the novel develops, and it is therefore not surprising that war becomes a central theme of the novel.

Zenia represents those aspects of the three other women that they wish to change, either to overcome or to intensify. Jennifer Enos writes that Zenia is a composite of the three women, not the people they are as adults, "but rather the names of the people they were in their youth, the names of their previous selves, the ones they think ought to be fixed. . . . The Z comes from the last part of Roz's name, the en from the last part of Charis's original name Karen and the ia from the last part of Tony's real name Antonia."[9] Moreover, Zenia accomplishes the other women's "dirty work," or actuates desires so secret that they are unaware of them. She rescues Roz from Mitch and Charis from the freeloading Billy, and her sexual threat is sufficient incentive for Tony to cherish West more fully (Aguiar, 5).

Tony searches for the derivation of Zenia's name: "Even the name Zenia may not exist. . . . Xenia, a Russian word for hospitable, a Greek one pertaining to the action of a foreign pollen on a fruit; Zenaida, . . . Zendic" (457). But what if this is also a code? Zenia's name moves in reverse alphabetical order from Z to A, suggesting that this is "a reversed allegory for writing itself."[10] Zenia is a touchstone, a kind of mirror. She unerringly finds each character's most vulnerable spot: Roz's ambivalence about her father's war profiteering, Charis's need to be a caretaker, Tony's interest in war and intrigue, Mitch's womanizing. Although Zenia's stories are suspect, her interactions with the characters reveal lessons each needs to learn. Roz and Charis blame Zenia for stealing their lovers, but, as Zenia points out to them, the men are making their own choices. And after all, the lecherous Mitch and the faithless Billy are unworthy mates for Roz and Charis.

The three friends believe that they are waging a battle with Zenia, and the theme of war is a central one in the novel. All the protagonists have been scarred by World War II, for it reshaped their families. Tony's mother calls herself a war bride because she met her husband during the war. In fact, her bitter quarrels with her husband turn Tony's home into a metaphorical battlefield, "raw sexes war." Charis is also a damaged war baby, abandoned by her mother and molested by her uncle. Roz feels guilt about her father's past as a profiteer in World War II.

Zenia's links to wars are intimate and dramatic. Indeed, she functions in the novel as a symbolic embodiment of war. "Like the history of war, she is without end and without an exact beginning."[11] She reappears on the eve of the Gulf War, her childhood stories are associated with war, and her connections with the three friends grow from war stories. To gain Roz's confidence, she tells her that her father (whom Roz believes to be a war profiteer) was in fact a war hero. She links up with Charis's lover, Billy, an American draft dodger, during the Vietnam War. Her faked death takes place during a guerrilla bombing raid in Lebanon, and she is reincarnated during a time of political upheaval. She tells Tony a story of her connections to Gerry Bull, developer of the Supergun. Tony perceives Zenia's relationship to the three protagonists as being a war over men.

In their last encounters with her, each of the women sets out with a plan to confront Zenia. Although (or because) their plans fail, each woman comes to terms with a lack in her life and finds new possibility for the future. Zenia tempts each of them with a story, asking for their help; each rejects the temptation. But Zenia is never at a loss for a story. When they resist her temptations, she confronts them with unpleasant stories about the men she stole from them.

To gain Charis's sympathy, Zenia claims she has AIDS and would welcome a rest at her island home. Charis almost invites her, but declines. Rebuffed, Zenia lashes out at her and admonishes her that her continuing despair over Billy is "just an excuse . . . [that] lets you avoid your life. . . . Forget about him" (423). Disappointed by this confrontation, Charis nevertheless finds that she can forgive Zenia and realizes that she can move on from her bereavement at the loss of Billy, and that she is now able to acknowledge her rejected other self, the angry and assertive Karen.

Tony plans her visit with murderous intent, packing a gun (and a cordless drill!) in her handbag (handbags in Atwood are often capacious). This time Zenia cloaks her request for help with a story of war and intrigue: she is in danger because she knows who murdered the ballistics expert Gerald Bull, and she needs a place to hide for two or three weeks. Tony at first believes Zenia, but then, suspecting the story is a fiction designed to bring her near West, refuses to hide her. When Tony leaves, she views her departure as a collapse; in point of fact, she has resisted the temptation to kill.

Roz fears Zenia is having an affair with her son, Larry. Zenia persuades her that this is the case and that furthermore, he is also a drug pusher. Zenia reminds Roz that she is not entirely to blame for Mitch's defection: "You should give me a medal for getting him off your back. . . . You always saw him as a victim of women, just putty in their hands. . . . Did it ever occur to you that Mitch was responsible for his own actions? He made his own decisions and maybe those decisions didn't have much to do with me, or with you either" (435–36).

Thus Zenia offers each a new story, a new interpretation of the past that may release each of them from the old stories that keep them in victim positions. That evening the three friends return to Zenia's hotel together and find her dead in the fountain. The ending of her life is as mysterious as its beginning. Did she commit suicide or was she murdered? And if murdered, by whom? Each of the friends had a motive and an opportunity, but there are multiple other suspects as well: apparently, each of Zenia's stories is partly true.

So the three friends attend another funeral for Zenia. They pour her ashes into the lake, a purification ritual, and then eat a ceremonial meal at Charis's house on the island. Roz thinks: "When Zenia goes into the lake Mitch will go too, finally; Roz will finally be a widow. No. She'll be something more, something beyond that. . . . She feels something else she never thought she would feel, towards Zenia. Oddly enough, it's gratitude" (463).

The novel ends with a ceremonial meal and with storytelling. The three friends will tell stories about Zenia that will commemorate their lives and cement their connection. The stories will be ongoing because Zenia, like all fictional characters, and like all people, remains complex, multiple, and ultimately indeterminate. Tony meditates on the meanings of history and stories, wondering if "the stories of history really teach anything at all?" and if anybody else cares about them. "Maybe it's just a hobby . . . . Or else it's an act of defiance: these histories may be ragged and threadbare . . . but to her they are also flags, hoisted with a certain jaunty insolence . . . glimpsed here and there through the trees . . . on the long march into chaos" (458). Stories, according to *The Robber Bride,* are the way we mark our journeys through the chaos of life.

Atwood's next novel, *Alias Grace,* uses the conventions of a nineteenth-century novel to tell the tale of another supreme storyteller, a woman with no family and no support system, whose release from prison depends on her storytelling.

Alias Grace (1996)

In *Alias Grace,* Atwood has written a novel in nineteenth-century style based on the story of Grace Marks, a housemaid accused of murdering her employer and his housekeeper in 1843. The novel combines social realism, comedy of manners, epistolary form, Gothic fiction, and even a ballad. At first blush this novel appears very different from Atwood's previous novels, because in contrast to her typically middle-class, contemporary, educated female protagonists, Grace Marks is an impoverished nineteenth-century woman who spends many years in prison. Yet this story manifests by-now familiar Atwoodian motifs, including social satire, attention to detail, a keen ear for dialogue, and wry humor. Moreover, the novel epitomizes central Atwood themes: the Gothic, victims and victimization, the slipperiness of identity, doubling of characters and plot, the complexities of sexual politics, the protagonist's imprisonment (literal here as it is in *Bodily Harm,* although metaphorical in other novels), the vexed questions of sanity and insanity, narrative authority, the protagonist as trickster/storyteller, and the teller's control of her story. Additionally, as she often does, Atwood uses a fictional genre (in this instance the historical novel) both to provide structure and to form a basis for metafictional interventions that parody and subvert the genre. In fact, this novel contains echoes of many genres in which Atwood has written: Jamesian ghost story, detective thriller, Gothic tale, autobiography, and Scheherazade's story. Atwood even wrote a ballad in nineteenth-century style about the murder.

The novel is replete with Gothic motifs centered on the infiltration of disorder and irrationality into society. There is a murder, and a notorious young woman, Grace Marks, who may be innocent or guilty of the deed, is imprisoned. There are supernatural elements, for Grace's supporters seek the aid of spiritism and hypnosis to learn more about her role in the murder. Dr. Simon Jordan, the young physician, tries to apply logic to solve the mystery of Grace's personality and to live by his reason, yet his life spins out of his control. Grace spends much of her life in prison, spends some time in the Provincial Lunatic Asylum in Toronto, and may have a split personality. And Grace herself, while seeming to reveal all, hides the secret of her role in the murder.

The historical Grace Marks, the daughter of a mother who died young and an abusive, alcoholic father, was a penniless Irish immigrant to Canada who became a housemaid at age 13. In 1843, when she was 16, she was accused of murdering her employer, Thomas Kinnear, and his mistress and housekeeper, Nancy Montgomery. The sensationalized trial created a stir in the United States and Canada, turning her into a "celebrated murderess," a notorious and enigmatic figure, another Lizzie Borden. Atwood first learned about Grace Marks through Susanna Moodie's account (in *Life in the Clearings,* 1853) of the story and of her visits to see Grace in both an insane asylum and a penitentiary. The story has continued to fascinate Atwood. In 1974 she wrote a CBC television play, *The Servant Girl,* based on Moodie's account, and in 1996 she published *Alias Grace,* a fictionalized account based on further research. The novel quickly became a best-seller. The audiotaped version followed suit, and in 1997 Jodie Foster's Los Angeles–based film company, Egg Pictures, secured movie rights to the novel.

As Atwood reports in her afterword to the novel, Thomas Kinnear and Nancy Montgomery were murdered on 23 July 1843. Grace Marks, under the alias Mary Whitney, and her fellow servant James McDermott ran away together to the United States. They were brought back to Canada, tried for the murder of Kinnear, found guilty, and sentenced to death. McDermott was hanged publicly on 21 November, but Grace's sentence was commuted to life in prison. Atwood researched the story extensively and found that "the written accounts are so contradictory that few facts emerge" with any certainty (465). "It was no help that she [Grace] herself gave three different versions of the Montgomery murder, while James McDermott gave two" (462).

Questions swirled around the trial in 1843 and captured the public interest. Was Grace an innocent victim, duped or abducted by the real murderer, James McDermott? Or was she the sinister mastermind who incited McDermott to murder Nancy Montgomery so that she might become Kinnear's mistress? Was Grace in love with Kinnear? Or was she pretending to be to gain personal advantage? Atwood introduces additional questions in the novel. Did the trauma cause Grace to forget the events surrounding the murder? Or did she feign forgetfulness? Was she clever or dull witted? Was she "possessed" by the spirit of the dead serving girl, her friend Mary Whitney? Or did Grace have a split personality? Atwood researched the trial and the period carefully and was intrigued by the many gaps in the record and the impossibility of resolving the remaining questions: "What made it much more interesting to me, as a novelist, is the fact that Susanna Moodie was wrong! Other people were just making the story up from the moment it happened. They were all fictionalizing. They were all projecting their own views onto these various people. It is a real study in how the perception of reality is shaped."[12] And of course, the issue of "how the perception of reality is shaped" is a major ongoing concern of Atwood's. With consummate skill, she re-creates the atmosphere of the period setting, creates a shrewd and interesting protagonist, invents several subplots, and contrives to keep the questions open.

Noting Atwood's research for this novel, a reviewer calls it the doctoral dissertation that Atwood did not complete, a tour de force rendition of nineteenth-century Canadian social life.[13] Although its subject matter differs from the dissertation she planned (a study of nineteenth-century fiction in the genre she termed "metaphysical romance"), the novel includes such Victorian fictive devices as a ballad based on the murders, letters written in the period style, and courtship subplots.

Atwood, of course, has interrogated twentieth-century courtship in other texts (such as *EW, PP,* and *BH*). Here in *Alias Grace* she depicts the nineteenth-century variety and its representation in social realist novels of the period. Because a woman's economic well-being depended chiefly on being born into a financially secure family and/or obtaining a stable and solvent husband, the heroine's great adventure was courtship and marriage. Accordingly, eighteenth- and nineteenth-century fiction, such as Jane Austen's, for example, often contains parallel stories of several women's quests for husbands.

In *Alias Grace* Atwood develops several courtship subplots. Grace Marks herself gets married in the book's denouement, in a plot twist worthy of one of Dickens's coincidences. Interestingly, her marriage seems to be the happiest relationship in the novel, perhaps because she has no romantic expectations.

In one subplot, Lydia, daughter of the prison governor, is married off quickly to Reverend Verringer to avoid suspicion after two of her flirtations fail to result in marriage. Grace observes shrewdly: "[I]t is not a good plan to marry a man you do not love, but many do and get used to it in time" (426). In another romance, Rachel Humphrey, the unfortunate wife of an alcoholic ne'er-do-well husband, takes in a boarder, Dr. Simon Jordan, to support herself. She relies increasingly on the susceptible Simon and pursues him romantically. He accedes to the affair but abandons her when her husband's return is imminent.

In the working-class subplots, two young women form romantic liaisons with men of higher social status. Grace's fellow servant (at the home of Alderman Parkinson) Mary Whitney succumbs to the flirtations of her employer's son, is repudiated when she becomes pregnant, and dies of a botched abortion. Nancy Montgomery is the mistress of her bachelor employer, Thomas Kinnear. Whether Grace was trying to achieve a similar liaison with Thomas Kinnear (or, more likely, trying to avoid his sexual advances) remains an open question.

Using the voices of characters from the working and middle classes, Atwood comments slyly on the social mores she depicts so carefully. Mary Whitney's tart commentary and Grace's shrewd observations offer the servant's wisdom, and Simon Jordan's thoughts present the views of a cynical man. Grace, for example, thinks: "Mrs. Alderman Parkinson said a lady must never sit in a chair a gentleman has just vacated, though she would not say why; but Mary Whitney said, Because, you silly goose, it's still warm from his bum. . . . So I cannot sit here without thinking of the ladylike bums that have sat on this very settee, all delicate and white, like wobbly soft-boiled eggs" (21).

Simon Jordan narrates the book as well as Grace, and his observations are a cynical reflection of social mores. One train of thought comments on his mother's machinations as she attempts to marry him off. Another train reflects his acerbic comments about social situations. For example, he notes at a dinner party: "Mrs. Quennell, in her huge crinoline-supported skirt, resembles a lavender-colored Bavarian cream" (82). Or he discovers that, whereas women often keep scrapbooks of beautiful scenes or of cards from friends, the prison governor's wife keeps a scrapbook about famous murders, including the murder of Nancy Montgomery.

Grace's predicament arises in part from the constraints on women in the mid-nineteenth century. Born into a working-class family in Ireland, she has practically no opportunities for formal education and only menial job possibilities. She takes a series of jobs as a servant in houses where she is treated relatively badly or well. In Alderman Parkinson's house she meets Mary Whitney, who becomes a confidant, friend, and alter ego. Mary's earthy wit deflates the pretensions of the gentry, and on one level she is for Grace what Zenia is for the three protagonists of *The Robber Bride,* a model of irreverent, outrageous behavior. Grace is a survivor, a shrewd and observant woman who maintains her dignity and refuses the victim role. Indeed, she comments that "the victims . . . are the ones who cause all the trouble. If they were only less weak and careless, . . . think of all the sorrow in the world that would be spared" (457).

Grace is an artist and a quilt maker as well as a storyteller. A quilt is a patchwork, an assemblage of pieces—often remnants of outworn or castoff clothing—cut and shaped into attractive patterns. In North America in the eighteenth and early nineteenth centuries, quilts were a kind of underground storytelling, conveying subtle or blatant messages: drunkard's path, log cabin, tree of life. Grace's story is also a kind of quilt, a patching together of memory, fantasy, and ideas to serve her own purposes. The chapter titles, named after quilt patterns, suggest mystery and menace: Jagged Edge, Rocky Road, Young Man's Fancy, Secret Drawer, Hearts and Gizzards, Pandora's Box. Grace makes a quilt for the governor's wife and one for herself after she is freed from prison. For her own quilt she uses the Tree of Life pattern and puts a border of snakes around it to indicate that evil is part of every story. She includes snips of Mary Whitney's petticoat, Nancy Montgomery's dress, and her prison dress, "so we will all be together" (460).

Grace is always acting a role and always conscious of her audience. As she explains: "I am a model prisoner, and give no trouble. That's what the [prison] Governor's wife says, I have overheard her saying it. I'm skilled at overhearing" (5). There is a suggestion that she feigned madness to be transferred to the asylum in hopes of better treatment there. Or, telling her story to Simon, she remarks: "I had now been a servant for three years, and could act the part well enough by that time" (224). She tries to tell him what he wants to hear but sets limits on what she will divulge. When he asks her what an apple reminds her of, she thinks: "He's playing a guessing game, like Dr. Bannerling at the Asylum. . . . The apple of the Tree of Knowledge is what he means. Good and evil. Any child could guess it. But I will not oblige. I go back to my stupid look" (40).

Grace's story is the novel's core, but it is always suspect. When Simon asks her to tell him her story, she says: "Perhaps I will tell lies" (41). She professes to be shocked that women would tell stories publicly.

When Simon tells her about the Lowell Mill girls who published stories in a magazine, she asks, "[W]ho would want a wife like that, writing down things for everyone to see, and made-up things at that, and I would never be so brazen" (68).

Grace's narrative has at least two versions: her stream of consciousness and the more controlled story she tells Simon; however, there are gaps in both versions. Additionally, there are several other versions: Susanna Moodie's story; the stories told at the trial by the defending and prosecuting lawyers, James McDermott, Jamie Walsh, and others; and the stories printed in the newspapers. Regarding the newspapers, Grace comments: "They did say some true things." But she remains silent on a crucial point: "But they called James McDermott my paramour. . . . I think it is disgusting to write such things down" (27). As for her confession, she claims: "That is not really my Confession, it was only what the lawyer told me to say, and things made up by the men from the newspapers" (101).

Grace is called a "notorious murderess," and her history as the child of a dysfunctional working-class Irish immigrant family leaves her defenseless and vulnerable. She is suspected of having illicit sexual relations with James McDermott and possibly having designs on Thomas Kinnear as well. In contrast, Dr. Simon Jordan is a respectable, upwardly mobile young professional from a good family. Yet their roles during the novel's present action are strangely reversed. He is the one who is obsessed by sex, particularly with working-class women and prostitutes. In his dreams and reveries he remembers his youthful trysts with the servant girls in his then-affluent household. He acquiesces passively in a shabby affair initiated by his landlady, Rachel Humphrey, even though he is not especially attracted to her. He has no intentions of sustaining the relationship and breaks it off in cowardly fashion. Although he is presumably investigating Grace's psychology, especially her memory of the Kinnear and Montgomery murders, almost the first question he blurts out when she is hypnotized is about her sexuality. In a melodramatic counterpoint to the Kinnear murder, Rachel tries to enlist Simon in a plot to murder her husband, so that they can be together. He seizes his opportunity to end his affair and hastily leaves town under the pretense that his mother is seriously ill. Such an escape would not have been possible for Grace if, as she asserts, James McDermott held her hostage when he plotted to murder Kinnear.

Thus Grace and Simon are foils to each other to an exaggerated degree. As Grace's fortunes rise, his fall. He hopes to restore her possibly faulty memory, but ironically, as a result of a battle injury he suffers in the Civil War, he loses his recent memory. And the strategy he used for jogging Grace's memory (showing her objects such as the apple that he hopes will elicit associations) is the very one his mother and fiancée use to jog his memory. Grace is eventually pardoned, leaves prison, marries, and leads a comfortable, conventional life. Indeed, when the novel ends, she believes she may be pregnant. In contrast, Simon never achieves his goals of establishing a private sanitarium and conducting further psychological research. Instead, he ends up a convalescent in the care of Faith Cartwright, a young woman his domineering mother chooses to be his bride.

Again, Atwood is playing with the conventions of genre, in this case the historical novel. Like much historical fiction, her novel seems to wrap up all the details in a neat package at the conclusion. All of the important characters are accounted for. Grace is married off, improbably, to Jamie Walsh, whom she knew at Kinnear's house. Simon Jordan's trajectory is almost directly opposite to Grace's. Jeremiah the peddler conveniently turns up in a variety of aliases, including Dr. Jerome DuPont, the hypnotist; Simon will marry Faith Cartwright (the woman his mother has been promoting against his wishes). All *seems* to be smoothly wrapped up as in the conventional historical novel, but at the heart of the story Grace herself remains a mystery.

Grace is the quintessential Atwoodian Scheherazade. Imprisoned for life, she has a temporary diversion and amelioration of her situation when Dr. Simon Jordan asks to interview her. Realizing that she can prolong his visits, and perhaps win his assistance in seeking release from prison, by spinning out her tale, she tells him in poetic and detailed language everything but the one thing he most wishes to know: what her involvement was in the murders of Nancy Montgomery and Thomas Kinnear. Thus, Atwood again shows us the gap between life and the stories we tell about it.

Chapter Six

Firestorms and Fireflies:
The Later Poems, 1978–1995

Atwood belongs to a small group of authors who have achieved equal preeminence in both poetry and fiction. The poems in these four volumes, *Two-Headed Poems* (1978), *True Stories* (1981), *Interlunar* (1984), and *Morning in the Burned House* (1995), display her expanding tonal, emotional, and thematic range and versatility while they continue to probe themes such as the power and duplicity of language, identity, and storytelling. The world of these poems is larger than that of the earlier poems. Whereas the early poems stress individual isolation, these poems speak of human connections and of family. Early poems portray winter's danger in a harsh Northern landscape; these poems visit the Caribbean (although that turns out to be a harsh landscape as well) and appreciate the summer and harvest, speaking of making jelly, gathering mushrooms, and picking plums. The most dramatic change is the maturation of the speaking subject. The narrator of the earlier poems often believed herself a victim, a Persephone bereft of her mother's protection, struggling or submerging in a frozen landscape. In contrast, the speaker here is a crone, a witness, an older and wiser woman who observes life's events with sympathy, humor, anger, indignation, and compassion.

While the early poems tend toward abstraction and myth, as in "A Place: Fragments" (*CG*) or *Power Politics,* the poems here embrace both myth and the concrete, the particular, as in the "Daybooks" (*THP*) that recount details of daily life. Characters in earlier books are often archetypal; here we find particular fathers, daughters, husbands. The mood frequently turns to elegy. Awareness of mortality suffuses these poems. We live in full knowledge of our imminent death, yet, like the beautiful cancer cell, we seek "more life, and more abundantly" (*MBH,* 48).

The books speak of both the personal and the political. *Two-Headed Poems* contains two centers, the personal and the political, merging the two in "Solstice Poem." *True Stories* reminds us of global atrocities and urges us to bear witness. Political undertones resonate in "Marsh Languages" (*MBH*).

Stories and storytelling continue to be central. Scheherazade figures speak here in the voices of Mary Webster in "Half-hanged Mary" (*MBH*) and Françoise Laurent of "Marrying the Hangman" (*THP*). Figures such as Orpheus, Persephone, and Ava Gardner from both classical and popular mythology tell their stories (*MBH*). The title poem of *Two-Headed Poems* examines language and meaning. "You Begin" welcomes the poet's daughter into the world of language. *True Stories* exposes the paradoxes of storytelling. The title poem declares that there is no true story, while "Notes Toward a Poem That Can Never Be Written" points to the difficulties of translating events into language and to the poet's dilemma of trying to use language to effect change. And the remarkable "Spelling" recuperates the danger and power of language as a gift the poet shares with her daughter.

Two-Headed Poems (1978)

As its title indicates, this book emphasizes doubling, a device Atwood often employs to explore issues such as the paradoxes and duplicity of language, identity, politics, storytelling, and human relationships. The duplicity of the self is embodied in "The Right Hand Fights the Left," which casts the conflict in imagery of battle; a mechanical, metal right hand warring against a "soft and smaller" left (57). A similar conflict confronts "The Woman Who Could Not Live with her Faulty Heart" for her heart beats out a contradictory message: "I want, I don't want" (16). While this poem suggests the ambiguity of the heart, the emotions, the 11 "Two-Headed Poems" speak of the doubleness of the head and its manifestations, including language and politics.

The first Canadian edition features a cover photograph by Graeme Gibson of two faces Atwood made out of flour and salt as Christmas tree ornaments. This cover signals a more personal, homier tone than, for example, the abstract spiral of dots on the first edition cover of *The Circle Game*. The tree ornaments reappear in "Solstice Poem," and references to other handicrafts such as making puppets or sewing a daughter's shirt figure in the book as well.

By the time this book appeared, Atwood's *Selected Poems* had already been published, and her preeminence as a poet was secure. In the four years since her previous poetry book (*YAH*), the prolific Atwood published a novel (*LO*), a book of short stories (*DG*), and a short work of Canadian history, *Days of the Rebels: 1815–1840*. "Four Small Elegies" incorporate some of the material she researched for the history project. She was now living near Alliston, Ontario, with Canadian novelist Graeme Gibson; their daughter, Eleanor Jessica Atwood Gibson (Jess), was born in 1976. Many of the 29 poems here reflect Atwood's new familial status. They cover a greater emotional range than previous poems, and they celebrate family and lineage. Where the people inhabiting previous books are often stereotypes, mythic, unidentifiable, there are real people here: family, grandmothers, daughters, politicians, historical figures.

The poems in this book fall into four main overlapping categories: nature, politics, language, and family. The mood of the book is elegiac, remembering and honoring others as in the four small elegies and the poem for her aging grandmother. In contrast to the obsessive, distanced relationships depicted in *Circle Game* and *Power Politics,* many of these poems describe a reassuringly ordinary household where people sew clothes and celebrate holidays together.

The nature poems recall the lyricism of *You Are Happy.* "Burned Space" emphasizes the new growth that follows a burn in a forest. "All Bread" speaks of bread in terms of the natural processes of growth and decay; to eat it in full awareness may be a consecration. The "Day-books," a journal-like series, position the poet and her family in the rural environment of marshes, fields, a farm. The narrator remembers the cooking that fills the emptiness of November, and the jelly making that preserves the memories of summer's abundance. These poems record daily life and the particulars of nature rather than its mythic aspects; summer and autumn are here as well as winter.

The family poems that form the core of the book are linked with the nature/landscape and the language motifs. In "A Paper Bag," the making of a paper bag mask to amuse a child raises serious questions of identity and language. The mask gives the poet the possibility of a new beginning, a fresh approach to language, for it provides multiple identities and the concomitant new stories. Another of the group, "Five Poems for Grandmothers," is a loving memoir of Atwood's aging and fearful grandmother and a farewell to the woman she once was. Women in families form a link of generations through which we learn about each other and ourselves. The poem is cast as a "charm" against the evils of growing old. But while words may help others to remember the grandmother, they have only limited efficacy. The grandmother has begun to lose her control of language; she has forgotten the names of people once important to her.

"The Bus to Alliston, Ontario" reminds us that traveling home is always a quest, fraught with danger. The travelers on the bus make small talk about disasters, dead relatives, the history of the place. Reminiscent of Elizabeth Bishop's "The Moose," the poem contrasts the stodgy, familiar world of the bus with the larger mystery of the world that surrounds us.

"Solstice Poem" marks the end of the year, a time of darkness and despair, but also the renewal of hope. The speaker wonders what advice, what lessons, what protection against future difficulties she can give her daughter. How can she "teach her / some way of being human / that won't destroy her?" (83). She would like to advise the daughter to dance and to love. Instead, her advice, offered in a "crone's voice" is "be / ruthless when you have to, tell / the truth when you can, when you can see it." This advice, she fears, is "ugly, but / more loyal than mirrors" (83).

In "A Red Shirt" the speaker and her sister participate in women's traditions of sewing, of caretaking and of building family connections. Yet in making a red shirt they defy contemporary social conventions that claim red is too passionate or assertive for young girls. But the poet asserts that red is women's color, defining their blood lineage. Aware of her connection to the world of "fables and charms," the poet secretly weaves her own charms and myths into the shirt. The daughter wears the vivid shirt, unaware of its historical weight of connotation but rejoicing in the warmth and energy of the primary color, "waving her red arms / in delight" (105).

First published in *This Magazine*, "Two-Headed Poems" is an 11-part series exploring duplicity and language. It starts with the idea of Siamese twins, a Gothic motif that suggests disorder. Twins are portentous, associated in myth and tribal traditions with magical powers to preserve or destroy. Siamese twins seem to be freaks of nature, simultaneously repellent and fascinating. The poet tells us that the poems here are a dialogue in which both twins speak, either together or separately. Who are the twins? They are the two faces of Canada, a country with two official languages and cultures, French and English. And they are the neighbors, the United States and Canada, who stereotype each other. Earlier, Atwood defined the conflicts facing a woman who is a writer as "Siamese twins pulling uneasily against each other" (*SW*, 172). The dialogue here is termed a "duet / with two deaf singers" (74).

The twins stand for duplicity, for the two-facedness of politicians (Pierre Elliott Trudeau, the "man of water," served as prime minister of Canada from 1968 to 1979), for the possibilities and limits of language. Because language is living, words have histories; thus they accrete multiple stories and often contradictory meanings. Sections six and nine describe words in anthropomorphic terms: they grow old and wrinkled, they swell, they die of various causes. In the face of this confusing multiplicity the poem's speakers wish to find a simpler language that can be both signified and signifier, so that the language becomes the thing itself, so that no translation is needed and no misunderstanding can occur. Because this clarity and directness of speech are not possible, language remains problematic, a paradoxical source of both hope and despair, desire and frustration, "a disease" and at the same time "the hospital that will cure us" (73). Atwood asserts that "language *is* a distortion" and that "most writers share this distrust of language . . . but language is one of the few tools we *do* have. So we have to use it. We even have to trust it, though it's untrustworthy. . . . There's something tricky about 'reality,' let alone language" (Hancock, 276–78).

"Marrying the Hangman" is a poem about the power of language, of the poet, of the storyteller to effect change. Based on a historical incident, the poem imagines a story to explain how a woman sentenced to death was able to save her life by talking, by telling stories. A Scheherazade, she prefigures similar figures such as Offred (*HT*) or Grace Marks (*AG*). As Atwood notes, the only way a person in eighteenth-century Quebec could be saved from a death sentence was for a man to become a hangman or for a woman to marry the hangman. Françoise Laurent, sentenced to death for stealing clothes from her employer, talked the man in the cell adjoining hers into becoming the hangman and marrying her. Atwood speculates on the ways in which this may have come about. What could the woman have said to convince a man who was not condemned to death to become a hangman? In prison the keepers strip away the prisoners' identities and remove all mirrors. The woman persuades the man by becoming a voice, a mirror for his thoughts. Atwood imagines the language of persuasion that would transform him. Her words are sensuous, alluring, soft: "nipple, arms, lips, wine, belly, hair, bread, thighs, eyes, eyes." His words are promises of a secure future, a comfortable home: "the end of walls, the end of ropes, the opening of doors, a field, the wind, a house, the sun, a table, an apple" (51). What future could the couple have? The man wants a woman who will take care of him, watch him admiringly, and perhaps be grateful. He seeks the woman who will, as Virginia Woolf said, be a mirror that reflects him back to himself larger than life. Does the woman escape from prison only to discover that she is entrapped in marriage?

As frequently happens in Atwood's texts, storytelling is a way for women to bear witness and to save their lives. But language is ambiguous and humans imperfect; it appears that the man and woman have not fully understood each other's words. After their marriage, he says "foot, boot, order, city, fist, roads, time, knife" (52). His words are now those of the soldier, policeman, ruler. Monosyllabic and curt, these words evoke rigid order and violence, the gray world of the city. Like the city planners (*CG*) or the pioneer of *The Animals in That Country*, he seeks a world of order, linearity, rules. In contrast, she says "water, night, willow, rope hair, earth belly, cave, meat, shroud, open, blood" (52). Her words are soft, mysterious, and sensuous, words of the natural world, of vulnerability and victimhood. There are psychological overtones to the poem: we are all locked in prisons of our own making, and the way out may be through becoming the hangman or marrying the hangman, confronting and accepting our own possibilities for both good and evil.

The book's concluding poem, "You Begin," links the family and language themes. The poem situates the poet's daughter in a world of rich and varied colors, forms, textures, and words. Richly alliterative, the poem knits repeated words (hand, learn, words, world) and sounds (w, r, m, l) into subtle sound patterns: "Once you have learned these words / you will learn that there are more / words than you can ever learn" (110). As the poet tells her child about the world's many colors and the plenitude of language, she holds her hand: "your hand is a warm stone / I hold between two words" (110). Through touch, she builds emotional connection as she introduces her daughter to the world and its words.

Atwood's next volume of poetry, *True Stories,* continues to deal with politics and to examine the issues of language and the possibilities and limits of poetry.

True Stories (1981)

True Stories starts paradoxically, disrupting the reader's expectations immediately, by warning that the concept of a true story is a pernicious illusion: "Don't ask for the true story. . . . The true story is vicious / and multiple and untrue" (9–11). After this dramatic beginning, how can the book continue? If there is no true story, what can the poet's message be? How is the reader to interpret the poems? Will they be untruths? But the book does not disappoint, for it continues to broach serious questions of language, epistemology, politics, the contrasting worlds of city and nature, the quest for a secure home in the world, relationships, stories and storytelling, and the power and limits of poetry.

Linda Wagner-Martin writes that *"True Stories* pounds relentlessly at the reader's sensibilities. Negating in every respect . . . Atwood's collection assails the reader during its first half and then creates a firestorm in the second."[1] But she finds that these poems are written in "a dulled, prose-like language" that flattens out the emotions (77).

Atwood composed most of these poems in a six-month period from mid-December 1979 through May 1980. She was writing several poems a day in mid-January. There were also several poems "left over from 'before' (i.e. the last time I was writing poetry in 1977 and early 1978)" (TF, 15.7). As the book evolved Atwood experimented with several different ordering plans, including one that started with a section called "Torture" (TF, 15.3–9). The order that emerged is indeed dramatic, as indicated by Wagner-Martin's response. The book starts with poems of the narrator's alienation and discomfort in a West Indian setting where nature seems hostile and disproportionate. Poems of civic disorder, of torture and violence follow. The stark "Notes Towards a Poem That Can Never Be Written" expresses the impossibility of writing poems commensurate with human suffering. Balanced against this "firestorm" are gentler poems of the narrator's familiar daily life, the mundane routines, the tensions and joys of relationships. Throughout, questions about poetry echo. What can poetry do?

Atwood's novel *Bodily Harm,* published the same year, is a companion piece to this book. In both, a tourist is uneasy in an alien Caribbean setting that is less picturesque and charming than expected (see "One More Garden," "Postcard," "Hotel," "Dinner") and in fact turns out to be dangerous. Both books describe political atrocities such as torture ("The Arrest of the Stockbroker," "Torture," "Trainride, Vienna-Bonn," "A Conversation," and "Notes Towards a Poem That Can Never Be Written") and violence done to women ("A Women's Issue," "Christmas Carol"). Both books speak of holding the hand of a wounded victim and hoping for rescue ("Last Poem"). And both point to the imperative of bearing witness to pain and violence.

After its paradoxical start, *True Stories* continues with a group of poems expressing a tourist's perspective of the West Indies. The tourist is a familiar figure to readers of Atwood; she is a displaced person, removed from her home and uncomfortable in her present surroundings. This lush tropical world of blue sky, golden sun, pink sand, and ocean is just as unnerving to the protagonist as the frozen Northern landscape is to other Atwood characters. In many of these poems the narrator ponders her relationship to the natural world. In the two

"Landcrab" poems, poet and crustacean eye each other warily, recognizing both kinship and difference. In "Petit Nevis" the speaker feels that it is humans who are out of place. In "One More Garden" she thinks she would be more in tune with the surroundings if she gives up the trappings of the urban world and becomes a gourd. "Hotel" and "Dinner" are the laments of displaced persons, transients.

The title poem initiates the book's central theme, the impossibility of ascertaining or communicating a "true story." How can a writer tell a true story or write a poem that will bear witness and bring about political change? The poet's desire for the true story is always thwarted by the impossibility of either knowing the truth or communicating it in words. As for language, poets and linguists argue that language is slippery; there are gaps between what we intend and what language permits us to say. "Two-Headed Poems" explains that the poet's dream of a language so pure that the words are the equivalent of the subject matter, needing no translation, is unattainable.

But the problem is also an epistemological one. There can be no single Truth. As we observe in criminal and civil trials, different storytellers will always have different versions of the story, because they approach it from different positions. Furthermore, what we perceive as "the true story" may change from moment to moment. In any event, other people are opaque to us; we can never really know them (see "Solstice" poem 12). "True Stories" elaborates these concepts in a series of striking metaphors.

Other poems here also explore the truth problem. The two "Landcrab" poems contrast two of many possible, equally valid views of reality, the human perspective and the crustacean's view. Similarly, "Vultures" tells the birds' story from both the narrator's and the vultures' points of view. "Postcard" points out the discrepancy between the pictured paradise and the reality of mosquitoes, crying children, bad plumbing, and mistreated prisoners. But it turns out that both sides of the postcard are fraudulent, because the lover to whom the poet is writing is so distant as to be unreal. She remembers him frozen in the pose in which she last saw him, and, of course, he is different now.

Nevertheless, the impetus for writing poems continues. And if this is so, what kind of poems need to be written? How can the poet write them? In "Small Poems for the Winter Solstice" the speaker confesses that it is difficult to justify "gentle" poems in a world suffused with suffering (section 9); the poems that need to be written are the ones most difficult to write, the poems about pain, suffering, and political atrocity. Who is to write them? How are such poems received? And what happens to the poets who produce such poems? *Interlunar* continues to ask these questions.

In a provocative juxtaposition, "Spelling" and "Notes Towards a Poem That Can Never Be Written" confront these issues. "Spelling" moves from the speaker's daughter playing with plastic letters to a contemplation of poetry and its history. Spelling means both making words and making magic spells. Because poetry is powerful, the makers of poetry, like the makers of spells, have often suffered for their words, being burned at the stake or put to death in other ways. Speaking in metaphors, the poet here thinks of the body uttering "the truth" and writing itself. Poetry must begin with naming, with representing what is here. In this poem the poet welcomes her daughter into the charged and complex world of language.

The powerful "Notes Towards a Poem That Can Never Be Written" takes up the difficult issue of naming that which we prefer to ignore—violence, pain, atrocities—and explores the predicament of the writer who seeks to have a political impact. "Notes" speaks to the Surrealist movement's belief that art can effect political change and to the Surrealist rejection of mimesis (imitation of reality) as a strategy. It declares that mimesis must fail, for the poet can never fully and accurately depict its subject, the people tortured and killed. The third section describes a tortured woman dying and claims that her body is writing the poem. This is clearly impossible; her poem is another one that can never be written. Section 4 presents a series of metaphors that may apply to both torture and artistic production. Frank Davey argues that "the city planner of *The Circle Game,* . . . the artist who writes an authoritative, analytic poem, and the torturer who regards the human body as an object to be manipulated . . . are engaged in aesthetically similar (though morally dissimilar) tasks. Atwood writes only 'notes toward a poem' because to pretend to do otherwise would be" manipulative and objectifying.[2] The fifth section describes in painful physicality the agony of seeing the "facts of this world" clearly and then declares, "Witness is what you must bear" (73). The last section exhorts the poet to write this poem, the very poem that the poet already proved can never be written. Michael Pugliese writes, "A poem that started out on apparently solid ground has been utterly destabilized, and it is up to the reader to negotiate the competing possibilities it offers. The poem rankles, its internal conflicts irritate, and because of this its content stays with the reader, increasing, however slightly, the possibility that a greater awareness has been established, that a potential witness . . . has been awakened."[3]

After this "firestorm" the book ends with gentler, more personal poems as the narrator, now in a more familiar Canadian environment, speaks about sunsets, plums, mushrooms, and her relationship with a partner. "Small Poems for the Winter Solstice" is a series of 14 poems set in a Northern climate, a world of slush, ice, and mud. The speaker wishes she could write poems that are simple and clear, "a bouquet of nice clean words" (32), but she can't, because the ordinary messiness and distractions of daily life intrude. Her relationship with a partner forms the focal point of these poems. There are occasional failures, missed connections, fatigue, and clutter as well as shining moments. In the 14th poem the poet accepts the multiplicity and complexity of their relationship.

The last poems in the book combine the motifs of nature, relationship, and poetry. In the lyrical "Variations on the Word Sleep" the speaker watches her lover sleeping and wishes to enter his sleep as a protector or guide: "I would like to be the air / that inhabits you for a moment / only. I would like to be that unnoticed / & that necessary." She is always aware of birth and death: the mushrooms she brings as a gift smell like newborns or like death; wild plums fall from the tree that seems the appropriate burial place for her partner.

The storytellers in these poems are increasingly conscious of their role in constructing the stories, and storytelling itself is at issue. The next book, *Interlunar,* is more muted, lit with softer lights, and it continues to explore what poetry can accomplish.

Interlunar (1984)

If *True Stories* is a "firestorm," *Interlunar* is the glimmering light of fireflies in a jar, the glow emanating from a marsh or a lake at night, the unexpected shining that occasionally lights up the ordinary, mundane world. The book is about paradoxes of light and dark, life and death. It asks whether language and poetry have the power to heal or to assuage our grief for our mortality. *True Stories* is about power used against others; *Interlunar* is about the power of myth, magic, and trust. *True Stories* is an assault; *Interlunar* is a gentle hand holding the reader's, leading her to numinous places, to the boundaries between light and dark, life and death, presence and absence, language and silence, vision and blindness. The poems are gentler and more personal than in *True Stories.* Many of these speak directly to the reader; they are the stories of two people, an "I" and a "you." Critical interpretations of these poems differ. Linda

Wagner-Martin reads them as "a stark testimony to disaster" (Wagner-Martin, 81); Sharon Rose Wilson reads them as the poet's "marriage to death, her gradual empowerment, and by extension, the empowerment of all artists and human beings" (Wilson, 229).

Interlunar refers to the time of the month when the moon is dark, the four-day period between the old moon and the new moon. Thus it reminds us that the passage from darkness to light recurs every month, a form of cyclical death and rebirth. The second part of this book, named "Interlunar," is a journey from darkness to light. Atwood's watercolor for the cover represents light rather than darkness; it is a reflection of a red sun (or moon) in the still water of a pale blue-gray lake.

The first section consists of 11 "Snake Poems" (7–23) that blend the real and the mythic, danger and power, reminding us of the earlier *Procedures for Underground*. The snake, because it sheds its skin as it grows, symbolizes renewal, rebirth; it is associated with goddesses, fertility, shape changing, and female power (Wilson, 232–39). Here are both real snakes and the snakes of legend, of our imagination—snakes that are transparent, white, deities, souls of the dead. Throughout Atwood's work, eating is linked in one way or another to power; here, eating the snake is a way to connect with power, especially the power of language. But in many of these poems ("The White Snake," "Eating Snake," "Quattrocento"), as in the earlier "Fishing for Eel Totems" or "Procedures for Underground" (*PU*), such power entails danger.

The second part of the book, "Interlunar," is divided into three sections that delineate a journey from darkness to light and explore poetry's power to heal or console. Section 1 describes stasis, unused or unwanted power, disease, unease, and dissatisfaction (29–52). The speaker of the first poem, "Doorway" (29), believes herself to be "without power" and identifies with the inert forms of a gray stone, a murdered girl's bone, or an unopened door. "The Healer" (38–39) finds that others no longer seek her power to cure. "The Saints" (40–41) are still sacred, but "now they seem to have no use." The section ends with movement, "A Sunday Drive" (51–52) in another urban wasteland, the hot and overcrowded Bombay.

Section 2 is a descent into hell, into darkness (55–80). In "Orpheus (1)" (58–59) Eurydice explains that Orpheus (himself a singer, a poet dismembered and resurrected) summoned her from death but couldn't trust that she was there, and therefore lost her again. This Orpheus, "The Robber Bridegroom" (62), and Genghis Khan (68–69) are narcissists, feeding cannibalistically on women to assuage their own pain.

They embody the "city planner" mentality that needs the linear, the rational, the solid fact rather than the imagination. The woman who sings to Genghis Khan (68–69), Eurydice (60–61), and the Persephone of "Letter from Persephone" (63–64) are the poets who bear witness to suffering but can't solve humanity's problems. "Orpheus (2)" (78), linked to the political poems of *True Stories,* tells the story of Victor Jara, a Chilean musician killed because his songs opposed political terrorism (Wilson, 248). The "Three Denizen Songs" (65–67) speak about a person (a woman? a poet?) who is feared and considered to be alien because she is different. The poems of this section point to the transformative power possible in poetry but indicate that we fear that power and the poets who might use it.

Section 3 (82–103) continues the journey from darkness toward light. It starts with "The Words Continue Their Journey" (82–83), in which a caravan of poets travel through desolate terrain "looking for water," that is, questing for spiritual sustenance, purpose. "Heart Test with an Echo Chamber," (86–87) describes the paradoxes of mortality; the heart is "a pear / made of smoke and about to rot," but as the speaker views it on the screen, she sees it suffused with light: life entails death, but momentary luminous moments are possible. "The White Cup" (89) is the poet's gift of "a quiet shining" that lights up the mundane objects we look at. "A Blazed Trail" (99–101) describes a walk through trees, at sunset, to the shore, and ponders death: "I would hold back your death if I could, / but where would you be without it?" Poetry may provide a momentary solace, but it is grounded in knowledge of suffering and death, for "We can live forever, / but only from time to time" (101).

The concluding poem is the elegiac, low-key, subtly muscial "Interlunar" (102–3), a walk to a lake in the dark, the culmination of one poet's journey to find water. "Trust me. This darkness / is a place you can enter and be / as safe in as you are anywhere." The poem starts with the word "darkness" and ends with "light" as the poet leads the other, the reader, to a lake shore:

> The lake, vast and dimensionless,
> doubles everything, the stars,
> the boulders, itself, even the darkness
> that you can walk so long in
> it becomes light.
>
> (103)

The poem's internal rhyme, alliteration, and consonance weave a tightly knit pattern of sounds. Complex and many-faceted, the book is a story of the journey we all undertake, the solaces we hope for, the struggles and suffering we face. *Morning in the Burned House* resonates with the same elegiac tone.

Morning in the Burned House (1995)

Morning in the Burned House describes a world in flux. The book is rich with memories and with a sense of moving through changes into an unknown future, to the ultimate end in death. The poems mix the present and past, memory and fear. There is a broad sweep of tone and mood here, ranging from the wry humor of sex icons reflecting on their lives, including Helen of Troy as a "counter dancer," to a moving sequence on the death of the narrator's father. Survival, the continuation of life, is a central motif. In "The Red Fox" (16–17), the poet comments that we all do what we need to survive; in "Cell" (47–48) the speaker notes that the cancer cell's desires are human ones as well: to eat, to grow, to live forever. In "A Fire Place" the poet notes that new growth comes to replace the old in a burned place, and only humans "regret [its] perishing . . . Only we would call it a wound" (117). If Atwood's early poems were the words of victims trapped in obsessive, narrow lives, these are the poems of a crone, a Hecate, a wise woman who has seen a great deal and now observes life's predicaments with sympathy and wry amusement.

Section 1 describes ordinary life with its frustrations, sadness, fears, and malaise. When the sad child mourns, "I am not the favorite child," the speaker comforts her by saying that at the end "none of us is / or else we all are" (5).

The eight poems in Section 2 are the voices of sex icons who turn out to be powerful women, telling their stories with irony and humor. As "Miss July Grows Older" (21–23) she gets more sophisticated and complex. "Manet's Olympia" (24–25) is tough despite her vulnerable pose. Helen of Troy warns, "This is a torch song. / Touch me and you'll burn" (36).

Section 3 is centered around the powerful poem "Half-Hanged Mary" (58–69), which recounts the story of Atwood's ancestor Mary Webster (one of the dedicatees of *The Handmaid's Tale*), who was hanged as a witch but survived and lived for 14 years. The poem presents her meditations during the night she is hanging. She thinks of the townsfolk who accuse her and those who are afraid to save her; she quarrels with God, she prays, she struggles, "because who the hell else could understand me? / Who else has been dead twice?" (69). Later, people fear her, and her words have great power because of her dramatic brush with death:

> The words boil out of me,
> coil after coil of sinuous possibility.
> The cosmos unravels from my mouth,
> all fullness, all vacancy.
>
> (69)

The internal rhymes of boil and coil, out and mouth, the hissing sibilants, and the tightly packed accents underscore the crone's power. She is both Scheherazade, arguing with God during the night, and the poet returned from the dead bearing an appropriately ambiguous message, encompassing both absence and presence.

"Marsh Languages" describes the politics of language. Because society is becoming more inhumane, language is changing as well. The "hard" languages of logic, of the isolated individual, of linearity and exploitation are gaining power, replacing the "soft" discourses of emotion, of human connections; for example, we are losing "the . . . syllable for 'I' that did not mean separate" (54) as conquering nations with their "language of metal" weapons and technology suppress the languages of the conquered.

An elegiac 12-poem sequence, the poems of Section 4 grow from Atwood's experience of her father's illness and death. There are memories of the family's history, old slides of the father as a young man. "Man in a Glacier" laments the impermanence of life, the changes, the aging all must experience, for the godmothers at our christening, Chemistry and Physics, "laid / the curse on us: You will not sleep forever" (82). The narrator remembers that she was often bored as a young child doing small chores to help her father, and thinks, "Now I wouldn't be bored. / Now I would know too much" (92). After his death, she dreams of him paddling his canoe "so skillfully / although dead:"

> He's heading eventually
> to the sea. Not the real one, with its sick whales
> and oil slicks, but the other sea, where there can still be
> safe arrivals.
>
> (104)

The series starts in the particulars of one family's experience of a father's death and ends in the mythic, for the canoe trip becomes the mythic journey of the soul after death.

Section 5 joins images and ideas that reverberate in Atwood's work: body, language, touch, human connections. "The Moment" (109) tells how one can't really own anything but remains a visitor. "Shapechangers in Winter" (120–25) and "The Girl Without Hands" (112–13) reaffirm the importance of touch as a means of human connection. "The Girl without Hands" reiterates a fairy tale that recurs in Atwood's work as the speaker addresses someone like the emotionally frozen persons in earlier poems, a "you" who is isolate, unable to touch others: "No one can enter that circle / you have made" (112). Only the girl without hands can understand this experience, and she would reach out to build a connection, to "touch you / with her absent hands" (113). "Statuary" (118–19) looks back to "Formal Garden" (DP) but reverses the idea: here the statues complain that people are trying to limit their power of flight. "Morning in the Burned House" (126–27) is built, like Cat's Eye, on paradoxes of memory and the passage of time. For we experience our memories, our stories, as if they are real.

"The Signer" (114–15) epitomizes the book's themes and elegiac tone as it links language to the body and describes the woman who signs for the deaf at poetry readings. In her hands the words turn "into bone," becoming solid and actualized in the body. The narrator explains that the signer and poet are both practicing "for the place where all the languages / will be finalized and / one; and the hands also" (115).

We are all practicing for that place, and poets such as Margaret Atwood remind us of the journey, with its dangers and its consolations.

Chapter Seven

Scarlet Ibises and Frog Songs: Short Fiction

Atwood's stories combine realism and whimsy, fairy tale, myth, and fantasy as they represent the lives of contemporary women and men struggling to cope with an often puzzling or difficult world. Many of the stories contain striking symbols that stand in dramatic counterpoint to the routine or dulled lives of the characters. These short fictions explore a range of situations, from playful or provocative meditations on language and on women's bodies to examinations of our darkest fears. Atwood is especially interested in the fictions characters invent about their lives and in the ways that these stories may become traps or self-fulfilling prophecies or may be rewritten to offer new possibility. Dramatic symbols drawn from the world of nature (a flock of scarlet ibises, a cistern, a hurricane, ancient bog people) often mark these stories. Characters who are locked in narrow, self-enclosed fantasy worlds cannot read these signs or they misinterpret them. In contrast, the characters who are receptive to the signs are vital, creative, and able to modify or learn from their stories.

Atwood's first short story collection, *Dancing Girls* (1977), depicts characters who are alienated from each other and sometimes even psychically alienated from themselves. Most of them face disasters, either real or imagined, but their alienation and isolation are in fact the worst disasters. The second collection, *Bluebeard's Egg* (1983), focuses on themes of sexual politics and storytelling as they relate to the Bluebeard story of the demon lover. In the Grimms' version of this story, the female protagonist saves herself from a dangerous suitor by telling the story that reveals the murders he has committed. The women here tell stories, but most of them remain locked in obsessive relationships with their demon lovers. *Murder in the Dark* (1983), published in the same year as *Bluebeard's Egg,* contains short fictions and prose poems that play a series of variations on themes of language, perception, stories, and sexual politics. *Wilderness Tips* (1991) is primarily about reclaiming lost women through storytelling and about the stories we tell ourselves and each other, out of our need for fictions to explain the often incomprehensible world. *Good Bones* (1992) is a series of playful meditations retelling popular myths.

Dancing Girls (1977)

Dancing Girls is Atwood's first collection of short stories. The 14 stories in this book, most of them previously published in a wide range of magazines in the United States and Canada, tell of difficult human relations, of missed connections, of failed communication, of loss. Most of the protagonists are victims in one way or another, although they usually do not recognize or admit that they are (Atwood claims in *Survival* that the first victim position is denial). Their lives are lackluster, boring, and unsatisfying. Yet dramatic symbols punctuate these stories: ancient sacrificial cisterns, timber wolves, the grave of a famous poet, a plate of cookies shaped like moons and stars. But the protagonists are unable to read these portents and thus cannot resolve their problems. Consequently, they remain isolated and emotionally frozen. Most of them live more deeply in fantasy than in the real world; their stories serve to isolate them even further.

Disaster, real or imagined, large or small, hovers over all the stories: one woman fantasizes about an unspecified apocalyptic event, another about rape; several experience the ends of romantic relationships; one woman is sent to a mental hospital; a plane crashes; a child dies at birth and leaves its parents' lives empty. Most of the women expect danger or disaster. Are they more aware than most people of the world's dangers? Or are they more paranoid? Or perhaps they are simply more used to being victims and thus continually expect the worst. And if the world is a dangerous place, how does one prepare for disaster? What would our responses to these situations be? Apart from the plane crash and the baby's death, these disasters are created by people rather than forces of nature. In fact, the most frequent disaster here is the isolation of individuals and their consequent entrapment in narrow lives of emotional paralysis.

As in "The Man from Mars," other people seem so alien as to be incomprehensible, fearsome, as if from other planets. Sometimes even the disparate parts of the self are alien to each other, as in "The War in the Bathroom." Central figures here are often tourists, aliens, foreigners, displaced persons. Although they travel, as tourists or travel writers, their journeys may lead them to unpleasant revelations but do not result in personal transformation. Locked in their separate worlds, the main characters lead lives of "quiet desperation," emotional flatness. They are split, schizoid, for they sustain public roles but keep their feelings private, hidden from others and even from themselves.

The first story, "The War in the Bathroom," sets the book's tone of claustrophobia and despair and introduces the first of its doubled protagonists who have minimal expectations and who experience isolation and alienation. It is narrated by an unpleasant, vindictive, and bossy woman who orders around the other unnamed woman in the story, proffering such advice as never to accept help from strangers. It turns out that the voice is a split self—the "I" is the ego or the mental function of the "she" who carries out the mechanical activities of her constricted daily routine: washing, dressing, marketing, eating. The narrating "I" is like a character in a Samuel Beckett story; she is obsessive about detail and locked into a minimal round of repeated daily chores. Compounding her vindictiveness, she achieves what she perceives as a small victory by arranging to lock an elderly man out of the shared bathroom.

This protagonist is explicitly split into two, a speaking voice and an acting person. But all the characters in this volume share her doubleness to some degree. They lead secret fantasy lives that contrast dramatically with their public lives. Often the fantasies are more compelling than their daily routines. As a result, they are unable to form deep connections with others, and they remain fragmented.

In "The Man from Mars" and in "Dancing Girls," foreign students cause consternation for women who see them as aliens, as if from other planets. Frightened by their differences, the women imagine that these young men from other cultures will endanger them. Their fears and fantasies produce emotional withholding. In "The Man from Mars," Christine is stalked by a small Asian man, "a person from another culture" (10). She is outwardly polite to him but avoids him and resists his attempts to become friends. After he is deported for stalking the Mother Superior of a convent in Montreal, Christine finds that she is obsessed with him and fantasizes about his fate in his home country. She realizes her similarity to him when she thinks that "he would be something nondescript, something in the background, like herself" (37). In "Dancing Girls," Ann observes her landlady, Mrs. Nolan, watching her new tenant, the foreign student. Mrs. Nolan is fascinated by his foreignness and asks him to dress up in his native costume for her children, but she is secretly terrified that he will be disruptive or violent. She uses the occasion of a party he holds to call the police to get rid of him.

"Polarities" tells of a graduate student, Louise, who attempts to create connections among a group of people that she knows. She enacts her wish in increasingly bizarre ways. At first she wishes to become friends with Morrison, but he is indifferent. She fantasizes building a "circle" of human linkage to counteract the alienation of a desolate and uncongenial urban environment. She repeatedly approaches Morrison, but he puts her off, remaining noncommittal. Reingard M. Nischik analyzes this story in terms of speech act theory and finds that Morrison speaks indirectly and insincerely, and that he uses questions to distance himself rather than to seek information or to establish communication: we learn repeatedly that he "lies," feigns interest he does not feel, and does not listen to Louise.[1] While Louise refers to herself and reveals her feelings, Morrison holds himself aloof.

The story is told from Morrison's point of view. He and a group of colleagues commit Louise to a mental hospital because of her bizarre behavior. Prying into her notebooks on the pretext of looking for the one she wants, they find that she has a clearer insight into Morrison than he has into himself; she has written, "Morrison is not a complete person. . . . he refuses to admit his body is part of his mind" (58). Morrison reluctantly comes to believe that he loves her, but he is uncomfortable because he realizes "it was only the hopeless, mad Louise he wanted. . . . A sane one, one that could judge him, he would never be able to handle" (62). Dismayed and at loose ends, Morrison drives to the zoo that he and Louise had once visited. He stands outside the pen where the wolves are now looking at him and senses that this is a portent he cannot understand. "Something was being told, something that had nothing to do with him, the thing you could learn only after the rest was finished with and discarded" (64). Yet he cannot comprehend what this might be.

A married couple who are likewise emotionally shut off, Sarah and Edward in "The Resplendent Quetzal" are unable to discuss their mutual grief and consequently face a loveless marriage after their baby dies at birth. Edward is a relentless tourist, a bird-watcher, a devotee of pre-Columbian ruins. He has planned their tour of ancient Mayan ruins in Mexico. His enthusiastic pursuits are a kind of quest for purpose, for meaning in a mundane life. Since the death of the baby, Sarah has not returned to school and "wouldn't get a job"; instead she "sat at home," listlessly, as if "waiting for something" (160). Sarah believes that after their baby's death Edward "had lost interest, he had deserted her" (169). Edward suggests that she try to become pregnant again, hoping that this will bring them comfort, but she secretly takes birth-control pills to prevent pregnancy.

Their life together is built of avoidance, indirection, evasion, and outright dishonesty. For example, Sarah pretends to see distant birds so as to get Edward to leave her alone for a few minutes. Although he knows her subterfuge, he pretends to believe her: "Her lie about the birds was one of the many lies that propped things up. He was afraid to confront her, that would be the end, all the pretenses would come crashing down and they would be left standing in the rubble, staring at each other" (158).

The exotic setting and a telling incident lend drama to the story. Sarah steals a figure of the infant Jesus from a crèche at a small restaurant, and she throws it into the cistern where formerly sacrificial victims were thrown to carry messages to the gods and to insure continuing fertility for the community. Her act is a symbolic sacrifice, an unconscious prayer for a restoration of her own fertility and engagement with life. Edward sees her standing on the brink of the cistern and fears that she is about to jump in. But when he reaches her and finds that she is crying silently, he is "dismayed . . . desperate," because he is unprepared to deal with her feelings, to confront the emotion beneath her pretense of control. The implication is that their marriage will continue, sterile and suffocating.

Physical disaster sets the stage for the human disasters that follow in "A Travel Piece." This is the story of Annette, a travel writer whose airplane crashes into the ocean while she is returning from her latest exotic excursion. Annette has increasingly felt as if her life is unreal and the places she visits for her job merely scenery, painted backdrops. "Real events happen to other people, she thinks, why not me?" (141). In the lifeboat with a small group of others she thinks, "[S]omething real had happened to her," then decides that after all, "[T]here is no danger here, it is as safe in this lifeboat as everywhere else" (147). The expected rescue does not come, and the stranded survivors contrive stratagems to remain alive, for it is indeed dangerous in the lifeboat (as dangerous as everywhere else?). They make sunshades out of plastic food trays and smear lipstick on their faces as sunscreen, causing them to look like interplanetary aliens. Annette thinks of taking a photo but does not, probably because she no longer believes they will be rescued. When one of the men on the boat becomes delirious and tries to jump overboard, Annette realizes that the group on the boat is considering the possibility of killing him and eating him for their own survival. She sees her

predicament as "stuck in the present with four Martians and one mad-
man waiting for her to say something" (153) and wonders, "Am I one of
them or not?" (153). Are other people like Martians or madmen? Is
there an "us" and a "them"? This is real life, not the game of lifeboat
played at Elizabeth Schoenhof's dinner party in *Life Before Man*. Cannibalism is a recurring motif in Atwood's work, sometimes treated humorously (as in Marian McAlpin's woman-shaped cake) but contemplated as
a terrifyingly real possibility in this story.

   The narrators of "The Grave of the Famous Poet," "Lives of the
Poets," and "Hair Jewellery" describe failing relationships as the couples
in each grow distant from each other and subside into emotional stagnation. The poet's grave does not bring redemption or inspiration to the
tourists who seek it out; indeed, the grave symbolizes the death of their
relationship. The narrator of "Hair Jewellery" enjoys her fantasies of
unrequited love, rationalizing that although she experiences the "emotional jolts of the other kind," she can continue to live her "meager . . .
and predictable" life (108). She and her partner romanticize and demo-
nize each other (as do the sparring pair in *Power Politics*). Yet when they
meet unexpectedly at a conference years later, they are both disappointed that the other "has sold out" and is leading a respectable academic life, complete with spouse and children. Julia Morse narrates "Lives
of the Poets," referring to herself in both the first and the third person as
she describes her travels to give poetry readings to support herself and
her partner, Bernie, an artist involved in a small and unlucrative cooper-
ative gallery. Julia has come increasingly to dislike these readings,
although she does not tell Bernie. As if her body is rebelling, she gets
headaches, colds, and swollen hands and ankles. At the current reading,
in Sudbury, Ontario, she develops a nosebleed. Waiting for the escorts
from the university to bring her to the reading, she calls Bernie. "Something is frozen," she thinks, reflecting on her life on the road; "Bernie,
save me" (206). When a woman answers the phone she realizes that
Bernie has been carrying on an affair. Furious, Julia determines that at
this poetry reading she will not be polite and decorous as usual. Instead,
at the start of the reading, "she will open her mouth and the room will
explode in blood" (195).

   "When It Happens" describes the apocalyptic fantasies of Mrs. Bur-
ridge, another woman who leads a double life. While she conducts her
daily routines of harvesting tomatoes, canning pickles, and writing marketing lists for the weekly trip to town, she has absorbing fantasies of a
national disaster that will prompt her to run away into the woods for

safety. Certain that a disaster will occur, although she is unsure of its nature, she mentally prepares for the event, hiding one of her husband's guns and thinking of her escape route. Again, as in the other stories here, she does not share her thoughts with her husband, for she believes he would not understand her fears. Thus she perpetuates their lack of communication. Is she intuiting an actual approaching catastrophe? Or is she becoming paranoid, as she continues to live more fully in her disaster fantasy than in her life?

In "Rape Fantasies" a young woman does share her fantasies of possible danger with a man, but the situation is complicated, and we are left to wonder if her stories protect her or endanger her. The story takes the form of a monologue of a young secretary out at a bar on a Friday night. Like Scheherazade she tells stories to a possibly threatening male in the hope that her narratives will intrigue him and establish a rapport so that he will not harm her. Her monologue talks about female fantasies of a disastrous event, rape. She is trying to debunk the notion that women find rape fantasies pleasurable, and to that end she describes her own nonsexual fantasies. In each of her scenarios she uses compassion as a vehicle to avoid becoming a victim. In each instance, she and/or the would-be rapist come to sympathize with and help each other, and each of the rapists is deterred from attacking her. In one of her fantasies the would-be rapist has a cold and she gives him a hot soothing drink; in another she tells the man that she is dying of leukemia, and it turns out that he has the same ailment, so they agree to spend their last months together. As she talks to the man she meets at the bar, she is trying to use conversation to build a connection so that he will not rape her: "I think it would be better if you could get a conversation going. Like, how could a fellow do that to a person he's just had a long conversation with, once you let them know you're human, you have a life too, I don't see how they could go ahead with it, right?" (104). The story ends with this question, a chilling one, for as we know, date rape is a common occurrence.

After the major and minor disasters, the losses and endings, the book ends with a story about a birth. Jeannie gives birth and, as a new woman, writes the story, and her life changes; as a mother, she becomes a different person.

Two of the stories in the Canadian edition of *Dancing Girls* ("The War in the Bathroom" and "Rape Fantasies") did not appear in the first American edition, although they are included in subsequent editions; instead, two more-recently published stories, "Betty" and "The Sin

Eater," appeared in their place. "The Sin Eater," a complex story with richly ambiguous symbolic overtones, deals with the subjects of redemption through storytelling and the responsibility of people for each other. Indeed, this story is the subject of a volume of essays entitled *The Daemonic Imagination* that presents a range of interpretive approaches and pairs critiques of Atwood's story with discussions of a New Testament passage, Mark 5:1–19, that tells the story of Jesus exorcising demons besieging a suffering man.[2]

In "The Sin Eater" the unnamed woman narrator recounts her memories of her therapist, Joseph, on the night after his funeral. She remembers his cynicism, his refusal to explain her dreams, his insistence that life is "a desert island . . . Forget about the rescue" (215). After he dies, the narrator laments his loss because for her he was the one person "who is there only to be told" (223). She also remembers a story he told her about the "sin eaters": in rural areas of Wales, food was placed on the coffin already prepared for dying people. The Sin Eater, an elderly person that Joseph believes was probably a woman, was invited to come and eat the food, thus symbolically transferring the sins of the dying person to herself.

The narrator attends Joseph's funeral, where his two ex-wives and his third, now widowed, wife are dressed in pastels rather than black, and where the guests eat rich chocolate cake and cookies in the shape of stars and moons. That night she dreams of being delayed at an airport, lacking her passport (again, the alien, the tourist, the displaced person), and meeting Joseph, who takes her to a restaurant where the first wife, in a waitress's uniform, serves them a plate of star and moon cookies. Joseph says wistfully, "My sins," and the narrator panics as she looks at the plate, thinking, "[I]t's too much for me, I might get sick" (224). But as the story ends the plate floats toward her, she reaches for the cookies, the table disappears, and she notes, "There are thousands of stars, thousands of moons, and as I reach out for one they begin to shine" (224).

The story, replete with richly ambiguous biblical and mythic symbols, tells of loss and its possible transformation. The biblical Joseph, the hero cast out by his brothers, interpreted the Pharaoh's dreams to save Egypt from famine, but the contemporary Joseph refuses to decipher the narrator's dreams. The Sin Eaters are linked to Jesus, who takes on sins to redeem repentant sinners. And, of course, communion food is symbolic of Christ's body just as the funeral food symbolizes resurrection and continuing life. Martha Burdette writes: "Joseph, the powerful male deity of her dream, associated with the moon, stars, and darkness, and with Dumuzi/Tammuz, the vegetation god of presence/absence mourned especially by women, refuses to stay buried" (164–65).[3]

Yet Atwood's story is complicated. The old women who eat sins are outcasts in their communities, women who "became absolutely bloated with other people's sins," although they had some "perks": it was bad luck to kill them (213–14). Moreover, the story reminds us that in Atwood's fiction the consumption of food is usually linked to power. And the nature of this power is ambiguous here. For example, Ann-Janine Morey compares the narrator to another Atwood protagonist who is linked with food, Marian McAlpin of *The Edible Woman*. Morey believes that in "The Sin Eater" the narrator has regressed. "We leave the nameless female narrator at some point of transformation, but we have no idea if, in reaching for the cookies, she enacts a triumph or a further loss. . . . Has this been a narrative about the loss of a therapist, or the loss of a self who never has a chance to appear?" (175).[4]

Other questions are raised as well. Who is the Sin Eater in this story? Is it the therapist, who listens to the sins and absolves the guilt of his clients? Or is it the narrator, whom Joseph is asking to absolve him from his guilt? And when the narrator recounts the story to the reader—who takes the place of Joseph as the one "who is there only to be told"—does the reader then become the Sin Eater, the one who consumes the story that the narrator tells in her search for absolution?

What are the sins that must be eaten to insure the sinner's redemption? In the world of *Dancing Girls* the sins are those of self-absorption, removing oneself from human connections. And if this is so, then storytelling may participate in the sin-eating process. For telling stories performs many functions. Stories may be exemplary, cautionary tales. A story may also be a confession, a seeking for absolution. And telling stories may become a means of making connections and of sharing experiences. Atwood, as a satirist, a moralist, is writing cautionary tales about the dangers of isolation and alienation, the human disasters of everyday life.

Bluebeard's Egg (1983)

These 13 stories, 12 of them narrated by women, focus on storytellers and storytelling and on the themes of sexual politics embedded in the Bluebeard fairy tale of the title story. In the one story narrated by a man, "Spring Song of the Frogs," Will speaks in a flat, unemotional voice. His marriage has ended, and he has had several affairs, but we learn nothing of the emotions and conflicts that characterized these relationships. In this story he tries to initiate or resume affairs with two women, but neither attempt succeeds. Self-absorbed and devoid of emotions, he is a Bluebeard figure, a man who brings emptiness rather than passion to his relationships.

Two types of women inhabit these stories. One type is the "ice maiden" so often encountered in Atwood's world—the narrator of *Surfacing* or of *Power Politics,* for example—a woman uncertain of her direction, frozen emotionally, a victim trapped in a difficult relationship with a Bluebeard-like male. These women (Alma, Becka, Christine, Sally) live in cities, gray urban wastes of alienation, and they are distanced from their own stories, locked into cliché and superficiality, failing to confront the deeper significance of their lives. The second type is "a creative non-victim," akin to Joan Foster's aunt, Louisa Delacourt, in *Lady Oracle,* a mature woman with a sense of purpose. The strong, purposeful Loulou, the fearless Emma, the self-contained artist Yvonne are approaching this state; the narrator's mother in the autobiographical fictions has achieved it. ("What is her secret?" the narrator keeps asking.) These women are more vital, associated with the life force, marked by their connections to nature's green world; they bake bread, watch the sunrise, take risks.

In this book, characters such as the narrator's mother who find meaning in natural symbols are engaged, open to life and to other people. When Christine views the flock of scarlet ibises, she and her husband feel closer than they have in some time, and she feels more solid, more grounded (224–25). When Yvonne watches the sunrise, her sense of order returns (298–99). In contrast, Will in "Spring Song of the Frogs" hopes to find pleasure and satisfaction (and romance) when the frogs sing, but he is thwarted: "The voices . . . sound thin and ill. There aren't as many frogs as there used to be, either" (201). Frogs symbolize transformation, the renewal of life. His inability to hear meaning in the songs reveals that he is cut off from the world of nature and from others.

The Bluebeard story forms a central motif in Atwood's work, providing a framework to explore heterosexual relationships. This tale, as is usually the case, exists in many versions and concerns the dangers of marriage. The "Fitcher's Bird" story typically involves three sisters. While the first two marry and are killed by the Bluebeard figure, the third outsmarts him, discovers his murderous secrets, and restores her sisters to life. The villain is a wizard who gives each successive wife an egg to carry wherever she goes but forbids her to enter one room in his castle. Of course, all of them do, finding murdered women in a basin of blood and causing their eggs to become bloodstained. When he finds out, he punishes them with dismemberment. The clever third sister leaves her egg outside, escapes from the wizard, and reassembles her siblings. In "The Robber Bridegroom" variant, the maiden foils the killer by telling what she has discovered, pretending that it is a fiction. The villain is then put to death. Thus, the young woman finds her power through storytelling, a frequent theme in Atwood.

While the Bluebeard tale casts the man as the villain, Atwood's texts suggest that women internalize social conventions that deny them power. Thus, social pressures contribute to the victims' problem. For example, Marian McAlpin opts to let her fiancé make all her decisions when they become engaged; the girls in *Cat's Eye* cut pictures out of an Eaton's catalogue and paste them in scrapbooks, thus learning how to become consumers. In contrast, the narrator's mother in "Unearthing Suite" resists social pressures. She considers her marriage "an escape [from convention]. . . . Instead of becoming the wife of some local small-town professional and settling down, in skirts and proper surroundings, to do charity work . . . she married my father and took off down the St. John's river in a canoe. . . . She . . . must have felt that she had been rescued from a fate worse than death: antimacassars on the chairs" (312).

Atwood takes a tongue-in-cheek look at sexual (and linguistic) politics in "Loulou, or the Domestic Life of the Language." Loulou is an earth mother whose house has become the gathering place for a group of free-loading poets. A potter, Loulou is absorbed in the physical world; she embodies the female "secret life—the life of pie crusts, clean sheets, . . . the loaves in the oven" (4). Loulou wedges her own clay, bakes bread, cooks casseroles. The poets, on the other hand, deal with abstractions, with language. They are comic Bluebeard wanna-bes. They write poems about Loulou, live in her house without paying rent, eat the food she cooks for them, tease her, and refer to her solidity and earthiness in big words she doesn't understand: marmoreal, geomorphic, chthonic, telluric. One teases her, "[W]hat existed in the space between Loulou and her name? Loulou didn't know what he was talking about" (66). Eleonora Rao explicates this story as exploring "women's marginal position within hegemonic [i.e., male-dominated] discourse. The story dramatizes woman's (self) exclusion from language, and the strategies of resistance and survival she adopts in a male-dominated context, where the power of naming is in the hands of male poets" (Rao, 167). Loulou chooses to reject the poets' abstract and arcane language, to live in the physical realm. But there is a delightful twist here. Because the story is told from Loulou's point of view, we see the poets through her eyes: they are quite helpless without her practical capability. And so she has "the last word" about them.

Repeatedly in Atwood, telling stories is an imperative, a way for a protagonist to achieve insight into her situation, to establish connections, or to make her voice heard. In "Bluebeard's Egg" Sally fails to achieve a positive outcome. Sally's problem is that she tells the wrong kinds of stories and doesn't tell her own story. Obsessed with her husband Ed, a cardiologist, "a heart man," she tells herself stories about him: that women are chasing him, hiding from him, then making sexual advances. She tells him these stories as well. Because she is the narrator, the reader may wonder: Is her repeated story a reflection of her personal insecurity? Is Ed innocently oblivious to the flirtations of women who approach him at parties to ask about their hearts? Is Sally aware (or suspicious) that he is a philanderer? Or do her repeated stories precipitate the very situation she fears? Moreover, when Sally repeatedly tells these stories to her new friend, the divorcée Marylynn, she may be setting up the very outcome she fears.

Because she focuses on her husband's story, Sally fails to learn her own story that could offer her greater self-awareness and release from her obsession. When she persuades Ed to examine her heart with a new machine at his office, she finds that her heart seems foreign and insubstantial to her: "a large gray object, like a giant fig" (161). She takes adult education courses to "concentrate her attention on other things," yet somehow her attention always returns to Ed. Her instructor tells the class to "explore your inner world," but Sally is "fed up with her inner world; she doesn't need to explore it. In her inner world is Ed . . . and in Ed is Ed's inner world, which she can't get at" (167). For her current course, Forms of Narrative Fiction, she has to tell a modern version of the Bluebeard tale from the point of view of one of the characters. To be creative, Sally decides to tell the story from the egg's point of view. But she doesn't know yet what her story will be. She identifies Ed with the egg, and he is a mystery to her.

Meanwhile, Sally hosts a party and sees Ed standing with his arm brushing her friend Marylynn's rump. What is the meaning of this gesture? Is it casual, unplanned, or does it signal a liaison between the two? Or has Sally imagined the gesture? In contrast to the inquisitive heroine of the "The Robber Bridegroom" fairy tale, she is afraid to find the answer to her question. The fairy tale heroine discovered the truth and confronted her prospective husband by telling the story in the guise of fiction, thereby saving her life. In contrast, Sally is hesitant and fearful; accordingly, she keeps quiet about her discovery. She lies beside Ed and thinks of her pale and "ghostly" heart, in contrast to her vibrant image of an egg, "glowing softly as though there's something red and hot inside it. It's almost pulsing; Sally is afraid of it. . . . the egg is alive and one day it will hatch. But what will come out of it?" We must wonder what the consequences will be for her marriage and for her understanding of her "inner world."

"Uglypuss" and "The Salt Garden" are also variants of the Bluebeard story, featuring men who are destructive and hostile to their partners. Joel in "Uglypuss" is self-centered and unfaithful, and Becka gets revenge. Alma in "The Salt Garden" is drifting, caught up in two complicated, overlapping romance triangles.

Four of the stories here, "Significant Moments in the Life of My Mother," "Hurricane Hazel," "In Search of the Rattlesnake Plantain," and "Unearthing Suite," purport to be autobiographical. Like the later *Cat's Eye,* these fictions blur the line between autobiography and fiction, and of course, all autobiography is to some degree fiction.

The mother in "Significant Moments" is a gifted storyteller, aware of her audience. She speaks with emotion, uses different voices and gestures, and dramatizes the stories. She tailors stories for different occasions and tells the more serious ones, about divorces and romantic tragedies, to women, because men need to be shielded from the unpleasant facts of life. The narrator explains that "the structure of the house [her mother grew up in] was hierarchical, with my grandfather at the top, but its secret life—the life of pie crusts, clean sheets, the box of rags in the linen closet, the loaves in the oven—was female" (4). The narrative here focuses on anecdotes the mother tells about her life, interspersed with the narrator's commentary. The significant moments are childhood memories: how her mother convinced her father (the narrator's grandfather) to allow her to get a haircut, how her pet chicks died, how she jumped from the barn rafters attempting to fly. Then there are stories about the narrator as a child: how she talked to her rabbit cookie at a tea party. What lesson am I to learn from this, she wonders.

"Hurricane Hazel" is another family story. The narrator is 14 and has her first boyfriend, the older Buddy. She tries to pretend to be "normal," but her family is different from the conventional suburban family because they live in the bush in the summers, where her father conducts entomological research. Buddy visits her at their cabin, and she spends the day with him. She accepts his ID bracelet even though she does not want it because "I felt that Buddy had something on me: that, now he had accidentally seen something about me that was real, he knew too much about my deviations from the norm. I felt I had to correct that somehow. It occurred to me, years later, that many women probably had become engaged and even married this way" (48). Sharon Rose Wilson comments wryly that here, as in much of Atwood's fiction, "[P]assing the test of socialization, being a conventionally 'true bride' or good date, is failing the test of being a human being" (Wilson, 266).

The volume's closing story, "Unearthing Suite," is cast as a memoir of the narrator's parents. In fact, Atwood reads a passage from this story as a voice-over in the videotape *Atwood and Family* as her parents enact the parts, her mother swimming in the lake and her father surveying the dock for repairs. In this story, the narrator contrasts herself with her more agile, active, and healthy parents. They are healthy; she has a cold. She would cling anxiously to the roof if she climbed it; her mother "clambers nimbly" to sweep off the leaves every fall. They are energetic and carry out projects; she does "as little as possible" (311). Among their projects, her parents build houses that she calls "earths" and explains, "[T]hey are more like stopping places, seasonal dens, watering holes on some caravan route which my nomadic parents are always following" (306).

The narrator finds that her vocation as a storyteller emerged from childhood patterns. When she was young, her parents exhorted her to be still so as not to tip a canoe, touch a tent in the rain, or unsettle the precarious balance of a heavily laden motorboat. "Perhaps it was then that I began the translation of the world into words. It was something you could do without moving" (311). And perhaps also, enforced stillness in natural surroundings taught her to observe carefully and to enjoy her imagination.

In contrast to the unmoving narrator, the mother is active, always moving—ice-skating, skiing, swimming, or organizing the family moves from house to house. The narrator explains: "Photographs have never done justice to my mother. This is because they stop time; to really reflect her they would have to show her as a blur" (303). Unlike the passive, frozen women, the mother cannot be "captured" by a camera.

Her mother is optimistic, unconventional; she asserts herself as a real person, lively, active, interesting, a full partner in the marriage. The unconventional, nomadic life she found in her marriage was a way to freedom—out of the stifling conventions of the parlor and drawing room, into the bush. She is a welcome counterpoint to the women who are figuratively Bluebeard's victims in the book's other stories (Sally, Alma, Becka).

The incident that ends the story, and the book, reveals the mother's character and is another "significant moment." When her mother was sweeping the roof, she found the droppings of an unusual animal, a fisher. The father finds this "an interesting biological phenomenon." For her mother; however, it is a "miraculous token, a sign of divine grace; as if their mundane, familiar, much-patched . . . roof has been visited and made momentarily radiant by an unknown but by no means minor god" (323). Thus, her mother, attuned to the green world, reads divine grace into animal droppings. Thus, the book's framing stories depict a comfortable, stable marriage and present a woman who escapes from restrictive social conventions to become her own person, a "creative nonvictim."

Murder in the Dark (1983)

This collection appeared in Canada in 1983 and was combined with *Good Bones* when published in the United States as *Good Bones and Simple Murders* (Doubleday, 1994). Many of the pieces here are about the writing and storytelling process. They are small snippets of stories: young children making poison, schoolgirls reading horror comics and throwing snowballs. Some are mental games: What if men did the cooking? What if words were tangible objects?

The title piece describes a party game in which the person taking the role of the murderer lies while the others tell the truth. The narrator claims that the writer is the murderer, and "by the rules of the game, I must always lie" (30). "Simmering" is a role-reversal fantasy. It retells the subversive stories told by women who have been exiled from the sacred mysteries of the kitchen and sent off by their husbands to work. There was a time when women's "kitchen envy" was treated by amputating the tips of their tongues. Now, women gather in living rooms and whisper the secret tales of a time when women did cook. "The Page" describes the terror and danger of entering the world beneath the blank page, for "beneath the page is everything that has ever happened, most of which you would rather not hear about" (45). "Happy Endings" details various plots that may be written, but the author notes that the endings are all the same: "John and Mary die" (40).

The book ends with "Instructions for the Third Eye," the eye that sees things we would rather not see. The third eye sees more, and more clearly: "The third eye can be merciless, especially when wounded. . . . Try not to resist the third eye: it knows what it's doing. Leave it alone and it will show you that this truth is not the only truth. One day you will wake up and everything, the stones by the driveway, ... each brick, each leaf . . . your own body, will be glowing from within, lit up, so bright you can hardly look. You will reach out . . . and you will touch the light itself" (62).

Wilderness Tips (1991)

This collection of 10 stories is unified through the themes of loss of innocence, difficult relationships, death, and storytelling. In particular, these stories reveal our need of storytelling as a way of discovering meaning, explaining our experiences, and coming to terms with ourselves and others. For the stories we tell often determine our survival. The stories counterpose ordinary life with our fantasies about it, which are often inadequate or misleading, such as the fashion magazine's fantasies of sexual allure ("Hairball"), the romance magazine's tales of sex and betrayal ("True Trash"), and Greek myths of transformation ("Isis in Darkness"). Particularly Canadian fantasies of the Northern landscape underlie three of these stories, "The Age of Lead," "Death by Landscape," and "Wilderness Tips." It is instructive to read these stories in tandem with Atwood's *Strange Things,* a discussion of Canadian popular myths about "the malevolent North." In Atwood's stories here, the focus is on the dangers humans cause rather than the dangers posed by the landscape. The Bluebeard story, the demon lover fairy tale, is an intertext of "Weight" and "Hack Wednesday." "Uncles" foregrounds the gap between our own fictions about ourselves and the way others see us.

Telling stories is a major theme here, especially in "True Trash," "Isis in Darkness," and "Death by Landscape," three stories about the reclamation of lost women through storytelling. The first story, "True Trash," is about the process of telling stories. Joanne, a freelance writer, is the perceiver who gives structure to the tale. When the story begins she is about 18 and a waitress at a boys' summer camp in the 1950s. The title is the waitresses' parody of the *True Romance* magazine that the waitresses read, snickering at the contrived melodramatic tales of forbidden lust and sex. Yet even as they are reading the tales, a similar story is unfolding among them: one of them becomes pregnant out of wedlock.

Joanne later discovers who the unsuspecting father of the child is and wonders if she should tell him: "The melodrama tempts her, the idea of a revelation, a sensation, a neat ending. But it would not be an ending, it would only be the beginning of something else. In any case, the story itself seems to her outmoded. . . . It's a story that would never happen now" (30).

"Hairball" is narrated by Kat, a fashion magazine editor who comes to realize that she has designed her life to mirror a slick magazine. She dresses at the height of fashion—tough, hard, edgy—and assumes a demeanor to match but discovers that what she really wants is comfort, marriage, security. Similarly, she chooses clothing to transform her lover into a sexier man but then realizes that she liked him better as he was before. The hairball of the title is her ovarian cyst, a benign growth that has been surgically removed. Kat comes to think of the hairy growth as the child she has never had. She keeps it in a jar and uses it to dramatic purpose at the story's conclusion.

"Isis in Darkness" is the title of a poem sequence written by the mysteriously alluring young woman Selena. Her poems recount the story of the Egyptian fertility goddess searching for the bones of her beloved Osiris, the vegetation god, and piecing them back together. The story tells of the transformations of myth and poetry and points to the missed opportunities for human transformation. Selena is named after the Greek goddess of the moon. But the contemporary Selena becomes an alcoholic and dies young, while the story's narrator, Richard, a less-talented poet who loves her from afar, lapses into a dull marriage, a divorce, and an uninspired career. Richard is in the position of Isis at the story's end, assembling his fragments of Selena's life on notecards and planning to write the book that will reveal her poetic genius and troubled life. In memorializing her he finally finds the subject that inspires him. In contrast to Richard, whose retelling of Selena's story enhances and magnifies her, Julie's story of Connor ("The Bog Man") diminishes him, for her memory of him dwindles over time.

"Death by Landscape" is a haunting tale of Lois, whose friend Lucy disappears on a canoe trip one summer at camp. A typical Canadian nature story, according to Atwood, is about being lost or killed in a dangerous landscape (*SV* 55). In this story, the focus shifts from the dangerous landscape to the characters' stories about it. The camp director needs to account for the inexplicable event and persuades herself that Lois pushed Lucy off a cliff. Lois finds the event inexplicable. She lacks a story about the accident and retreats into her memories of Lucy. She collects landscape paintings by Tom Thomson and the Group of Seven and believes that "every one of them is a picture of Lucy" (118).[5] Interestingly, Tom Thomson himself was drowned while canoeing on one of his painting expeditions.

"The Age of Lead" juxtaposes two seemingly unrelated narratives: a TV documentary describing the death of John Torrington, a young sailor on the ill-fated Franklin expedition of 1845, and the story of Jane's friend Vincent. As Jane tells the story, the links between the two narratives emerge. The documentary recounts a scientific expedition led by Owen Beattie, a Canadian forensic anthropologist, in 1984 and 1986 to exhume Torrington's body from the permafrost. In 1845, Captain John Franklin of the British Royal Navy led a group of 134 men in two specially equipped ships to search for a Northwest Passage that would link England and northern Europe with the Pacific through the Arctic Ocean. The entire expedition died, the cause of their deaths a mystery: "At the end those that had not yet died in the ships set out in an idiotic trek across the stony, icy ground, pulling a lifeboat laden down with toothbrushes, soap, handkerchiefs, and slippers, useless pieces of junk" (161). It has taken more than one hundred years to develop the story that explains their deaths. Jane learns that Franklin and his explorers were poisoned by the lead solder in their cans of provisions: "It was what they'd been eating that had killed them" (161).

Jane juxtaposes the documentary with memories of Vincent, who died recently at age 43 of an unidentified disease and who had joked that his disease "must have been something I ate" (160). Jane thinks about "the sidewalk that runs past her house . . . cluttered with plastic drinking cups, crumpled soft-drink cans, used take-out plates," very like the "useless pieces of junk" left behind by the Franklin expedition (162). Sherrill E. Grace writes: "[W]e are positioned to perceive that the moral . . . is that we, like Franklin and his men, are being poisoned by what we eat or by what we are doing to the environment upon which we depend for food. . . . If [they] could not read the signs connecting their destruction with the conveniences of their world in time to save themselves, why should we? If they were not safe in their science and technology, why should we be safe?"[6] Thus, interestingly, the danger lies more in technology than in the Northern landscape that proved so dangerous in Atwood's early poems. And perhaps we need to revise our own stories about contemporary technology.

Two stories tell of the demon lover, the deathlike male. In "Weight" the gentle and forgiving Molly clings to romantic hopes for redeeming her obsessively jealous husband and is murdered, while her friend, the pragmatic and cynical narrator, survives to commemorate Molly with a battered women's shelter. For Molly and the narrator, telling the right stories is a life-or-death imperative. "Hack Wednesday" is a comic variant, a day in the life of a middle-aged newspaper columnist, Marcia, and her political activist husband, one of the rigid, "straight-line" personalities whose version of political correctness imposes artificial and needlessly constraining rules of behavior.

"Wilderness Tips," the title story, is narrated by George, an immigrant to Canada, whose polite surface charm belies his amoral behavior. The story is a complex one, alluding to actual and invented stories of the North as it questions the meanings of wilderness for Canadian identity (Howells, 32–37). Each of the characters has a set of assumptions about the values implicit in wilderness, and in the course of the story, these values are destabilized, turned upside down: again, humans prove more treacherous than the wilderness.

In each of the stories here, the characters must reevaluate the fictions on which they have based their lives. In her next collection of short fiction, *Good Bones,* Atwood plays with a variety of popular myths, rewriting them from unusual points of view.

Good Bones (1992)

The 27 short fictions and prose poems collected in this book are confections, jeux d'esprit, stories told with wit from unusual points of view, wryly revising cultural myths although often carrying sly undertones, as in "The Female Body" and "Making a Man." The bat tells of its fear of humans in "My Life as a Bat." The moth in "Cold-Blooded" reports to its home planet about a race of strange and backward "blood-creatures." When "The Little Red Hen Tells All," she explains that, being henlike, she shared the loaf of bread with all the lazy animals who never helped her. When "Gertrude Talks Back," she tells her son Hamlet that he is an "awful prig sometimes," just like his father.

"Let Us Now Praise Stupid Women" tells us that the wise, smart, careful women lead wise, ordered lives, but the stupid ones are endearing because "they make even stupid men [and women] feel smart" (32). Moreover, the stupid women, because of their general innocent ineptness, generate the plots of narratives; they are the ones "who have given us Literature" (37). And where would we be without stories, for, as the narrator exclaims, "No stories! Imagine a world without stories!" (32).

The pieces here, like those in *Murder in the Dark,* have been called fables, speeded-up short stories, and prose poems. They blur the boundaries between fiction and poetry, thus "expanding the brackets" of the genres. They are testaments to Atwood's love of story and to her continuing exploration of the complex, multiple, ambiguous fictions we invent in our ongoing quest for survival.

Chapter Eight
Poets and Princesses: An Atwood Miscellany Literary Criticism, Reviews, and Children's Books

Atwood's fictions and poems explore a range of concerns and "expand the brackets" of traditional literary genres, establishing Atwood's stature as a major author in Canada and internationally. In addition to these achievements, her works of literary criticism are important texts as well. To write such texts is to participate in the work of building and sustaining a cultural community. Atwood explains that reviewers form a bridge between writers and readers and that their work arises from our love of language.[1] Compiling literary collections is another gesture of community building, and Atwood has edited *The New Oxford Book of Canadian Verse in English* (1982), and coedited three collections of short stories. She compiled *The CanLit Foodbook* (1987), a collection of food-related literary excerpts and recipes from Canadian writers, originally intended as a fund-raiser for P.E.N. Atwood carries out these serious literary tasks with wit and humor. Playfulness is also a significant factor in her children's storybooks, probably growing out of stories she made up for her daughter, Jess. And stories are one way to introduce children to the life of our human community. In these projects Atwood continues to share with a wide audience her passion for ideas, for language, and for story.

Atwood has been writing literary criticism since her high school days, when she wrote reviews, parodies, and other critical essays. Many of her essays have been collected in *Second Words*; others have been delivered as papers at a wide variety of conferences, public lecture series, artistic events, and other venues. Like her fiction and poetry, her essays combine seriousness and humor, pointed insights and provocative questions.

Survival (1972)

Survival: A Thematic Guide to Canadian Literature (1972) is one of Atwood's early forays into literary criticism. "Foray," with its connotations of venture into new territory or military advance, is an apt description, for the book has proved to be surprisingly controversial, giving rise to such acrimonious debate that one critic summed up the responses as "The *Survival* Shoot-Out."[2] The furor signaled the book's impact. Coming as it did at a time of strong national feeling and literary ferment, it became a focal point of critical debate about the meaning of Canadian literature. The book is intended to be a guide and introduction for students and teachers, because the field of Canadian literature as an academic subject was in its early stages. Many critics applauded the book's brilliance, wit, and pithiness.

Survival begins with several disclaimers, asserting that it is not academic, and it does not attempt to be evaluative or exhaustive or to provide a historical survey. Its primary intent is to identify recurring thematic patterns that characterize Canadian literature. Yet despite the disclaimers, some critics took the book to task for failing to be more historical or more exhaustive. Some felt that thematic studies are inherently exclusive, for they do not take into account those works that deal with themes outside of the studies' frameworks. It was also noted that many of the works discussed or listed in the bibliography were published by a small publishing house for which Atwood served on the board of directors, the independent House of Anansi Press. Perhaps some of the critical discomfort with the book was caused by its intent to be a popular rather than a scholarly study. No doubt, *Survival*'s focus on themes of victimhood and failure was disconcerting.

The book sold well, partly because it filled a need; partly because it is well written, thoughtful, succinct, and interesting; and partly because of its notoriety. Over 70,000 copies were sold by 1980, making it "the most visible, widely read critical work on Canadian literature in Canada's history" (Rosenberg, 135). Lively and provocative, the book argues that survival itself is the main theme of Canadian literature, largely because the land is a difficult one. It portrays Canadian literature as dealing primarily with victims, both people and animals, and proposes four victim positions: one, denial; two, resignation; three, recognition and anger; and four, creative nonvictimhood. Each chapter provides an overview of how the theme of survival or victimhood pervades one aspect of Canadian literature. For an indication of Atwood's epigrammatic style, let us look, for example, at her discussion of "Nature the Monster." Summing up nineteenth-century nature poetry written by authors who wish to find in the Canadian wilderness a replica of their English birthplaces, she writes: "Pretending that Nature is the all-good Divine Mother when you're being eaten by mosquitoes and falling into bogs is [victim] Position One. It can't really stand up very long against the Canadian climate and the Canadian terrain, measured against which Wordsworth's Lake District—Divine Mother country—is merely a smallish lukewarm pimple" (61). The book's chapter titles indicate its range of concerns, for example, "Nature the Monster," "Animal Victims," "Early People: Indians and Eskimos as Symbols," "Ancestral Totems: Explorers, Settlers," "The Paralyzed Artist," and "Ice Women vs. Earth Mothers." At the end of each chapter are suggestions for further reading, organized into short and longer lists of readily available paperbacks.

Frequently, an author's literary theories provide insight into his or her writing. Atwood observes that some of the patterns she discovers "were first brought to [her] attention by [her] own work" (14), and critics find her analysis a useful tool for examining her writings, as, for example, I use *Survival*'s discussion of victims to read *Surfacing*.

Second Words (1982)

Second Words compiles a selection of Atwood's essays, talks, and reviews. Atwood divides it chronologically into three sections. She explains: "When you begin to write, you deal with your immediate surroundings; as you grow, your immediate surroundings become larger" (14). This is true of the material in her essays and of the world depicted in her fiction and poetry as well. Starting with reviews of Canadian writers in Part I, this book grows to include essays on U.S. writers, on Canadian-American relations, on the role of the writer and the reading public in democracy, and on human rights. As editors sought her out to write reviews, Atwood avoided the "woman writers ghetto" by seeking to review the work of male authors as well. Part I contains essays written from 1960 to 1971; all of them are reviews of Canadian writers (including Margaret Avison, Eli Mandel, and Al Purdy) except for a reprinted article, "Superwoman Drawn and Quartered: The Early Forms of *She*," based on Atwood's work for her (uncompleted) dissertation on H. Rider Haggard.[3]

Part II consists of essays written between 1972 and 1976. In addition to reviews of Canadian writers (including Audrey Thomas and Marie-

Claire Blais) and American authors (including Adrienne Rich, Kate Millett, and Erica Jong), this section contains Atwood's response to Robin
Mathews's review of *Survival* and essays on Canadian self-deprecatory
humor, on Canadian mythological beings such as the wendigo and the
wabeno (later elaborated in *Strange Things*), and on being a woman
writer. In "On Being a Woman Writer: Paradoxes and Dilemmas,"
Atwood describes the tendency of reviewers and interviewers to characterize women writers in terms of gender. She explains that "writers are
eye-witnesses, I-witnesses" (203), a position that many of Atwood's protagonists assume. In "The Curse of Eve—Or, What I Learned in
School," she lists stereotypes attributed to female fictional characters
("Old Crones, Delphic Oracles . . . Mad Mothers, . . . Rapunzel and her
tower, Cinderella and her sackcloth and ashes," 219–20) and the tendency of female characters to be "static," natural forces. In contrast to
these, Atwood presents "a simple plea; women, both as characters and
as people, must be allowed their imperfections," their full range of qualities, their personhood (227).

In Part III, essays written between 1977 and 1982, there is a greater
range of reviews and topics. Included here is "An Introduction to *The
Edible Woman.*" Governmental politics and human rights become
increasingly important topics. "Witches" includes an anecdote about
Atwood's ancestor Mary Webster, who was hanged as a witch but survived. The essay warns about witch-hunting and argues in favor of free
speech. "An End to Audience?" stresses the importance of literature for
democracy. "Canadian-American Relations: Surviving the Eighties" ends
with the reminder, "[T]here are boundaries and borders, spiritual as well
as physical. . . . But there are values beyond national ones. Nobody
owns the air; we all breathe it" (392). "Amnesty International: An
Address" cites the writer's imagination, "the power to communicate;
and hope" as our best defenses against oppression (397).

Strange Things (1995)

Strange Things consists of a series of four lectures presented at Oxford
University. Again, Atwood starts with a disclaimer. She reassures her
audience that these lectures are not academic and avoid academic jargon. They are about the legends of the Canadian North and trace some
of the literature based on these legends. In these talks Atwood returns
to the Canadian world of *Survival* and proves that her "literary vision is
in every way her country's."[4]

Her first lecture is on the disastrous Franklin expedition of 1845 in search of the Northwest Passage. The entire expedition died of hunger, cold, and, it later turned out, of lead poisoning from the solder in their tin cans of provisions. Atwood traces a genealogy of poems and stories about the expeditions, from E. J. Pratt to Mordecai Richler. She herself drew on it for her story "The Age of Lead"(*WT*). Earlier retellings of the Franklin story inscribe the myth of the malevolent North, "Nature as Monster," a devouring and jealous female figure. Atwood, on the other hand (profiting from recent scientific discoveries about the expedition's fate), by focusing on the lead poisoning information, uses the story to critique our reliance on technology, which often turns out to have unexpected consequences.

"The Grey Owl Syndrome" describes the Westerner's romantic vision of the native people as "noble savages" and their attempts to "go native." "Eyes of Blood, Heart of Ice; the Wendigo" traces the literary history of two monster cannibal figures, the wendigo and the wabeno. The last lecture, "Linoleum Caves," derives its title from Alice Munro's novel *The Lives of Girls and Women* (1971) to suggest the juxtaposition of domesticity and wildness. In the last talk Atwood considers the use women writers have made of the myths of the Canadian North, starting with E. Pauline Johnson, who gave poetry readings dressed in an evening gown in the first half and in a buckskin-and-fur costume, as an Indian princess, in the second half. The talk mentions Susanna Moodie and her sister, Catherine Parr Traill; Ethel Wilson's *Swamp Angel* (1954); and Marian Engel's *Bear* (1976) and ends with a discussion of the comic use of the wendigo motif in *Winter Hunger* (1990) by Ann Tracy. Atwood concludes by warning her audience that the real North is in danger and needs preservation.

Children's Books

Margaret Atwood has written four children's books, *Up in the Tree* (1978), *Anna's Pet* (1980), *For the Birds* (1990), and *Princess Prunella and the Purple Peanut* (1995). These tales have subtle moral underpinnings, as is often the case with children's literature, but Atwood handles the themes with restraint and humor.

Up in the Tree, illustrated by Atwood with round-eyed, curly-haired, androgynous-looking children, is the rhymed story of two children who play in a treehouse. The round-faced children with their halos of short curls look very much like Survivalwoman, the comic strip character Atwood created for *This Magazine* under her pen name of Bart Gerrard.

Anna's Pet, illustrated by Atwood's aunt, children's-book author Joyce Barkhouse, concerns Anna's quest for a pet she can bring from her grandparents' home on a farm to her city apartment. Most of the animals are inappropriate—for example, the snake might slither away—and each time she finds one she lets it go. Anna relinquishes all of the animals she has found, conceding that they are better off where they live. Anna is a lively girl who is comfortable handling snakes, lizards, and other animals.

For the Birds is an ecological fable. After throwing a rock at a crow, the heroine is temporarily changed into a crow herself and must undergo the struggles of a wild bird to find food, avoid human predators (including malicious children), and survive.

In *Princess Prunella,* illustrated by Maryann Kovalski, Atwood indulges her love of wordplay, playing with the deliciously explosive sounds of the letter "p," as Princess Prunella wears "puffy petticoats sprinkled with sparkling pink sequins, a peculiar pilly polo-necked pullover, a pair of pale purple pumps with peonies on the insteps" and wreaks havoc in the palace because she never "picks up her playthings, plumps her pillows, or puts away her pens, pencils and puzzles." Even reviewers get caught up in the game; the reviewer for the *Library Journal* called it "perfectly peachy."

The story is a humorous moral fable: Prunella is reformed through the agency of a Wise Woman and meets an unlikely Prince Charming. Atwood explains that in fairy tales, "[T]here were a lot of quite active female characters. . . . there are active princesses. And if anybody is passive, it's the prince. You know, he goes home and his mother casts some sort of spell on him, and the Princess has to go through all these interesting machinations to get him back. She rescues him; she's the one that has the magic powers" (Lyons, 224–25). And indeed, Princess Prunella rescues the prince in this fable.

The spoiled and selfish princess learns her lesson when a Wise Woman casts a spell that mars her pretty face until she is able to perform three good deeds. After she successfully performs two, Prunella meets her perfect mate, a "pear-shaped, pinheaded prince . . . [wearing] a plaid pajama top and a pair of preposterous plum-colored polka-dotted pants." Her third good deed is to rescue the prince from plunging into a polluted pond full of carnivorous pike. The prince recognizes her (newly acquired) kindness and promises, "[W]hen you are older perhaps I might be prepared to propose." Prunella's appearance is restored, and her parents are pleased to find her behavior greatly improved.

Conclusion

Atwood continues her prolific production. Her most recent book of poems, *Eating Fire: Selected Poems 1965–1995,* just appeared in England; she is at work on a novel, and she is listed as a speaker at a variety of venues. Her remarkable literary achievements continue to inform, entertain, and intrigue. How better to end this study than with quotes from Atwood herself on reading and writing.

"All writers believe, must believe, that if you can only get the right words into the right order, once anyway, the world will be miraculously transformed."[6]

Through reading and writing, we join "a community that is transnational, trangenderal . . . that crosses, in fact, all borders . . . . Anyone can be a member of it; all you need is love, the love of reading and writing, of words—the love of language, which has been with us for at least 35,000 years, and which helped to make us human in the first place" ("Pretty Face," 7).

"If writing novels—and reading them—has any redeeming social value, it's probably that they force you to imagine what it's like to be somebody else. Which, increasingly, is something we all need to know" (*SW,* 430).

"Writing is what we *choose* to say to one another. It can be a prayer or a curse; it can be our anger, but it can also be our love. It can keep on speaking to others, even after we die. It's a shared song, and it's also what we whisper to one another, out of our deepest and most unique and private solitudes in the dark" ("Pretty Face," 7).

Notes and References

Chapter One

1. Peter Dale Scott, "The Difference Perspective Makes: Literary Studies in Canada and the United States," *Essays on Canadian Writing* 44 (Fall 1991): 23.

2. See Barbara Hardy, "Narrative as a Primary Act of Mind," in *The Cool Web,* ed. M. Meek, A. Warlow, and G. Barton (London: Bodley Head, 1977). Hardy explains that we "dream in narrative, daydream in narrative, remember, anticipate, hope, despair, believe, doubt, plan . . . learn, hate and live by narrative" (13).

3. *Atwood and Family* (short version), prods. Michael Rubbo, Barrie Howells, dir. Michael Rubbo, 29 min., National Film Board of Canada, 1995, videocassette.

4. Sandra Djwa, "The Where of Here: Margaret Atwood and a Canadian Tradition," in *The Art of Margaret Atwood: Essays in Criticism,* ed. Cathy N. Davidson and Arnold E. Davidson (Toronto: Anansi, 1981), 21.

5. Beatrice Mendez-Egle, "A Conversation with Margaret Atwood," in *Margaret Atwood Reflection and Reality,* Living Author Series no. 6, ed. Beatrice Mendez-Egle (Edinburg, Tex.: Pan American University, 1987), 175. Interview took place in November 1983.

6. Geoff Hancock, *Canadian Writers at Work* (Toronto: Oxford University Press, 1987), 260; hereafter cited in text.

7. Sharon Rose Wilson, *Margaret Atwood's Fairy-Tale Sexual Politics* (Toronto: ECW Press, 1993); hereafter cited in text.

8. George Woodcock, *Introducing Margaret Atwood's Surfacing,* (Toronto: ECW Press, 1990), 15–16; hereafter cited in text.

9. Sherrill Grace, *Violent Duality: A Study of Margaret Atwood* (Montreal: Vehicule, 1980); Lorraine M. York, ed., *Various Atwoods* (Concord, Ontario: Anansi, 1995); J. Brooks Bouson, *Brutal Choreographies* (Amherst: University of Massachusetts Press, 1993), hereafter cited in text; Camille Peri, "Witchcraft," *Mother Jones* 14, no. 3 (April 1989): 30; Coral Ann Howells, *Margaret Atwood* (Houndmills, England: Macmillan, 1996), 9, hereafter cited in text; Eleonora Rao, *Strategies for Identity: The Fiction of Margaret Atwood* (New York: Peter Lang, 1993), hereafter cited in text; Gayle Greene, *Changing the Story* (Bloomington: Indiana University Press, 1991), hereafter cited in text.

10. Marilyn Patton, "Tourists and Terrorists: The Creation of *Bodily Harm,*" *Papers on Language and Literature* 28 (Spring 1992): 165; hereafter cited in text.

154 NOTES AND REFERENCES

Chapter Two

1.   Northrop Frye, conclusion to *Literary History of Canada: Canadian Literature in English,* ed. Carl F. Klinck and Alfred G. Bailey (Toronto: University of Toronto Press, 1965), 826. Hereafter cited in text.

2.   Fredric Jameson, *Postmodernism, or, the Cultural Logic of Late Capitalism* (Durham, N.C.: Duke University Press, 1991).

3.   Kathryn VanSpanckeren, "Shamanism in the Works of Margaret Atwood," in *Margaret Atwood: Vision and Forms,* ed. Kathryn VanSpanckeren and Jan Garden Castro (Carbondale: Southern Illinois University Press, 1988), 189; hereafter cited in text.

4.   Frank Davey, "Atwood's Gorgon Touch," in *Critical Essays on Margaret Atwood,* ed. Judith McCombs (Boston: G. K. Hall, 1988), 146; hereafter cited in text.

5.   Judith McCombs, "Atwood's Haunted Sequences: *The Circle Game, The Journals of Susanna Moodie,* and *Power Politics,*" in *The Art of Margaret Atwood: Essays in Criticism,* ed. Cathy N. Davidson and Arnold E. Davidson (Toronto: Anansi, 1981), 35–54; hereafter cited in text as McCombs 1981.

6.   Eli Mandel, "Atwood Gothic," in *Critical Essays on Margaret Atwood,* ed. Judith McCombs (Boston: G. K. Hall, 1988), 119.

7.   Louis Dudek, "Poetry in English," in *The Sixties: Writers and Writing of the Decade,* ed. George Woodcock (Vancouver: University of British Columbia Publications Center, 1969), 117.

8.   Margaret Atwood, "Why I Write Poetry," *This Magazine* 29, no. 6/7 (1 March 1996), 44. Hereafter cited in text as "Why I Write."

9.   Eli Mandel, "Seedtime in Dark May," *Alphabet* 4 (June 1962): 69–70; Peter Dale Scott, "Turning New Leaves," *Canadian Forum* 41 (February 1962): 259–60; Milton Wilson, "Letters in Canada, 1961: Poetry," *University of Toronto Quarterly* 31, no. 4 (July 1962): 448–49. Because so little poetry was published, every work was reviewed at least once.

10.   Charles Pachter, "An Atwood/Pachter Duet," in Margaret Atwood and Charles Pachter, *The Journal of Susanna Moodie* (Boston: Houghton Mifflin Company, 1997), xxix; hereafter cited in text.

11.   Judith McCombs, "From 'Places, Migrations' to *The Circle Game*: Atwood's Canadian and Female Metamorphoses," in *Margaret Atwood: Writing and Subjectivity,* ed. Colin Nicholson (New York: St. Martin's Press, 1994), 51–67; hereafter cited in text as McCombs 1994.

12.   Michael Ondaatje, review of *The Circle Game. Canadian Forum,* April 1967, 22–23, reprinted in *Critical Essays on Margaret Atwood,* ed. Judith McCombs (Boston: G. K. Hall, 1988), 29–32.

13.   Judith McCombs, "Politics, Structure, and Poetic Development in Atwood's Canadian-American Sequences: From an Apprentice Pair to 'The Circle Game' to 'Two-Headed Poems,' " in *Margaret Atwood: Vision and Forms,* ed.

Kathryn VanSpanckeren and Jan Garden Castro (Carbondale: Southern Illinois University Press, 1988), 148–49; hereafter cited in text as McCombs 1988.

14.   Abraham Moses Klein, "Portrait of the Poet as Landscape," in *The Rocking Chair and Other Poems* (Toronto: Ryerson, 1948).

15.   Judith McCombs, "Country, Politics and Gender in Canadian Studies: A Report from Twenty Years of Atwood Criticism," in *Literatures in Canada*, ed. Deborah C. Poff (Montreal: Association for Canadian Studies, 1989), 28; Mona Van Duyn, "Seven Women," *Poetry* 115, no. 6 (March 1970): 432–33.

16.   Colin Nicholson, "Living on the Edges," in *Margaret Atwood: Writing and Subjectivity*, ed. Colin Nicholson (New York: St. Martin's Press, 1994), 34–37.

17.   Linda Sandler, "Interview with Margaret Atwood," in *Margaret Atwood: Conversations*, ed. Earl G. Ingersoll (Princeton, N.J.: Ontario Review Press, 1990), 46; hereafter cited in text as Sandler 1990.

18.   From "Writing Susanna," on Margaret Atwood's web site, 31 January 1998, http://www.web.net/owtoad/toc.html.

19.   Jerome H. Rosenberg, *Margaret Atwood* (Boston: Twayne, 1984), 49; hereafter cited in text.

20.   Michael A. Peterman, "Susanna Moodie," in *Canadian Writers and Their Works*, Fiction Series, ed. Robert Lecker, Jack David, and Ellen Quigley. Vol. 1 (Downsview, Ontario: ECW Press, 1983), 67.

21.   Judith McCombs, "Crossing Over: Atwood's Wilderness *Journals* and *Surfacing*," in *Essays on the Literature of Mountaineering*, ed. Armand E. Singer (Morgantown: West Virginia University Press, 1982), 106–117; hereafter cited in text as McCombs 1982.

22.   Peter Stevens, "Dark Mouth," *Canadian Literature* 50 (Autumn 1971): 91–92.

23.   Margaret Kaminski, "Preserving Mythologies," in *Margaret Atwood: Conversations*, ed. Earl G. Ingersoll (Princeton, N.J.: Ontario Review Press, 1990), 31; hereafter cited in text.

24.   Mary Greer, *Tarot for Your Self* (North Hollywood, Calif.: Newcastle, 1984), 212.

25.   Arthur Edward Waite, *The Pictorial Key to the Tarot* (New York: Carol Publishing Group, 1995), 116–19.

26.   Linda Sandler, "Interview with Margaret Atwood," *Malahat Review* 41 (January 1977): 14; hereafter cited in text as Sandler 1977.

27.   Dennis Cooley, "Nearer by Far: The Upset 'I' in Margaret Atwood's Poetry," in *Margaret Atwood: Writing and Subjectivity*, ed. Colin Nicholson (New York: St. Martin's Press, 1994), 68–93.

28.   Christine Downing, *The Goddess: Mythological Images of the Feminine* (New York: Crossroad, 1989).

29.   Judith Yarnall, *Transformations of Circe: The History of an Enchantress* (Urbana: University of Illinois Press, 1994); hereafter cited in text.

30.   Jane Lilienfeld, "Circe's Emergence: Transforming Traditional Love in Margaret Atwood's *You Are Happy*," in *Critical Essays on Margaret Atwood*, ed. Judith McCombs (Boston: G. K. Hall, 1988), 124.

Chapter Three

1.   Valerie Miner, "Atwood's Metamorphosis: An Authentic Canadian Fairy Tale," in *Her Own Woman: Profiles of Ten Canadian Women*, ed. Myrna Kostash, Melinda McCracken, Valerie Miner, Erna Paris, Heather Robertson (Toronto: Macmillan, 1975), 173–94.

2.   D. J. Dooley, "In Margaret Atwood's Zoology Lab," in *Moral Vision in the Canadian Novel* (Toronto: Clarke, Irwin & Co. 1979), 138, hereafter cited in text; Robin Skelton, "Review of *The Edible Woman*," *Malahat Review* 13 (January 1970): 108–9; Jane Rule, "Life, Liberty, and the Pursuit of Normalcy: The Novels of Margaret Atwood," *Malahat Review* 41 (January 1977): 44–45; W. J. Keith, *Introducing Margaret Atwood's* The Edible Woman (Toronto: ECW Press, 1989); T. D. MacLulich, "Atwood's Adult Fairy Tale: Lévi-Strauss, Bettlelheim, and *The Edible Woman*," in *Critical Essays on Margaret Atwood*, ed. Judith McCombs (Boston: G. K. Hall, 1988), 179–97; David Harkness, "Alice in Toronto: The Carrollian Intertext in *Edible Woman*," *Essays on Canadian Writing* 37 (Spring 1989): 103–11; Glenys Stow, "Nonsense as Social Commentary in *Edible Woman*," *Journal of Canadian Studies* 23, no. 3 (Fall 1988): 90–101.

3.   Dell Texmo, "The Other Side of the Looking Glass: Image and Identity in Margaret Atwood's *The Edible Woman*," *Atlantis* 2, no. 2 (Spring 1977): 74.

4.   Catherine McLay, "The Dark Voyage: *The Edible Woman* as Romance," in *The Art of Margaret Atwood: Essays in Criticism*, ed. Cathy N. Davidson and Arnold E. Davidson (Toronto: Anansi, 1981), 123–38.

5.   Graeme Gibson, "Margaret Atwood," *Eleven Canadian Novelists*, ed. Graeme Gibson (Toronto: House of Anansi Press, 1973), 25.

6.   Margery Fee, *The Fat Lady Dances: Margaret Atwood's* Lady Oracle (Toronto: ECW Press, 1993), 20; hereafter cited in text.

7.   Judith McCombs, "Atwood's Nature Concepts: An Overview," *Waves* 7 (Fall 1978): 68–77 and "Atwood's Fictive Portraits of the Artist: From Victim to Surfacer, from Oracle to Birth," *Women's Studies* 12 (February 1986): 69–88; Sherrill E. Grace, "In Search of Demeter: The Lost Silent Mother in *Surfacing*," in *Margaret Atwood: Vision and Forms*, ed. Kathryn VanSpanckeren and Jan Garden Castro (Carbondale: Southern Illinois University Press, 1988), 34–47, hereafter cited in text as Grace 1988; Robert Cluett, "Surface Structures: the Syntactic Profile of *Surfacing*," in *Margaret Atwood: Language, Text and System*, ed. Sherrill Grace and Lorraine Weir (Vancouver: University of British Columbia Press, 1983), 67–90, hereafter cited in text.

8. Richard Lane, "Anti-Panoptical Narrative Structures in two Novels by Margaret Atwood," *Commonwealth* 1, no. 16 (Autumn 1993): 63–69.

9. Robert Lecker, "Janus through the Looking Glass: Atwood's First Three Novels," in *The Art of Margaret Atwood: Essays in Criticism,* ed. Cathy N. Davidson and Arnold E. Davidson (Toronto: Anansi, 1981), 193–94.

10. Kate Ferguson Ellis, *The Contested Castle: Gothic Novels and the Subversion of Domestic Ideology* (Urbana: University of Illinois Press, 1989).

11. Karen F. Stein, "Speaking in Tongues: Margaret Laurence's *A Jest of God* as Gothic Narrative," *Studies in Canadian Literature* 20, no. 2 (Winter 1995): 74–95.

12. Karla Hammond, "Defying Distinctions," in *Margaret Atwood: Conversations,* ed. Earl G. Ingersoll (Princeton, N.J.: Ontario Review Press, 1990), 107.

13. J. R. (Tim) Struthers, "Playing Around," in *Margaret Atwood: Conversations,* ed. Earl G. Ingersoll (Princeton, N.J.: Ontario Review Press, 1990), 64; hereafter cited in text.

14. Molly Hite, *The Other Side of the Story: Structures and Strategies of Contemporary Feminist Narrative* (Ithaca, N.Y.: Cornell University Press, 1989), 127–67, hereafter cited in text; Roberta Rubenstein, *Boundaries of the Self: Gender, Culture, Fiction* (Urbana: University of Illinois, 1987); Roberta Sciff-Zamaro, "The Re/membering of the Female Power in *Lady Oracle," Canadian Literature* 112 (Spring 1987): 37.

Chapter Four

1. Jill LeBihan, *"The Handmaid's Tale, Cat's Eye,* and *Interlunar*: Margaret Atwood's Feminist (?) Futures (?)," in *Narrative Strategies in Canadian Literature,* ed. Coral Ann Howells and Lynette Hunter (Philadelphia: Open University Press, 1991), 93–107.

2. Gregory Fitz Gerald and Kathryn Crabbe, "Evading the Pigeonholders," in *Margaret Atwood: Conversations,* ed. Earl G. Ingersoll (Princeton, N.J.: Ontario Review Press, 1990), 131–39.

3. Bonnie Lyons, "Using Other People's Dreadful Childhoods," in *Margaret Atwood: Conversations,* ed. Earl G. Ingersoll (Princeton, N.J.: Ontario Review Press, 1990), 224–25; hereafter cited in text.

4. Adele Freedman, "Happy Heroine and 'Freak' of CanLit," *Globe and Mail* (Toronto), 25 October 1980, El.

5. Carol Beran, *Living Over the Abyss: Margaret Atwood's* Life Before Man (Toronto: ECW Press, 1993), hereafter cited in text; Ildiko de Papp Carrington, "Demons, Doubles, and Dinosaurs: *Life Before Man, The Origin of Consciousness,* and 'The Icicle,'" in *Critical Essays on Margaret Atwood,* ed. Judith McCombs (Boston: G. K. Hall, 1988), 229–245, hereafter cited in text; Paul Goetsch, "Margaret Atwood's *Life Before Man* as a Novel of Manners," in *Gaining Ground: European Critics on Canadian Literature,* ed. Robert Kroetsch and Reingard M. Nischik (Edmonton, Alberta: NeWest Press, 1985), 137–49, hereafter cited in text.

6. Elizabeth Meese, "An Interview with Margaret Atwood," *Black Warrior Review* 12 (Fall 1985): 89. Interview conducted April 1985.

7. Annette Kolodny, "Margaret Atwood and the Politics of Narrative," in *Studies on Canadian Literature,* ed. Arnold E. Davidson (New York: Modern Language Association, 1990), 95.

8. Sherrill Grace, " 'Time Present and Time Past': *Life Before Man.*" *Essays in Canadian Writing* 20 (Winter 1980–81): 168; hereafter cited in text as Grace 1980–81.

9. John Berger, "Why Look at Animals?" in *About Looking* (New York: Pantheon, 1980), 1–26.

10. Linda Nochlin, *Realism* (Harmondsworth, Middlesex, England: Penguin, 1971).

11. Lorna Irvine, *Collecting Clues: Margaret Atwood's* Bodily Harm (Toronto: ECW Press, 1993), hereafter cited in text; Jennifer Strauss, " 'Everyone Is in Politics': Margaret Atwood's *Bodily Harm* and Blanche d'Alpuget's *Turtle Beach*: Being There, Being Here" in *Australian/Canadian Literatures in English: Comparative Perspectives,* ed. Russell McDougall and Gillian Whitlock (Melbourne: Methuen Australia), 111–19; Helen Tiffin, " 'Everyone Is in Politics': Margaret Atwood's *Bodily Harm* and Blanche d'Alputget's *Turtle Beach*: Voice and Form," in *Australian/Canadian Literatures in English: Comparative Perspectives,* ed. Russell McDougall and Gillian Whitlock (Melbourne: Methuen Australia), 119–32; Roberta Rubenstein, "Pandora's Box and Female Survival: Margaret Atwood's *Bodily Harm,*" *Journal of Canadian Studies* 20, no. 1 (1985): 120–35.

12. Grace Epstein, "*Bodily Harm*: Female Containment and Abuse in the Romance Narrative," *Genders* 16 (Spring 1993): 80–93.

13. Jo Brans, "Using What You're Given," in *Margaret Atwood: Conversations,* ed. Earl G. Ingersoll (Princeton, N.J.: Ontario Review Press, 1990), 148.

14. Diana Brydon, "Atwood's Postcolonial Imagination: Rereading *Bodily Harm,*" in *Various Atwoods,* ed. Lorraine M. York (Concord, Ontario: Anansi, 1995), 111.

15. Lee Briscoe Thompson, *Scarlet Letters: Margaret Atwood's* The Handmaid's Tale (Toronto: ECW Press, 1997), hereafter cited in text; Sharon R. Wilson, Thomas B. Friedman, and Shannon Hengen, ed., *Approaches to Teaching Atwood's* The Handmaid's Tale *and Other Works* (New York: Modern Language Association, 1996); hereafter cited in text.

16. For further discussion of the contrasts between the novel and the film, see Mary R. Kirtz, "Teaching Literature through Film: An Interdisciplinary Approach to *Surfacing* and *The Handmaid's Tale,*" in Wilson, Friedman and Hengen, 140–45; Glenn Willmott, "O Say, Can You See: *The Handmaid's Tale* in Novel and Film," in *Various Atwoods,* ed. Lorraine M. York (Concord, Ontario: Anansi, 1995), 167–90.

17.   Michele Lacombe, "The Writing on the Wall: Amputated Speech in Margaret Atwood's *The Handmaid's Tale*," *Wascana Review* 21, no. 2 (Fall 1986): 3–20.

18.   Karen F. Stein, "Margaret Atwood's *The Handmaid's Tale*: Scheherazade in Dystopia," *University of Toronto Quarterly* 61, no. 2 (Winter 1991/92): 269–70, 275; hereafter cited in text as Stein 1991/92.

19.   Madonne Miner, " 'Trust Me': Reading the Romance Plot in Margaret Atwood's *The Handmaid's Tale*," *Twentieth Century Literature* 37, no. 2 (Summer 1991): 148–68; Sandra Tomc, " 'The Missionary Position': Feminism and Nationalism in Margaret Atwood's *The Handmaid's Tale*," *Canadian Literature* 138/39 (Fall/Winter 1993): 73–87.

20.   Stephanie Barbé Hammer, "The World as It Will Be? Female Satire and the Technology of Power in *The Handmaid's Tale*," *Modern Language Studies* 20, no. 2 (Spring 1990): 39–49.

21.   Joseph Andriano, "*The Handmaid's Tale* as Scrabble Game," *Essays on Canadian Writing* 48 (Winter 1993): 89–96.

Chapter Five

1.   Earl G. Ingersoll, "Waltzing Again," in *Margaret Atwood: Conversations,* ed. Earl G. Ingersoll (Princeton, N.J.: Ontario Review Press, 1990), 236.

2.   Jill Ker Conway, *When Memory Speaks: Reflections on Autobiography* (New York: Knopf, 1998), 7; hereafter cited in text.

3.   Nathalie Cooke, "Reading Reflections: The Autobiographical Illusion in *Cat's Eye*," in *Essays on Life Writing: From Genre to Critical Practice.* ed. Marlene Kadar (Toronto: University of Toronto Press, 1992), 162–70; Jessie Givner, "Names, Faces and Signatures in Margaret Atwood's *Cat's Eye* and *The Handmaid's Tale*," *Canadian Literature* 133 (Summer 1992): 56–75. See also Paul de Man, "Autobiography as De-Facement," in *The Rhetoric of Romanticism* (New York: Columbia University Press, 1984).

4.   Alice Palumbo, "Class, Gender, and the Birth of the Suburbs in Margaret Atwood's *Cat's Eye*," *Newsletter of the Margaret Atwood Society* 19 (Fall/Winter 1997), 2–3.

5.   R. D. Lane, "Cordelia's 'Nothing': The Character of Cordelia and Margaret Atwood's *Cat's Eye*," *Essays on Canadian Writing* 48 (Winter 1992–93): 73–88.

6.   Michelle Gadpaille, "Odalisques in Margaret Atwood's *Cat's Eye*," *Metaphor and Symbolic Activity* 8, no. 3 (1993): 221–26.

7.   On the iconography of the fallen woman in Victorian art, see Linda Nochlin, *Women, Art and Power* (New York: Harper and Row, 1988).

8.   Linda Hutcheon, "Universal Soldiers," review of *The Robber Bride. The Nation* 257, no. 20 (13 December 1993), 734–37; Sarah Appleton Aguiar,

"Good Girls and Evil Twins: Constructing Zenia in Margaret Atwood's *The Robber Bride*," *Newsletter of the Margaret Atwood Society* 19 (Fall/Winter 1997): 5–6, 15–16, hereafter cited in text.

    9. Jennifer Enos, "What's in a Name? Zenia and Margaret Atwood's *The Robber Bride*," *Newsletter of the Margaret Atwood Society* 15 (Fall/Winter 1995): 14.

    10. Arnold Davidson, "The Mechanics of Mirroring in *The Robber Bride*," *Newsletter of the Margaret Atwood Society* 13 (Fall 1994): 5.

    11. Robyn Younkin, "Decoding History in Margaret Atwood's *The Robber Bride: Y NOT?*," unpublished paper, May 1995, 19.

    12. Laura Miller, "Interview with Margaret Atwood," *Salon* (January 1977), 2.

    13. Elspeth Cameron, *Alias Grace,* book review, *The Canadian Forum* 75, no. 856 (January-February 1997), 39.

Chapter Six

    1. Linda Wagner-Martin, "Giving Way to Bedrock: Atwood's Later Poems," in *Various Atwoods,* ed. Lorraine M. York (Concord, Ontario: Anansi, 1995), 76; hereafter cited in text.

    2. Frank Davey, *Margaret Atwood: A Feminist Poetics.* (Vancouver: Talonbooks, 1984), 49.

    3. Michael Pugliese, "Surrealism and the Possibilities of Art in 'Notes Towards a Poem That Can Never Be Written,' "unpublished paper, May, 1998, 4. For my reading of this poem I am indebted to Michael Pugliese.

Chapter Seven

    1. Reingard M. Nischik, "Speech Act Theory, Speech Acts, and the Analysis of Fiction," *Modern Language Review* 88, no. 2 (April 1993): 297–304.

    2. Robert Detweiler and William G. Doty, *The Daemonic Imagination: Biblical Text and Secular Story* (Atlanta: Scholars Press, 1990); hereafter cited in text.

    3. Martha Burdette, "Sin Eating and Sin Making: The Power and Limits of Language" in Detweiler and Doty, 159–68.

    4. Ann-Janine Morey, "The Old In/Out," in Detweiler and Doty, 169–80.

    5. The Group of Seven was a group of Canadian painters formed in 1920. Influenced by Tom Thomson (1877–1917), the group was eager "to develop a new style of Canadian painting" featuring landscapes and Northern scenes. "In constrast to the farmers and industrialists who sought to conquer the land and to prosper from it, these artists saw in the untamed terrain a reflection of the country's spirit." Members of the group were Franklin Carmichael, Lawren Harris, A. Y. Jackson, Frank Johnston, Arthur Lismer,

J. E. H. McDonald, and F. J. Varley. Anne Newlands, *The Group of Seven and Tom Thomson* (Willowdale, Ontario: Firefly Books, 1995), 6.

6.   Sherrill E. Grace, " 'Franklin Lives': Atwood's Northern Ghosts," in *Various Atwoods,* ed. Lorraine M. York (Concord, Ontario: Anansi, 1995), 159–61.

Chapter 8

1.   Margaret Atwood, "Not Just a Pretty Face," *The Women's Review of Books* 11, no. 4 (January 1994): 6–7; hereafter cited in text as "Pretty Face."

2.   T. D. MacLulich, "The *Survival* Shoot-Out," *Essays on Canadian Writing* 1 (Winter 1974): 14–20. See also Rosenberg, 135–43; Atwood, "Mathews and Misrepresentation" (*SW* 129–50).

3.   Margaret Atwood, "Superwoman Drawn and Quartered: The Early Forms of *She,*" *Alphabet* 10 (July 1965): 65–82.

4.   Tom MacFarlane, *"Strange Things,"* *New York Times* (18 April 1996).

Selected Bibliography

Primary Sources

Dates of the first major press publication, followed by details of the editions cited in this study.

Novels

The Edible Woman. 1968; New York: Bantam, 1991.
Surfacing. 1972; New York: Ballantine, 1987.
Lady Oracle. 1976; New York: Ballantine, 1991.
Life Before Man. 1979; New York: Ballantine, 1990.
Bodily Harm. 1981; New York: Bantam, 1983.
The Handmaid's Tale. 1985; New York: Ballantine, 1987.
Cat's Eye. 1988; New York: Doubleday, 1989.
The Robber Bride. New York: Doubleday, 1993.
Alias Grace. New York: Doubleday, 1996.

Poems

The Circle Game. 1966; Anansi, 1978.
The Animals in That Country. Boston: Atlantic Little-Brown, 1968.
The Journals of Susanna Moodie. Toronto: Oxford University Press, 1970.
Procedures for Underground. Boston: Atlantic Little-Brown, 1970.
Power Politics. Toronto: Anansi, 1971.
You Are Happy. 1974; New York: Harper & Row, 1975.
Selected Poems. 1976; New York: Simon & Schuster, 1978.
Two-Headed Poems. Toronto: Oxford University Press, 1978.
True Stories. New York: Simon & Schuster, 1981.
Interlunar. Toronto: Oxford University Press, 1984.
Selected Poems II: Poems Selected and New 1976–1986. Toronto: Oxford University Press, 1986; Boston: Houghton Mifflin, 1987.
Selected Poems 1966–1984. Toronto: Oxford University Press, 1990.
Morning in the Burned House. Toronto: McClelland & Stewart, 1995.
Eating Fire: Selected Poems 1965–1995. London: Virago, 1998.

Short Fiction

Dancing Girls and Other Stories. 1977; New York: Bantam, 1989.

162

Murder in the Dark. Toronto: Coach House, 1983.
Bluebeard's Egg. 1983; New York: Ballantine, 1990.
Wilderness Tips. 1991; New York: Bantam, 1996.
Good Bones. Toronto: Coach House, 1992.

Children's Books

Up in the Tree. Toronto: McClelland & Stewart, 1978.
Anna's Pet. Toronto: Lorimer, 1980.
For the Birds. Douglas & McIntyre, 1990.
Princess Prunella and the Purple Peanut. New York: Workman, 1995.

Nonfiction

Survival: A Thematic Guide to Canadian Literature. Toronto: Anansi, 1972.
Days of the Rebels: 1815–1840. Toronto: Natural Science of Canada, 1977.
Second Words: Selected Critical Prose. 1982; Boston: Beacon Press, 1984
Strange Things: The Malevolent North in Canadian Literature. Oxford: Oxford University Press, 1995.

Edited

The New Oxford Book of Canadian Verse in English. Toronto: Oxford University Press, 1982.
The Oxford Book of Canadian Short Stories in English (with Robert Weaver). Toronto and New York: Oxford University Press, 1986.
The CanLit Foodbook. Toronto: Totem Books, 1987.
The Best American Short Stories 1989 (with Shannon Ravenel), New York: Houghton Mifflin, 1989.
The New Oxford Book of Canadian Short Stories in English (with Robert Weaver). Toronto and New York: Oxford University Press, 1995.

Recordings

"The Poetry and Voice of Margaret Atwood," Caedmon, 1977.
"Margaret Atwood Reads from *The Handmaid's Tale,*" Caedmon.
"Margaret Atwood Reads Unearthing Suite," American Audio Prose Library, 1985.

Film

The Handmaid's Tale screenplay by Harold Pinter. Dir. Volker Schlondorff, (Cinecom, 1989).

Web site

http://www.web.net/owtoad/

Secondary Sources

Bibliographies

McCombs, Judith, and Carole L. Palmer. *Margaret Atwood: a Reference Guide.*
    Boston: G. K. Hall, 1991.
"Current Atwood Checklist," *Newsletter of the Margaret Atwood Society,* 1986–
    present.

Biographies

Cooke, Nathalie. *Margaret Atwood: A Biography.* Montreal: ECW Press, 1998.
Sullivan, Rosemary. *The Red Shoes: Margaret Atwood/Starting Out.* Toronto:
    Harper Flamingo, 1998.

Book-length Studies in English

Beran, Carol. *Living Over the Abyss: Margaret Atwood's Life Before Man.* Toronto:
    ECW Press, 1993. Introduction to the novel. Emphasizes chronology
    and ethnicity.
Bouson, J. Brooks, *Brutal Choreographies.* Amherst: University of Massachusetts
    Press, 1993. Study of family, politics and "oppositional strategies" in the
    novels.
Davey, Frank. *Margaret Atwood: A Feminist Poetics.* Vancouver: Talonbooks, 1984.
    Focuses on dichotomies between male/female, line/curve, space/ time.
Davidson, Arnold E. *Seeing in the dark: Margaret Atwood's* Cat's Eye. Toronto:
    ECW Press, 1997.
Davidson, Cathy N., and Arnold E. Davidson, eds. *The Art of Margaret Atwood:
    Essays in Criticism.* Toronto: Anansi, 1981. Essays on the novels, poetry,
    and criticism.
Fee, Margery. *The Fat Lady Dances: Margaret Atwood's Lady Oracle.* Toronto:
    ECW Press, 1993. Introduction to the novel. Discussion of Joan Foster,
    Gothic and "anti-Gothic," and the Toronto milieu.
Grace, Sherrill. *Violent Duality: A Study of Margaret Atwood.* Montreal: Vehicule,
    1980. Emphasis on the duality of Atwood's work.
Grace, Sherrill, and Lorraine Weir, eds. *Margaret Atwood: Language, Text and Sys-
    tem.* Vancouver: University of British Columbia, 1983. Essays on
    Atwood's work and the social and cultural contexts.
Hengen, Shannon. *Margaret Atwood's Power: Mirrors, Reflections and Images in
    Select Fiction and Poetry.* Toronto: Second Story, 1993. Provides contexts of
    Canadian feminism and nationalism.
Howells, Coral Ann. *Margaret Atwood.* London: Macmillan, 1996. Studies pri-
    marily the novels and *Wilderness Tips;* treats shifts of emphasis in
    Atwood's treatment of politics over time.

Irvine, Lorna. *Collecting Clues: Margaret Atwood's* Bodily Harm. Toronto: ECW Press, 1993. Introduction to the novel, emphasizing the detective genre. Annotated bibliography.

Keith, W. J. *Introducing Margaret Atwood's* The Edible Woman. Toronto: ECW Press, 1989. Introduction to the novel. Annotated bibliography.

McCombs, Judith, ed. *Critical Essays on Margaret Atwood.* Boston: G. K. Hall, 1988. Reprints reviews and critical studies of the novels and poetry. Introductory bibliographic essay reviews the reception of Atwood's works.

Mendez-Egle, Beatrice, ed. *Margaret Atwood Reflection and Reality.* Living Author Series no. 6. Edinburg, Tex.: Pan American University, 1987. Includes interview with Atwood.

Mycak, Sonia. *In Search of the Split Subject: Psychoanalysis, Phenomenology, and the Novels of Margaret Atwood.* Toronto: ECW Press, 1996.

Nicholson, Colin, ed. *Margaret Atwood: Writing and Subjectivity.* New York: St. Martin's Press, 1994. Essays on the fiction and poetry from a postcolonial perspective.

Rao, Eleonora. *Strategies for Identity: The Fiction of Margaret Atwood.* New York: Peter Lang, 1993. Postmodernism and paradox in Atwood's work.

Rigney, Barbara Hill. *Margaret Atwood.* Totowa, N.J.: Barnes and Noble, 1987. Study of Atwood's texts, emphasis on failed artist figures.

Rosenberg, Jerome H. *Margaret Atwood.* Boston: Twayne, 1984. Introduction to Atwood's texts. Annotated bibliography.

Staels, Hilde. *Margaret Atwood's Novels: A Study of Narrative Discourse.* Tubingen, Germany: Francke Verlag, 1995.

Thompson, Lee Briscoe. *Scarlet Letters: Margaret Atwood's* The Handmaid's Tale. Introduction to the novel. Annotated bibliography.

VanSpanckeren, Kathryn, and Jan Garden Castro, eds. *Margaret Atwood: Vision and Forms.* Carbondale: Southern Illinois University Press, 1988. Essays on novels, poetry, and criticism. Autobiographical foreword by Atwood and interview. Reproductions of Atwood paintings.

Wilson, Sharon Rose. *Margaret Atwood's Fairy-Tale Sexual Politics.* Jackson: University of Mississippi Press, 1993. Detailed study of fairy-tale motifs in Atwood's fiction and poetry. Reproductions of Atwood paintings. Appendix lists folklore types and motifs.

Wilson, Sharon R., Thomas B. Friedman, and Shannon Hengen, eds. *Approaches to Teaching Atwood's* The Handmaid's Tale *and Other Works.* New York: Modern Language Association, 1996. Includes bibliographical essay. Focus on teaching strategies and useful materials for the study of Atwood.

Woodcock, George. *Introducing Margaret Atwood's* Surfacing. Toronto: ECW Press, 1990. Introduction to the novel. Annotated bibliography. Focus on birth imagery.

York, Lorraine M., ed., *Various Atwoods.* Concord, Ontario: Anansi, 1995. Critical essays chiefly on the more recent poetry and fiction.

Interviews with Atwood

Aronoff, Phyllis, and Howard Scott, trans. *Two Solicitudes: Conversations/Margaret Atwood, Victor-Lévy Beaulieu.* Toronto: McClelland and Stewart, 1998.
Ingersoll, Earl G., ed., *Margaret Atwood: Conversations.* Princeton, N.J.: Ontario Review Press, 1990.

Web site

The Margaret Atwood Society http://www.cariboo.bc.ca/atwood

Index

"Age of Lead, The" *(Wilderness Tips)*, 140, 142, 149
Aguiar, Sarah Appleton, 99, 100
Ainsley *(Edible Woman)*, 46, 47, 49
Alias Grace: discussion of, 103–109; Grace Marks, 86, 103–109, 114; James McDermott, 104, 108; Jamie Walsh, 108, 109; Mary Whitney, 86, 104–107; Nancy Montgomery, 104, 106–109; Rachel Humphrey, 106, 108; Reverend Verringer, 105; Scheherazade figure, 87; Simon Jordan, 86, 104, 106–108, 109; themes in, 85–86. *See also* Kinnear, Thomas
Alice in Wonderland, 43–45, 47
"All Bread" *(Two-Headed Poems)*, 112
Alliston, Ontario, 34, 111, 112
Amnesty International, 4, 71, 75, 148
Anansi. *See* House of Anansi Press
Andriano, Joseph, 82
Animals in That Country, The, discussion of, 18–22
Anna *(Surfacing)*, 51, 54, 56
Anna's Pet, children's book, 149
"Arctic syndrome: dream fox" *(The Animals in That Country)*, 20
"Arrest of the Stockbroker, The" *(True Stories)*, 116
Arthur *(Lady Oracle)*, 31, 57, 60, 61, 78
artist: as creator, 21, 29; compared to torturer, 118; Elaine Risley *(Cat's Eye)*, 87, 88, 91, 92, 93; empowerment, 120; Grace Marks *(Alias Grace)*, 107; invisible in society, 17; Joe *(Surfacing)*, 56; in "Lives of the Poets," *(Dancing Girls)*, 130; Realist, 68; trickster as, 6; as visionary, 28, 42; Yvonne *(Bluebeard's Egg)*, 134, 145;
artist books, 3, 15, 19, 23. *See also* Pachter, Charles
"at first I was given centuries" *(Power Politics)*, 33
"At the Tourist Center in Boston" *(The Animals in That Country)*, 20

Athena, 100
"An Attempted Solution for Chess Problems" *(The Circle Game)*, 16
"Attitudes Towards the Mainland" *(The Animals in That Country)*, 22
Atwood and Family, videotape, 2, 138
Atwood, Carl (father), 2
Atwood, Harold (brother), 2
Atwood, Margaret Dorothy (Killam) (mother), 2
Atwood, Margaret Eleanor: childhood, 2; college, 2–3; comic strips, 1; daughter Jess, 2, 112, 145; marriage, 34, 43; on her works: *Second Words,* 5; *Double Persephone,* 13; *The Journals of Susanna Moodie,* 21; *Cat's Eye,* 88; *The Robber Bride,* 90, 95–96, 99; *Alias Grace,* 104–5; *True Stories,* 116; on writing, 113, 114, 47–48, 151; pseudonyms, 97, 149. *See also* Atwood, Carl; Gibson, Graeme; Polk, James; *titles of individual works.*
Aunt Lou *(Lady Oracle)*, 59–61
Austen, Jane, 105
Autobiography, 89, 90
Avison, Margaret, 147
"Axiom" *(The Animals in That Country)*, 20, 22

"Backdrop Addresses Cowboy" *(The Animals in That Country)*, 20, 21
Ballantyne, Sheila, 58
Barkhouse, Joyce, 150
Beckett, Samuel, 127
Beran, Carol, 67
Berger, John, 68, 71
"Betty" *(Dancing Girls)*, 131
Billy *(The Robber Bride)*, 98, 100, 101, 102
Birney, Earle, 19
Bishop, Elizabeth, 113
Blais, Marie-Claire, 148
"Blazed Trail, A" *(Interlunar)*, 121
Bluebeard, fairy tale, 30, 133–39, 140

"Bluebeard's Egg" *(Bluebeard's Egg)*,
    136–37
Bluebeard's Egg, 125, 133–39
Bodily Harm, 71–78; Jake 73–76. *See also*
    Daniel Luoma; Lora; Paul; Rennie
    (Renata) Wilford
"Bog Man, The" *(Wilderness Tips)*, 141
"Book of Ancestors" *(You Are Happy)*, 39
boundary, between U. S. and Canada, 148
boundary (ies), crossing; art forms, 4;
    between autobiography and fiction,
    89; between fiction and poetry, 144;
    in *The Edible Woman*, 46; in *Interlunar*,
    119; in *The Journals of Susanna Moodie*,
    26; in *Surfacing*, 51–56; tricksters, 6
Bouson, J. Brooks, 6; on *Bodily Harm*, 77;
    on *Cat's Eye*, 95; on *Edible Woman*, 44;
    on *Life Before Man*, 66; on *The Robber
    Bride*, 99
Brydon, Diana 77
Buckley, Jerome, 3
"Buffalo in Compound: Alberta" *(Proce-
    dures for Underground)*, 28
Burdette, Martha, 132
"Burned Space" *(Two-Headed Poems)*, 112
"Bus to Alliston, Ontario, The" *(Two-
    Headed Poems)*, 112

cake: in *Edible Woman*, 42, 44, 45–49,
    130; in "The Sin Eater" *(Dancing
    Girls)*, 132
camera, 15, 17, 32, 138
Canadian Literature, 146
canadian literature, 12
Canadian nationalism, 4, 57
CanLit Foodbook The, 1, 145
cannibalism, 44, 47, 130
caricature, Atwood's style, 4, 5; of
    Canada *(Bodily Harm)*, 84; in *Edible
    Woman*, 43; of Gothic *(Lady Oracle)*,
    75; of popular art *(Lady Oracle)*, 70; of
    quest *(Surfacing)*, 57
"Carrying Food Home in Winter" *(Proce-
    dures for Underground)*, 29
Cat's Eye, 85; and autobiography, 137;
    Carol Campbell, 88, 91; and con-
    sumerism, 135; discussion of, 86–95;
    Elaine Risley 86–95; Grace Smeath,

    88, 91; memory in, 88–89, 124; Mrs.
    Smeath, 91, 92, 94; Stephen, 89
"Cell" *(Morning in the Burned House)*,
    122
"Chaos Poem" *(You Are Happy)*, 35
Charis *(The Robber Bride)*, 96–102
Chris Beecham *(Life Before Man)*, 69
"Christmas Carol" *(True Stories)*, 116
Chuck Brewer *(Lady Oracle)*, *See* Royal
    Porcupine
Circe, 34–39
"Circle, Game, The" *(The Circle Game)*,
    16–17; and *Power Politics*, 30; touch
    in, 22
Circle Game, The: compared to *Procedures
    for Underground*, 29; compared to *Two-
    Headed Poems*, 111; discussion of,
    13–18; Northern landscape in, 9; and
    Selected Poems, 40; and *True Stories*, 118;
    and underground 28; won Governor
    General's Award, 13, 43
"City Planners, The" *(The Circle Game)*,
    16; compared to "Marrying the
    Hangman," 115; compared to "Pro-
    gressive insanities of a pioneer," 21
city, and bush: Atwood's childhood, 2; in
    The Animals in That Country, 21; in
    Anna's Pet, 150; in *The Circle Game*,
    16, 18; in *The Journals of Susanna
    Moodie*, 23; in *Life Before Man*,
    64–70; in "Marrying the Hangman"
    (Two-Headed Poems), 115; in *Surfacing*,
    50–55; as theme, 4, 6, 10, 42. *See
    also* north, Canadian
Cixous, Helene 7, 71
claustrophobia, 16, 127
clothing: in *Edible Woman*, 47; in *The
    Handmaid's Tale*, 82; in *Power Politics*,
    31; in *The Robber Bride*, 99; used
    in quilts, in *Alias Grace*, 107; in
    Wilderness Tips, 141. *See also* masquer-
    ade
Cluett, Robert, 51, 52
"Cold-Blooded" *(Good Bones)*, 143
Commander *(The Handmaid's Tale)*, 79,
    80–84
consumerism, 5, 6, 51
Conway, Jill Ker, 89, 90

Cooke, Nathalie, 90
Cooley, Dennis, 33
Cordelia *(Cat's Eye)*, 88, 90–95
costume. *See* clothing
courtship theme, 41, 45; in *Alias Grace*, 105–106; in *Cat's Eye*, 90; in *Edible Woman*, 48–50; in *Lady Oracle*, 57, 61. *See also* romance
crone: in "Double Persephone," 14; in *The Journals of Susanna Moodie*, 27; in *Lady Oracle*, 59; in *The Robber Bride*, 100; in *Two-Headed Poems*, 110, 113; in *Morning in the Burned House*, 122, 123

Dancing Girls, 125, 126–133
"Dancing Practice" *(Procedures for Underground)*, 29
Daniel Luoma *(Bodily Harm)*, 74
Davey, Frank, 11, 118
Davidson, Arnold E., 67
Davidson, Cathy N., 67
Davies, Paul, 89
Davies, Robertson, 24
"Daybooks" *(Two-Headed Poems)*, 110, 112
"Death by Landscape" *(Wilderness Tips)*, 140, 141
"Death of a Young Son by Drowning" *(The Journals of Susanna Moodie)*, 27, 40
"Delayed Message" *(The Animals in That Country)*, 28
Delilah, 95
De Man, Paul, 90
Demeter, 51, 52, 83, 100
"Departure From the Bush" *(The Journals of Susanna Moodie)*, 26
"Dinner" *(True Stories)*, 116
"Disembarking at Quebec" *(The Journals of Susanna Moodie)*, 26
disguise. *See* clothing; masquerade
dissertation, Atwood's, 3, 19, 105, 147; *See also* Haggard, H. Rider
Djwa, Sandra 3
Dooley, D. J. 44, 49
"Doorway" *(Interlunar)*, 120
double characters, 4; in "The War in the Bathroom" *(Dancing Girls)*, 127, 130. *See also* mirror

double perspectives, 6; in *The Journals of Susanna Moodie*, 25, 27; in *The Robber Bride*, 94, 96; in *Two-Headed Poems*, 111. *See also* mirror
"Double Persephone," 9, 13, 14
"Double Voice, The" *(The Journals of Susanna Moodie)*, 27
Dr. Minnow *(Bodily Harm)*, 74–76, 78
Dracula, 30
"Dream: Bluejay or Archeopteryx" *(Procedures for Underground)*, 28
"Dreams of the Animals" *(Procedures for Underground)*, 28

"Eating Snake" *(Interlunar)*, 120
Eaton catalogues, 90
Eden, 29, 52, 64, 76
"Eden is a Zoo" *(Procedures for Underground)*, 29
Edible Woman, The: and advertising, 16, 18; Atwood's introduction, 148; Clara, 46; courtship as hunt, 22; discussion of, 41–50; Duncan, 42, 46–49; femininity as masquerade, 82; Marian McAlpin compared to "The Sin Eater," 133; Peter Wollander, 24, 29, 42–49, 76. *See also* Marian McAlpin
egg: in *Alias Grace*, 106; in "Bluebeard's Egg," 136, 137; in *Edible Woman*, 46
E.J. Pratt Medal, 3, 13
Eliot, George, 63, 66
Elizabeth Schoenhof *(Life Before Man)*, 65–70, 113, 130
Engel, Marian, 149
Enos, Jennifer, 100

fairy tale: in *Bluebeard's Egg*, 133, 134, 137; in *Bodily Harm*, 73; in *Cat's Eye*, 88, 91, 92; in *Edible Woman*, 44; influence on Atwood, 5, 6; in *Morning in the Burned House*, 124; in *Princess Prunella and the Purple Peanut*, 150; in *The Robber Bride*, 97; in *Surfacing*, 56; in *Wilderness Tips*, 140
Fee, Margery, 55, 58, 59, 75
"Female Body, The" *(Good Bones)*, 143
feminism, 3, 6, 44, 45, 50

feminist: art theory, 88, 92, 93; in *Bodily Harm,* 72; in *The Handmaid's Tale,* 80, 84; issues, 30, 44, 47, 64; movement, 4; on pornography, 71; theorists on language, 7; and women's friendship, 65

"Fire Place, A" *(Interlunar),* 122

"First Prayer" *(You Are Happy),* 39

"Fishing for Eel Totems" *(Procedures for Underground),* 28, 120

"Fitcher's Bird," variant of the Bluebeard fairy tale, 134

"Five Poems for Grandmothers" *(Two-Headed Poems),* 112

For the Birds, children's book, 149, 150

"Four Auguries" *(You Are Happy),* 39

"Four Small Elegies" *(Two-Headed Poems),* 111

French feminists, 7, 71

Friedan, Betty, 45

friendship, 42, 65; in *The Handmaid's Tale,* 78, 83; in *Cat's Eye,* 86–95; in *The Robber Bride,* 95–103

Frye, Northrop, 3, 10, 17, 52

garden, 14, 54, 64, 76, 100

Gardner, Ava 111

"Gertrude Talks Back" *(Good Bones),* 143

Gibson, Eleanor Jessica Atwood (Jess), 2, 112, 145

Gibson, Graeme, 2; cover photograph for *Two-Headed Poems,* 111; dedicatee of *Bodily Harm,* 72; moves with Atwood to Alliston, Ontario 34, 112; interview with Atwood about *Edible Woman,* 50

Gilead *(The Handmaid's Tale),* 65, 78, 79, 81–85

"Gingerbread Boy" fairy tale in *Edible Woman,* 44

"Girl Without Hands, The" fairy tale, 73; *(Morning in the Burned House),* 124

Givner, Jessie, 90

Good Bones, 126, 139, 143–44

Good Bones and Simple Murders, 139

Gothic: in *Alias Grace,* 103; in *The Circle Game,* 15, 18; in *Edible Woman,* 45–49; in *The Handmaid's Tale,* 80–86; in *Lady Oracle,* 41, 57–63,

70; Northern Gothic, 9–13; themes, 5, 14, 34, 38, 78; in "Two-Headed Poems," 113

"Gothic Letter on a Hot Night" *(You Are Happy),* 38–39

Gotlieb, Phyllis, 12

Governor General's Award, 13, 14, 43, 78

Grace, Sherrill; on *The Circle Game,* 15, 18; on *The Journals of Susanna Moodie,* 25; *Life Before Man,* 67–68; on *Surfacing,* 50, 51

"Grave of the Famous Poet, The" *(Dancing Girls),* 130

Greene, Gayle, 7, 67, 68, 70

Greer, Germaine, 81

Gribbin, John, 89

"Hack Wednesday" *(Wilderness Tips),* 140, 143

Haggard, H. Rider, 3, 147

"Hair Jewellery" *(Dancing Girls),* 130

"Hairball" *(Wilderness Tips),* 140, 141

"Half-Hanged Mary" *(Morning in the Burned House),* 122–23

Halloween, 69

Hamlet, 95, 143

Hammer, Stephanie Barbé, 81

Handmaid's Tale, The: dedicated to Mary Webster, 122; discussion of, 64–65, 78–85; Luke, 79; Nick, 79, 80, 84, 85; on power and silencing, 33; Serena Joy, 64, 80, 84; and textual authority, 62, 94. *See also* Commander; Gilead; Moira; Offred; Ofglen

Hanged Man, Tarot card, 31

"Happy Endings" *(Murder in the Dark),* 139

Harkness, David, 44

Harvard University, 3, 19, 23, 82

Hawking, Stephen, 89

"Healer, The" *(Interlunar),* 120

"Heart Test with an Echo Chamber" *(Interlunar),* 121

Helen of Troy, 122

"Highest Altitude" *(Procedures for Underground),* 29

Hite, Molly 59, 60

Hopkins, Elizabeth, 25
"Hotel" *(True Stories)*, 116
Howells, Coral Ann, 7; on *Bodily Harm*,
74; on *Cat's Eye*, 90, 91; on *Edible
Woman*, 43, 49; on *Lady Oracle*, 58; on
Life Before Man, 66; on *The Robber
Bride*, 99; on *Surfacing*, 55; on
"Wilderness Tips," 143
"Hurricane Hazel" *(Bluebeard's Egg)*,
137
Hutcheon, Linda, 99

"Immigrants, The" *(The Journals of
Susanna Moodie)*, 27
"I Was Reading a Scientific Article, *(The
Animals in That Country)*, 22
"In Search of the Rattlesnake Plantain"
(Bluebeard's Egg), 137
Ingres, Jean: and Elaine Risley's paint-
ings, *Cat's Eye*, 93–94
"Instructions for the Third Eye" *(Murder
in the Dark)*, 140
Interlunar, 110, 118, 119–22
"Interview with a Tourist" *(Procedures for
Underground)*, 28
Irigaray, Luce, 7, 71
Irvine, Lorna, 71, 72, 76
"Isis in Darkness" *(Wilderness Tips)*, 3,
140, 141
"It is dangerous to read newspapers" *(The
Animals in That Country)*, 20, 21

Jameson, Frederic, 10
Jara, Victor, 121
Jiles, Paulette, 81
Joan Foster *(Lady Oracle)*: as Gothic storyteller, 32, 41–42, 78; discussion of,
57–63; compared to Zenia *(The Robber Bride)*, 99
Johnson, E. Pauline, 149
Jong, Erica, 148
Journals of Susanna Moodie, The,
22–27
journey; in *The Animals in That Country*,
19–22; in *The Circle Game*, 9–13, 92;
in *Dancing Girls*, 126; David, 51, 54;
in *Interlunar*, 120–122; in *The Journals
of Susanna Moodie*, 26; in *Life Before*

Man, 66; in novels, 41; in *Morning in
the Burned House*, 124; in *Procedures for
Underground*, 28–29; in *Surfacing*,
50–52;
"Journey to the Interior" *(The Circle
Game)*, 10, 18

Kaminski, Margaret, interview with
Atwood, 30, 36
Keith, W. J., 44
Kimber, William, 31
King Lear, 88, 93
Kinnear, Thomas *(Alias Grace)*, 104, 106,
108, 109
Klein, A. M., 17
Kovalski, Maryann, 150

Lacan, Jacques, 18
Lacombe, Michelle 79
Lady Oracle, 5; Aunt Lou as nonvictim,
134; discussion of, 57–63; Joan Foster
as Gothic storyteller, 32, 41–42, 78;
Joan Foster compared to Zenia *(The
Robber Bride)*, 99; open-ended, 41–42;
parody of Gothic, 70, 99; part of a
unit of three novels, 50. *See also* Joan
Foster; Royal Porcupine
"Landcrab" *(True Stories)*, 117
landscape, Atwood's Northern, 9, 11, 16,
18, 110; in *The Animals in That Coun-
try*, 19, 22; contrasted to city, 10, 15;
in "Double Persephone," 14; in The
Journals of Susanna Moodie, 24, 27;
linked to power and death, 17; in *Pro-
cedures for Underground*, 28–29; in *Sur-
facing*, 53; in *Two-Headed Poems*, 112;
in *Wilderness Tips*, 140–42. *See also*
north; city, and bush
Lane, Richard, 56
Larry *(The Robber Bride)*, 97, 100, 102
"Last Poem" *(True Stories)*, 116
"Late August" *(You Are Happy)*, 39
Lecker, Robert, 56
Lee, Dennis, 3
Lesje Green *(Life Before Man)*, 65–70
Lessing, Doris, 58
"Let Us Now Praise Stupid Women"
(Good Bones), 143

Levi-Strauss, Claude, 44
Life Before Man, 63–71, 81, 130; Nate
    Schoenhof, 65–71. *See also* Chris
    Beecham; Elizabeth Schoenhof; Lesje
    Green
Lilienfeld, Jane, 37, 39
"Little Red Hen Tells All, The" (*Good
    Bones*), 143
Livesay, Dorothy, 19
"Lives of the Poets" (*Dancing Girls*), 130
Lora (*Bodily Harm*), 65, 76, 77
"Loulou, or the Domestic Life of the Lan-
    guage" (*Bluebeard's Egg*), 135

MacEwen, Gwendolyn, 12
MacLulich, T. D., 44
Macpherson, Jay, 3, 14
"Making a Man" (*Good Bones*), 143
"Man from Mars, The" (*Dancing Girls*),
    126, 127
"Man in a Glacier" (*Morning in the Burned
    House*), 123
Mandel, Eli, 12, 14, 19, 147
"Manet's Olympia" (*Morning in the Burned
    House*), 122
Marian McAlpin (*Edible Woman*): and can-
    nibalism, 130; compared to Joan Fos-
    ter, 57; compared to narrator of "The
    Sin Eater," 133; denial of power, 135;
    discussion of; 41–50; and romance
    conventions, 32;
"Marrying the Hangman" (*Two-Headed
    Poems*), 40, 111, 114
"Marsh Languages" (*Morning in the
    Burned House*), 110, 123
masquerade, 47, 49, 64, 82. *See also* cloth-
    ing
Mathews, Robin, 148
McClelland and Stewart, publishers, 43
McCombs, Judith: on *Cat's Eye*, 91; on
    The Circle Game, 15, 16, 17; on Gothic
    in early poems 12; on *Power Politics*,
    33; on reviews of *The Animals in That
    Country*, 19; on Susanna Moodie as
    wendigo, 26; on *Surfacing*, 50, 53;
McLay, Catherine, 49
Medusa, 99
"Meal, A" (*The Circle Game*), 16

"Memory" (*You Are Happy*), 35
metafiction, 7, 85, 103
Miller, Perry, 3
Millett, Kate, 30, 148
Miner, Madonne, 81, 84
Miner, Valerie, 43
mirror: in *Cat's Eye*, 91, 92; in *The Circle
    Game*, 17; in *The Journals of Susanna
    Moodie*, 26; in *Lady Oracle*, 59, 61; in
    The Robber Bride, 95, 98, 100; in *Sur-
    facing*, 52, 55; in *Two-Headed Poems*,
    113, 114; in *You Are Happy*, 35–37,
    39. *See also* camera; double characters;
    double perpectives; photograph
Mirror Stage, 18
"Miss July Grows Older" (*Morning in the
    Burned House*), 122
Mitch (*The Robber Bride*), 98, 100, 101,
    102
Moers, Ellen, 58
Moira (*The Handmaid's Tale*), 61, 65, 79,
    82, 83
"Moment, The" (*Morning in the Burned
    House*), 124
Morey, Ann-Janine, 133
Morning in the Burned House, 110,
    122–124
Munro, Alice, 149
Murder in the Dark, 125, 139–40,
    144
"My Life as a Bat" (*Good Bones*), 143
myth: in English and Canadian poetry, 3;
    and nature, 110, 112, 140, 149;
    opposed to realism, 8, 10, 18; as sub-
    text, 5, 6, 8, 9, 65, 71

IN WORKS
The Circle Game, 15, 17
Interlunar, 119, 120
Life Before Man, 66, 71
Morning in the Burned House, 124
Proceedings for Underground, 28
Surfacing, 52, 56
Two-Headed Poems, 113
Wilderness Tips, 140, 141
You Are Happy, 37
See also Circe; fairy tale; north; Pandora;
    Persephone; realism; Siren

New Oxford Book of Canadian Verse in English, The, 145
Nischik, Reingard M., 128
Nochlin, Linda, 68
nonvictim, 33, 34, 134, 139, 146. *See also* victim
north, Canadian; in *Strange Things,* 148–49; in *Surfacing,* 53; in *Wilderness Tips,* 143. *See also* landscape; myth; *Survival;* winter
"Notes from various pasts" *(The Animals in That Country),* 20
"Notes Toward a Poem that Can Never Be Written" *(True Stories),* 40, 111, 116
"November" *(You Are Happy),* 35

O. W. Toad, 97
Odysseus, 35, 36, 37, 38, 39
Offred *(The Handmaid's Tale):* discussion of, 78–85; female friendships, 65; her story edited by a scholar, 87, 94; as Scheherazade, 114
Ofglen *(The Handmaid's Tale),* 65, 82, 83
"On the Streets, Love" *(The Circle Game),* 16
Ondaatje, Michael, 15
"One More Garden" *(True Stories),* 116, 117
Ophelia, 95
Orpheus, 111, 120, 121
Orwell, George, 78

Pachter, Charles, 3; *The Circle Game* 15; 19; *The Journals of Susanna Moodie,* 23, 24
"Page, The" *(Murder in the Dark),* 139
Palumbo, Alice, 91
Pandora, 71, 107
"Paper Bag, A" *(Two-Headed Poems),* 112
Patton, Marilyn, 7, 72
Paul *(Bodily Harm),* 72, 73, 74, 75
Paul *(Lady Oracle),* 60
Peri, Camille, 7
Persephone, 9, 13, 14, 43, 45, 52, 83, 100, 110, 111, 121
"Persephone Departing" *(Double Persephone),* 14
Peterman, Michael, 24

Petit Nevis, 117
photograph, 15; in *Bluebeard's Egg,* 138; in *The Circle Game,* 17–18; cover of *Two-Headed Poems,* 111; in *Edible Woman,* 45; of Susanna Moodie, 27; 28. *See also* camera, mirror
Pieixoto, Professor James Darcy *(The Handmaid's Tale),* 79, 85
Pioneers, 19
"Place: Fragments, A" *(The Circle Game),* 9, 11, 16, 18, 110
Plath, Sylvia, 45
"Polarities" *(Dancing Girls),* 128
politics, 5, 30; in *Bodily Harm,* 71. *See also* power
Polk, James, 34, 43
pornography, 64, 71, 75, 84
"Postcard" *(True Stories),* 116, 117
power, 4, 5, 6; in *The Animals in That Country,* 21; in *Bodily Harm,* 74, 75; in *Cat's Eye,* 92; in *Edible Woman,* 44; in fairy tales, 150; in *The Handmaid's Tale,* 82, 85; in *Interlunar,* 119, 120; in *The Journals of Susanna Moodie,* 27; and journey, 10; in *Lady Oracle,* 59, 60; of language, 7, 110, 114, 119, 120; in *Morning in the Burned House,* 123; of nature, 10, 18, 19; in *The Robber Bride,* 97–99; of storyteller, 87, 110, 115, 135; in *Surfacing,* 52; in *True Stories,* 119; in *You Are Happy,* 36–38. *See also* crone; politics; *Power Politics;* victim
Power Politics: abstract quality of, 110; discussion of, 30–34; obsession in, 112
Pratt, E. J., 3
Princess Prunella and the Purple Peanut (children's book), 149
Procedures for Underground, 9, 27, 28–29, 120
"Projected Slide of an Unknown Soldier" *(Procedures for Underground),* 28
"Provisions" *(The Animals in That Country),* 20, 22
Pugliese, Michael, 118
Purdy, Al, 19, 147

"Quattrocento" *(Interlunar),* 120

Rao, Eleonora, 7, 89, 135
"Rape Fantasies" *(Dancing Girls)*, 131
Rapunzel, 88, 91, 95, 148
rationality, 6, 10, 14, 16, 21, 42, 65, 103
ravine, 91, 92, 94
realism, 5, 8; in *Alias Grace*, 103; in *Edible Woman*, 48; in *Life Before Man*, 63, 66–69; in short fiction, 125
rebirth: in *Bodily Harm*, 77; in *Edible Woman*, 48, 49; in fairy tales, 73; in *Interlunar*, 120; in "Isis in Darkness," 141; in *Life Before Man*, 65–66; in *Surfacing*, 52, 54, 56;
"Red Fox, The " *(Morning in the Burned House)*, 122
"Red Shirt, A" *(Two-Headed Poems)*, 113
Red Shoes, The, 61, 62
Rennie (Renata) Wilford *(Bodily Harm)*: connection with Lora, 65; discussion of, 71–78; observed by men, 81; in toxic relationship, 32
"Repent" *(You Are Happy)*, 35
"Resplendent Quetzal, The" *(Dancing Girls)*, 128
Rich, Adrienne, 85, 147
"The Right Hand Fights the Left" *(Two-Headed Poems)*, 111
Robber Bride, The, 95–103. *See also* Billy; Charis; Mitch; Roz; Tony; West; Zenia
"Robber Bridegroom, The" 7, 73, 120, 135
romance; in *Alias Grace*, 106; in *Bluebeard's Egg*, 134, 137; in *Edible Woman*, 43, 49–50; English metaphysical, 3, 105; in *The Handmaid's Tale*, 78–81, 84; in *Lady Oracle*, 59–63; in *Life Before Man*, 69; and traditional women's plot, 5, 41, 89–90, 140. *See also* courtship theme
Rosenberg, Jerome, 23, 59, 146
Royal Porcupine, aka Chuck Brewer *(Lady Oracle)*, 57, 60, 61
Roz, (Roz Grunwald, Rosalind Greenwood; *The Robber Bride*), 96–102
Rubbo, Michael, 2
Rubenstein, Roberta 59, 71
Rule, Jane, 44

Sagan, Carl, 89
"Saints, The" *(Interlunar)*, 120
"Salt Garden, The" *(Bluebeard's Egg)*, 137
satire, 4, 6, 41, 78, 80,
Schaeffer, Susan Fromberg, 58
Scheherazade: in *Alias Grace*, 87, 103, 109; figures, 2, 7, 86, 87, 111; in *The Handmaid's Tale*, 79, 81; in "Marrying the Hangman," 114; Mary Webster, 123; in "Rape Fantasies," 131
Schlafly, Phyllis, 80
Sciff-Zamaro, Roberta, 59
Scott, Peter Dale, 1, 14
Scrabble; in *The Handmaid's Tale*, 82
Second Words, 4, 5, 145, 147
Selected Poems, 12, 13, 40, 87, 111
Seltzer, Richard, 72
sexism, 5, 6
"Shapechangers in Winter" *(Morning in the Burned House)*, 124
Shearer, Moira, 61
Shields, Carol 25
Shelley, Mary, 21, 33
"Signer, The" *(Morning in the Burned House)*, 124
"Significant Moments in the Life of My Mother" *(Bluebeard's Egg)*, 137
"Simmering" *(Murder in the Dark)*, 139
"Sin Eater, The" *(Dancing Girls)*, 132–33
Siren *(You Are Happy)*, 11, 36, 38
Skelton, Robin, 19, 44
"Small Poems for the Winter Solstice" *(True Stories)*, 117, 119
"Snake Poems" *(Interlunar)*, 120
"The Snow Queen," fairy tale, 88, 91, 95
"Solstice Poem" *(Two-Headed Poems)*, 110, 111, 113
"Songs of the Transformed" *(You Are Happy)*, 35, 36
"Soul, Geologically, A" (Procedures for Underground), 29
Souster, Raymond, 19
"Speeches for Dr. Frankenstein" *(The Animals in That Country)*, 21–22
"Spelling" *(True Stories)*, 111, 118
"Spring" *(You Are Happy)*, 35

"Spring Song of the Frogs" (Bluebeard's
    Egg), 133, 134
Staines, David, 24
"Statuary" (Morning in the Burned House),
    124
Stein, Karen, 58, 85
storyteller: Atwood as, 1; in The Hand-
    maid's Tale, 80; in The Robber Bride, 96;
    Zenia as, 86. See also Joan Foster;
    Offred; Siren; Scheherazade; Zenia
Stow, Glenys, 44
Strange Things, 140, 148–49
Strauss, Jennifer, 71
Struthers, J. R. (Tim) 59, 63
"Sunday Drive, A" (Interlunar), 120
sunrise (Bluebeard's Egg), 134, 145
Surfacing, 50–57; Anna, 51, 54, 56;
    David, 51, 54; Joe, 51, 54–56
Survival, 1; theme of victim, 5, 12, 33,
    34, 53, 126; image of cold north, 9,
    19; and pioneer, 21; discussion of
    146–47
Survivalwoman, 1, 149
Susanna Moodie, 22–27; and Grace
    Marks, 104, 105, 108; in Strange
    Things, 149

Tarot, 30, 31, 56, 99
Texmo, Del, 49
Thackeray, William Makepeace, 96
"There are Two Islands" (You Are Happy),
    39
"There is Only One of Everything" (You
    Are Happy), 35, 39
"They eat out" (Power Politics), 32
"This is a Photograph of Me" (The Circle
    Game), 17, 18, 27
This Magazine, 1, 113, 149
Thomas, Audrey, 147
Thompson, Lee Briscoe, 79, 83
"Three Denizen Songs" (Interlunar), 121
"Three Desk Objects" (Procedures for
    Underground), 28
Tiffin, Helen, 71
Tomc, Sandra 81
Tony (Antonia Fremont, The Robber Bride),
    86, 96–102

Toronto Arts Award, 78
"Torture" (True Stories), 116
touch: in Bodily Harm, 73, 76, 78; in The
    Circle Game, 22; in "Double Perse-
    phone," 14; in Interlunar, 122, 124; in
    Murder in the Dark, 140; in Power Poli-
    tics, 33; in Two-Headed Poems, 115; in
    You Are Happy, 39.. See also "The Girl
    Without Hands"
tourist, 9; in The Animals in That Country,
    19, 20; in Dancing Girls, 126, 128,
    130, 132; in Surfacing, 52, 53; in True
    Stories, 116. See also journey
Tracy, Ann, 149
Traill, Catherine Parr, 149
"Trainride, Vienna-Bonn" (True Stories),
    116
transformation; in Bodily Harm, 77; in
    fairy tales, 5; in Wilderness Tips, 141
trap, 13, 15, 26, 62, 125
"Travel Piece, A" (Dancing Girls), 129
Tree of Knowledge, 107
"Tricks With Mirrors" (You Are Happy), 35
trickster; storyteller as, 103; writer as 6,
    42, 52; Zenia as 86, 96, 98. See also,
    Scheherazade, storyteller,
triple goddess, 59, 100
"True Stories," 4
True Stories, 4; themes, 21; discussion of,
    115–119; mentioned, 33, 71,
    110–111, 121
"True Trash" (Wilderness Tips), 140–41
twins, 93, 113
"Two Fires, The" (The Journals of Susanna
    Moodie), 26
Two-Headed Poems, 110–115, 117

"Uglypuss" (Bluebeard's Egg), 137
Ulysses, 34
"Uncles" (Wilderness Tips), 140
"Unearthing Suite" (Bluebeard's Egg), 2,
    135, 137–38
University of Toronto, 2
Up in the Air So Blue, unpublished novel,
    3, 43
Up in the Tree, children's book 149
"Useless" (You Are Happy), 35

Van Duyn, Mona 19
Vanity Fair, 96; Becky Sharp, 96
VanSpanckeren, Kathryn 10
"Variation on the Word Sleep" *(True Stories),* 119
victim, 4–8; in *Alias Grace,* 103, 104, 107; in *Bluebeard's Egg,* 143; in *Dancing Girls,* 131; in *Edible Woman,* 49; in *Power Politics,* 34; in *The Robber Bride,* 95, 97, 99, 102; as storyteller, 12, 33, 78, 119, 122; in *Surfacing,* 54–55; victim positions, 33, 99, 146; in *You Are Happy,* 37–39. *See also* non-victim
Virgin Mary *(Cat's Eye),* 92
"Vultures" *(True Stories),* 117

Wagner-Martin, Linda, 116, 120
Waite, Arthur Edward, 31, 56
"War in the Bathroom, The" *(Dancing Girls),* and alienation, 126; doubled protagonist, 127; not in first U. S. edition, 131
"We Don't Like Reminders" *(Procedures for Underground),* 28
Webster, Mary *(Morning in the Burned House),* 111, 122, 148
"Weight" *(Wilderness Tips),* 81, 140, 142
Wendigo, 149
West *(The Robber Bride),* 97, 99, 100, 102
"When it Happens" *(Dancing Girls),* 130
"White Cup, The" *(Interlunar),* 121
"White Snake, The" *(Interlunar),* 120
Whitman, Walt, 20
Wilderness Tips: and storytelling, 125; discussion of, 140–143
Wilson, Ethel, 149
Wilson, Milton, 14
Wilson, Sharon Rose, 5; on *Bodily Harm,* 73; on *Cat's Eye,* 91; on *Edible Woman,* 44; on "Hurricane Hazel," 138; on

Interlunar, 120, 121; on *Lady Oracle,* 61; on *Life Before Man,* 66, 67
winter: in *Cat's Eye,* 91; in *The Circle Game,* 11, 110; in *Life Before Man,* 69; in *Procedures for Underground,* 29; in *Surfacing,* 53; theme in Canadian literature, 19, 149; in *Two-Headed Poems,* 112; in *You Are Happy,* 39. *See also* north, landscape
witness: in *Interlunar,* 121; as preferred role 7, 65, 77, 110, 114; Rennie Wilford as, 73; in *True Stories,* 116–118; writer as, 148
Wizard of Oz, 66
"Woman Skating" *(Procedures for Underground),* 29
"Woman Who Could Not Live with her Faulty Heart, The" *(Two-Headed Poems),* 111
"Women's Issue, A" *(True Stories),* 116
Woodcock, George: editor of *Canadian Literature,* 6, 12; on *Surfacing,* 50, 52, 55
Woolf, Virginia, 35, 65, 67, 83, 114
"The Words Continue Their Journey" *(Interlunar),* 121
World War II, 4, 60, 87, 101
Writers' Union of Canada, 1

Yarnall, Judith, 36–37
You Are Happy: relationship of story and teller; 33–40; Siren, 11, 12, 36, 38
"You Begin" *(Two-Headed Poems),* 40, 111, 115
"Younger Sister, Going Swimming" *(Procedures for Underground),* 29
Yvonne, "Sunrise, The," *(Bluebeard's Egg),* 134–35

Zenia *(The Robber Bride),* 86; storyteller; 95–102, 107; trickster, 87

The Author

Karen F. Stein received her B.A. from Brooklyn College, her M.A. from the Pennsylvania State University, and her Ph.D. from the University of Connecticut. She teaches at the University of Rhode Island and writes about contemporary North American women writers.

The Editor

Robert Lecker is professor of English at McGill University in Montreal. He received his Ph.D. from York University. Professor Lecker is the author of numerous critical studies, including *On the Line* (1982), *Robert Kroetch* (1986), *An Other I* (1988), and *Making It Real: The Canonization of English-Canadian Literature* (1995). He is the editor of the critical journal *Essays on Canadian Writing* and of many collections of critical essays, the most recent of which is *Canadian Canons: Essays in Literary Value* (1991). He is the founding and current general editor of Twayne's Masterwork Studies and the editor of the Twayne World Authors Series on Canadian writers. He is also the general editor of G. K. Hall's Critical Essays on World Literature series.